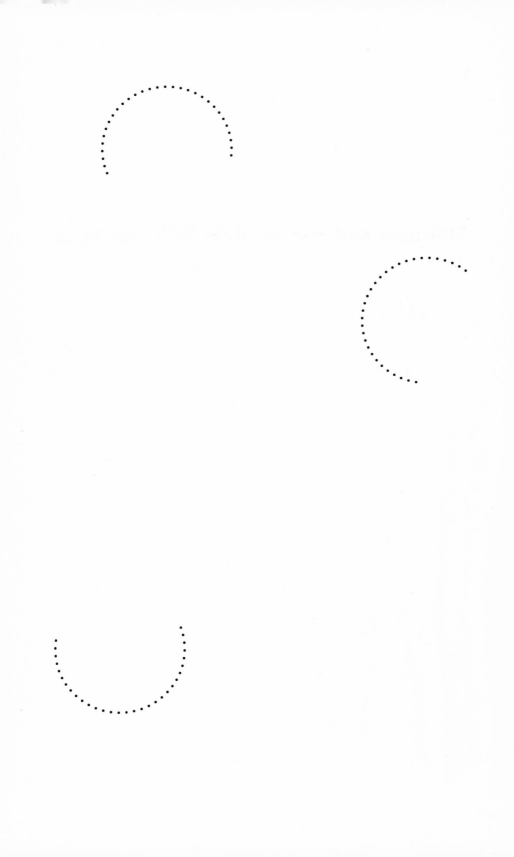

Strangers
and Friends
at the Welcome Table

Contemporary Christianities
in the
American South

JAMES HUDNUT-BEUMLER

THE UNIVERSITY OF NORTH CAROLINA PRESS

Chapel Hill

This book was published with the assistance of the
Fred W. Morrison Fund of the University of North Carolina Press.

Set in Arno and Scala by codeMantra

Manufactured in the United States of America

The University of North Carolina Press has been a member
of the Green Press Initiative since 2003.

Jacket illustration: © Tatiana Badaeva, 123RF Stock Photo.

LIBRARY OF CONGRESS CATALOGING-IN-PUBLICATION DATA
Names: Hudnut-Beumler, James David, author.
Title: Strangers and friends at the welcome table : contemporary
Christianities in the American South / James Hudnut-Beumler.
Other titles: Contemporary Christianities in the American South
Description: Chapel Hill : The University of North Carolina Press, [2018] |
Includes bibliographical references and index.
Identifiers: LCCN 2017044541| ISBN 9781469640372 (cloth : alk. paper) |
ISBN 9781469640389 (ebook)
Subjects: LCSH: Christianity—Southern States—21st century.
Classification: LCC BR535 .H83 2018 | DDC 277.5—dc23
LC record available at https://lccn.loc.gov/2017044541

For my son,

ADAM,

born in the South, now returned
to study American religion
in its most lively region

CONTENTS

Introduction   Christianities in the Now South   *1*

PART I   *Rock of Ages Cleft for Me: Southern Traditions Revised*

1   I Was Hungry, and You Gave Me Something
to Eat: Hospitality, Scarcity, and Fear
in Southern Christianity   *15*

2   The Religion of the Lost Cause, Reloaded   *42*

3   Rattlesnakes, Holiness, and the
Nearness of the Holy Spirit   *63*

4   Washed in the Blood in the Red States:
Religion and Politics   *84*

PART II   *Gulf Coast Disaster: Religion Is Only
as Good as What It Does*

5   Our Church Is Cleaning Up after Katrina   *107*

6   Mississippi Flooding   *131*

PART III   *Brand New Start: Southern Religious Innovations*

   7   Megachurches and the Reinvention of
        Southern Church Life   *153*

   8   The Changing Face of the Catholic South   *177*

   9   Christian Homeschoolers   *201*

   10   Southern, Christian, and Gay   *215*

Conclusion   Southern Christianities in Harmony and Conflict   *243*

Acknowledgments   *249*

Notes   *251*

Index   *271*

FIGURES, TABLES, AND MAP

Figures

1. "Slave Cabin," Rippavilla Plantation, Spring Hill, Tennessee *46*

2. The Reverend William J. Barber II addresses supporters at Moral Monday 11, July 15, 2013 *98*

3. Statue of Saint Roch, Saint Roch Cemetery Chapel, New Orleans *121*

4. Saint Roch Cemetery, with Our Lady: Star of the Sea in the distance, New Orleans *122*

5. Our Lady of Fatima at Ave Maria Grotto, Cullman, Alabama *180*

6. Saint Bernard Boys Memorial, Ave Maria Grotto, Cullman, Alabama *181*

7. Father William Bishop, "Missionary Map of the United States," showing priestless counties, 1938 *184*

8. Ten Commandments, Blessed Virgin, and Beatitudes, Shrine of the Most Blessed Sacrament, Hanceville, Alabama *186*

9. Entrance to the Shrine of the Most Blessed Sacrament, Hanceville, Alabama *186*

10. Virgin of Guadalupe with Juan Diego surrounded with lighted rosary, Iglesia Catolica Nuestra Señora de Guadalupe, Nashville, Tennessee *197*

Tables

1. States with Fastest-Growing Hispanic Populations, 2000–2010   *200*

2. Gay-Affirming Congregations in Southern States   *228*

Map

Megachurch Location by Region   *154*

INTRODUCTION

Christianities in the Now South

I have been studying to write this book my entire life. My mother was from New England stock and my father from Appalachian. Every time we traveled down from Michigan to see our relatives along the Ohio River in tiny South Webster, Ohio, my brothers and I marveled at their twanging accents. We would get back in the car to head north and try for days to talk that way ourselves until we crossed the line from affection into mockery and were corrected. We also asked questions, lots of questions—why did the little church need a song leader, a piano player, and an organist? Why were there so many churches on the same little main street? Why did people go to church at night on Sundays and Wednesdays, with each church's bell ringing at a slightly different time? And unsurprisingly, I asked most of those questions.

As much as I thought that I knew something about the upper rural South, I still had a lot to learn when, in 1993, Columbia Theological Seminary in Decatur, Georgia, called on me to be dean of its faculty. Early on in my tenure, I again became a somewhat bewildered student of southern religion and culture when a colleague who hailed originally from Mississippi visited me and soon left me baffled. For a full two minutes, he proclaimed his close friendship with a person he had gone to seminary with, including the detail that said person had been best man at his wedding. He then stated, however, that he disagreed with what his friend had recently said in public regarding urban ministry. For a full six months after that, I was under the impression that our conversation had been all about how much my colleague loved and admired his seminary classmate. But a half-year later, it occurred to me that all of his protestations of love and fealty were just so much boilerplate before the real message—that he sharply disagreed with his associate—and that I was to ignore everything up to the "however."

Not until two years into my southern sojourn did I begin to get a proper feel for the common rhetoric of "So and so is my closest friend and the dearest person in the world, but . . . " and to realize that disagreement was being

1

expressed within a larger pattern of Christian communal love and respect in a way that simply would not figure quite so much any place else in the country. So it is with me, as a historian writing and teaching about the South today. I have come to love and respect this region, which in some ways seems to have a soul of a church, and I desire to depict it lovingly and critically within that frame of mind, so that it might be seen for its strengths and weaknesses by those both within and beyond its all-too-fuzzy borders.

Thanks to Columbia Theological Seminary and, later, Vanderbilt Divinity School, I have been privileged to travel throughout the South to preach, teach, eat the local food, and learn people's stories and their communities' histories. I have found that the American South remains a place with a deep sense of its past. The southern present—the Now South, I am calling it—is thickly constituted by its relations to race, place, kinship (real or imagined), faith, myths, and stories.

Still, I began to wonder how long this cultural distinctiveness will last and whether it has already been so homogenized with the rest of American culture that the differences we observe are more vestigial than essential. As I contemplated this question, I increasingly felt that I could write deeply about what I saw of contemporary southern religiosity. This feeling came to a head when my Minnesota and New York Republican relatives, during the run-up to the 2008 presidential caucuses in Iowa, could not make sense of what Mike Huckabee was saying. They opined, "Nobody will vote for him—he's crazy. Nobody will fall for a fanatic minister-politician who keeps playing the bass in churches and talks like that. What's that about?" Now living in Nashville, my wife and I, and even our teenage children, though no great fans of Huckabee, nevertheless found ourselves translating for our northern relatives his southern evangelical speech and appeal, including how playing bass in church makes you a regular guy—not a goof—where we live. Huckabee, of course, won Iowa that year, if little else.

The 2008 election cycle turned out to be a crucial year for hardening the political-cultural differences between the South and other states (particularly reflected in congressional representation and control of southern statehouses), but where I wanted to go with a book about Christianity in the Now South was to peer under and through the big red Republican-dominated political map to seek out and look directly at the considerable variations of faith, belief, and practice that exist there under the rubric "Christian" in the first years of the twenty-first century. What I found, as chronicled in this book, is that the contemporary South is still religiously distinct and dominantly

Christian, yet it is steadily and inexorably changing and becoming more diverse in the forms of expression that claim that name.

Understanding religious life in the Now South is important for those both inside the region and beyond, I believe. Those who think that they know what a southern Christian is from watching politicians stumping through Liberty University every four years are at risk of flattening their comprehension from outside to a caricature in which all southern Christians are white, evangelical, and politically conservative. This book complicates that picture. Even southern Christians themselves have the tendency, I think, to believe that most others are just like themselves, because they live and move in lifestyle enclaves. This book unveils the considerable variety in ideology, practice, and outlook among southern Christians today but also demonstrates that they all derive considerable support for their respective worldviews from their common faith.

In a word, then, you cannot understand the South, a region home to a quarter of the U.S. population, without developing a subtle sense of the many melodies that attend the South's predominant religion and the cultural and political forms it takes there.

This book is also an answer to a question that has preoccupied anyone interested in the state of American religion—from church people to journalists to scholars—ever since legalized segregation ended and air conditioning and interstate highways hit the South. The question goes, "Is there still a distinctively southern religious life?" or, as journalist John Egerton and, later, historian Grant Wacker asked, "Has American religion been southernized and southern religion Americanized to the extent that the boundaries are now hard to discern?"[1] Three decades later, characteristics and markers of southern religious difference remain strong.[2] Though Christianity is, of course, America's dominant faith, this book grapples with how Christian dominance in the South is particularly and differently (at times) expressed so strongly as to create a religious imaginary. What I mean by "religious imaginary" is a collective sense of what matters and why, which provides meaning, identity, and purpose. Even if individuals rebel against it, the fact and effects of Christian social dominance are real. The visitor's or newcomer's impression that churches are everywhere in the South is not false. The South is, for example, home to more megachurches as a function of population than any other region—more than five times as many such churches as in the Northeast, for example.[3] Meanwhile, those churches, and the smaller ones, too, are well used. The region is home to the denominations that the 2014 Pew Landscape

Study found had the people who were most highly involved with their congregations. Groups like the Church of God (Cleveland, Tennessee), the Churches of Christ, the Southern Baptist Convention (SBC), the Church of God in Christ, and the National Baptist Convention all call the South home and feature memberships who are "highly involved" at the 44–57 percent range as measured by frequent attendance and involvement in small groups associated with their churches. By contrast, only 16 percent of Catholics and 19 percent of Evangelical Lutherans in America nationally reach these levels of involvement.[4] The other signs of this religious imaginary abound in the South—prayer at suburban Little League games is common, as is the sight of families praying in restaurants, and Christian billboards along the highways offer all manner of services. Religion is not just a private matter, as it is in more cosmopolitan parts of the nation—though there are other places (Utah and Colorado Springs, Colorado, come to mind) where religion is comparably palpable in public (and, not surprisingly, Mormons outpace all other groups in absolute levels of personal involvement in church activities). Still, of the top twenty American cities, the South's largest and most cosmopolitan city, Atlanta, has the second most Christians (76 percent), exceeded only by Dallas (78 percent). This compares with Boston (57 percent), Seattle (52 percent), and San Francisco (48 percent), where involvement rates are also much lower.[5]

The statistics confirm that the South is highly religious and Christian. But the stories that fill the chapters that follow break down any sense that the Christian South is just one thing. There is no essential southern form of Christianity. The Christians of the South today are sufficiently varied in their understanding and practice of their faith to merit using the word "Christianities" to characterize the variety of views, and even levels of dissent, about important matters when it comes to how to love their neighbors, construe sin, and constitute their fellowships. Today's southern Christians may all join in singing the words of the hymn "I Want to Eat at the Welcome Table," but when they all show up to eat, some will be friends and others strangers according to the way they have been reckoning.

Three of my all-time favorite books about American religion are written about the South: Charles Reagan Wilson's *Baptized in Blood: The Religion of the Lost Cause, 1865–1920* (1980), Dennis Covington's *Salvation on Sand Mountain: Snake Handling and Redemption in Southern Appalachia* (1995), and Charles Marsh's *God's Long Summer: Stories of Faith and Civil Rights* (2008) are all classics now. My book is like them insofar as it follows religion inside churches and outside into spaces that do not at first blush look very holy. But mine treats the Now South. I try to seek to understand what it means to speak of southerners and their varieties of Christianity in the first decades of the twenty-first century. As such, I have benefited immensely from travel and talking with and interviewing dozens of people in the South who practice and think about religion in the here and now. I have also enjoyed visiting other places via the Internet and have benefited from the southern Christians and groups who wished to share what they were doing with the rest of the world. As immediate as these sources are, I gratefully draw on other thinkers and writers who have explored aspects of southern religious life in the contemporary period.[6]

I have chosen to focus on a range of the fascinating varieties of Christian expression. When I first set out to explore the South systematically, I had expected that I would find more diversity in the religious traditions represented. What I discovered was that, in large measure, Christianities continue to dominate the culture of the southern states. If you exclude Florida south of I-4 and "NOVA" (the area of northern Virginia near Washington, D.C.), there is no non-Christian group that forms more than 0.6 percent of a southern state's population.[7] Politically, state legislatures, school boards, and citizens themselves often act as though religious minorities do not exist—or are threats.

I have taken it as my interpretive task to get inside the practices of the dominant majority while being profoundly grateful for other scholars whose work takes us inside the contemporary religious experience of other traditions.[8] Not all southern religion is Christian, it is good to remember, and we must work hard to avoid making the error committed by many earlier interpreters of religious life in the American South of mistaking the majority for the totality.

CHRISTIANITIES, PLURAL

As I have suggested, the forms of Christianity practiced in the contemporary South are so varied as to deserve the plural designator: Christianities. This is important for interpretive purposes and also to remind readers from the start that my mode of analysis is American religious history, not theology. I provide accounts of various forms of religious life that exist in the early twenty-first century in the southern United States under the name Christian, and I explain their origins and internal contradictions. I purposefully do not choose among them according to any standard of theological truth—that would not be the best service a historian could provide, even when working on contemporary culture. In this respect also I am indebted to my religious studies colleagues who, throughout my scholarly life, have been pluralizing the religions they study when heuristically useful to do so (for example, speaking of plural Buddhisms or Indian religions).

I have also learned along the way that I was writing a fresh take on contemporary southern Christian phenomena when I was asked, "How's your book about the southern church coming?" and I was at pains to explain how much of the action in the so-called Christianities was outside of churches per se. When Sam Hill wrote his landmark *Southern Churches in Crisis* in 1967, there really were white churches in deep division over segregation, and the institutional church really was the major site for religious activity in the South.[9] A half-century later, by way of remarkable contrast, those trained in religious studies can see many other sites of religious activity. Living religion and religion in practice is visible in politics, culture, education, social services, law, voluntary groups, and sexual mores, while churches are less powerful for some and less monolithic for all. So I ask readers to begin to see and hear, in terms of Christianities—and not Christianity—in the South.

Another matter of interest in setting up my journey is: How do I delimit the South? What's in and what's out, and why? In this book, I define the South culturally and religiously rather than politically (on the basis of state lines) or geographically (on the basis of rivers and mountains, for example). The South, I contend, shares religious commonalities that are distinct in varying degrees from other parts of the country. A religious culture definition of the region's states and portions of states leads us to see the South as characterized by an overwhelming Baptist presence—as a place where white and black Baptists of various conventions are the most numerous people of faith in nearly every county, except in southern Louisiana, Mississippi, and Alabama. Alongside the Baptist churches are the Churches of Christ, Methodist, Presbyterian, and Episcopal churches on main streets in towns across the South and the Pentecostal, Apostolic, Holiness, and nondenominational churches on the back streets and the big roads leading out of town. Catholics are present in the South—especially on the coasts—but not in numbers as great as they are in New England or the Midwest. Nor are Lutherans, the mainline Protestants of the Midwest and Pennsylvania, to be found in large concentrations, except in particular counties in the Carolinas.

As I've found, however, one does not have to be a member of a dominant faith group to be affected by its faith practices. Therefore, the South displays a culture of religious practice, where, even in big companies in big cities, people routinely ask coworkers where they go to church and promise to pray for them in their sorrows. In the South, the sound of a gospel choir provides comfort, and it is not uncommon to see people briefly bowed in prayer at a business lunch or even in a fast food restaurant.

So where does this South, religiously and culturally defined, start and stop? The South defined by religious cultures includes all of the states that broke from the Union, and it also follows the Baptists and Churches of Christ into Kentucky and West Virginia. This southern Christian religious cultural influence is lessened in NOVA and in Florida below Orlando, but even in these places, the statewide political environment is shaped by a conservative, Bible-based agenda.

A HARMONY OF CHRISTIANITIES IN THE NOW SOUTH

In the South today, as sometimes happens with a song, not everyone is singing the same tune or words, yet nevertheless the singers think on good warrant that they are singing "the song." In the case of southern religion, the song has a distinctively Christian tune, and each harmonized version makes its claim to be *the* tune, but emphatically what the song is not is a single-note chant or a unison hymn.

I was pointed to the first fundamental feature of southern Christianity—its variegated nature—by my former colleague Erskine Clarke of Columbia Theological Seminary. The author of the National Book Award–winning history *Dwelling Place: A Plantation Epic*, Clark never cared for treatments of southern history, and still less of the contemporary South, that flattened people into caricatures in which all southern religion was basically evangelical and the only question of note was its denominational label and its skin color.[10] Diversity, though not always easy to see, is an old story in southern religion, and so the many varieties that make up today's harmony of Christianities are both linked to the past and, I hope to show, totally remarkable for their proliferation in the present.

The second key feature of this southern harmony is that it is *not* usually a cacophony. Rather, it layers, adds up, builds, and coheres much like the mountain music or blues or gospel or jazz that are all native to the region. This has become only clearer and more striking for me over time as I have worked with a rich array of sources, as I describe below. The overwhelmingly Christian character of formal religious life in the South continues to fund a vocabulary of redemption, sin, sacrifice, a mother's love, and prodigal sons that finds its way into politics, common speech at work, and coaches' pep talks, not to mention country songs. Not many words rhyme with "Christian," but Christian concepts form the rhyming thoughts of southern religious life and culture.

The third and final fundamental aspect of this southern harmony is the capacity of the old forms of southern music—and Christianity—when played together in proximity to generate new forms, new harmonics, new sounds that were not played by any one instrument and yet create a haunting tune that listeners may take up in their minds again and again. Out of the mixture of voices come still other voices and themes. One of the most popular of all biblical quotations in Baptist churches, "There is none righteous, no, not one" (Rom. 3:10 KJV), has over time been shortened in popular usage to "No. Not One," and today it is commonly used to mean, variously, "Quit being a hypocrite," "Love the sinner, hate the sin," or, in some places, "Let's welcome gay and lesbian worshippers since we are all in a fallen state and no human dare judge another's soul." The old hymns and scriptural texts beget new faith and forms.

STUDYING SOUTHERN CHRISTIANITIES UP CLOSE

This book is the fruit of a decade of wide-ranging research. I dived deep into historical archives of many types, from libraries to churches to Civil War sites. I got out into the field, visiting cities and rural areas throughout the South. I interviewed religious leaders, religious practitioners, scholars of religion, and many other people I met along my path. (Sometimes I was fortunate enough to travel and interview people with my wife, Heidi, who provided additional ears and observations. Whenever I slip into "we" in my narrative as I describe an interaction, readers will know that I had this extra assistance at that point.)

Inevitably this book will be limited by where I went, whom I talked with, what I read, and what I missed. I may have missed something that turns out to be important, and I may have picked up on facets of religious life that seem minor now yet will read as prescient in the future. To those who care about representation and interpretation of religion and culture, this book is an invitation to do more such work and not the last word. I came away from my travels and studies with the clear impression that religious music was in the air. Witnessing firsthand the varieties of contemporary southern religiosity, I saw it performed and enacted in so many ways and in so many registers. I therefore invite readers to approach southern religion with their ears open. For instance, the argument in chapter 4 between the Rev. William Barber in North Carolina and former Alabama chief justice Roy Moore over what it means to be Christian, American, and free in the twenty-first century is no mere exercise in discursive reasoning; it is a passionate sing-off between believers who belong putatively to the same faith but who enact that faith in opposing political directions. I am not suggesting that political views are all the same or that they do not matter, of course, but I am suggesting that hearing the diverse musicalities of the religious actors in the following chapters will enable you to hear how southern religious life continues to bind its members to one another—sometimes uncomfortably—despite this accelerating diversity. These tonalities and techniques that political opponents employ along the southern Christian spectrum also indicate the grounds of their disagreements. They use common terms—love of neighbor, justice, God's intentions, family—to mean such different things that at various points the sound threatens to break down into just so much noise, yet it never quite does.

THE OLD WAYS MADE NEW AND INNOVATIONS BEGUN

The three-part structure of this book grew directly out of my findings and observations as I studied Christianity in the South. In Part I, "Rock of Ages Cleft for Me: Southern Traditions Revised," we encounter some of the oldest themes in southern life and Christian practices—hospitality and feeding the hungry, the vexed meanings of the Civil War, the Pentecostal tradition, and the way politics and religion inevitably mix. In each of this part's four chapters there is a twist and sometimes several as we learn that underneath the most characteristically southern Christian practices and traditions, change and reinterpretation is vigorously buzzing. In Part II, "Gulf Coast Disaster: Religion Is Only as Good as What It Does," we spend two chapters traveling between the very different southern contexts of New Orleans and coastal Mississippi as Christians, with the help of many others, recover from Hurricane Katrina. At least in part due to massive government and insurance company failures, the hurricane tested the faith of leaders and people affected by flooding, but the response of religious groups and individuals was unprecedented and still amazes survivors more than a decade later. In Part III, "Brand-New Start: Southern Religious Innovations," we come face to face with four trends no one could have predicted by looking at the southern Christianity of forty years ago. In this section we see how the megachurch movement—an offspring of the prosperity gospel—is affecting long-standing ways southerners worship. We see how Latino worshippers have turned what was once called No Priest Land, U.S.A., into growing Catholic enclaves in the deep South. We see how Christian homeschooling is feeding off the white-flight-derived Christian academies movement of the 1970s. And we see how lesbian, bisexual, gay, and transgender congregations, including evangelical gay congregations, are establishing significant presences in larger southern cities. Together all of these new developments are producing a religious South that is less Baptist, less denominationally connected, more entrepreneurial, and more fragmented. New Christian expressions for LGBT and Hispanic persons in this fragmented setting are offset on the Christian right by prosperity gospel megachurches; we are a long way from church as depicted on *Mayberry R.F.D.* in 1968–71.

My grandmother outlived her son—my father—by eight years, a terribly sad occurrence in any generation. When my grandmother died, just short of her ninety-sixth birthday, I returned to her, and my father's, Appalachian hometown—South Webster, Ohio—to preach at her funeral. Among the mourners were few people from her generation. You do not have many friends your own age left at ninety-five. But imagine the impact on me and the congregation as one man or woman after another introduced him or herself as my father's classmates in the school from which he had been graduated in 1950 in a town to which he never returned except for brief vacations. This is a town where I could walk into a hardware store for the first time in my life and be recognized by the way I looked. One of the great differences between this Appalachian community and the upstate New York village where I once served as a pastor is the almost scary willingness to ask (or assert) who you are and thereby lay a claim on you: "You're Arthur's son, aren't you?" So I am. Sometimes, there's just a declarative: "You're Mildred's grandson." Just as in a scene from a Wendell Berry novel, community is suddenly much more formidable than an individual's plans. This kind of closeness, which has inspired writers from Jean Toomer, William Faulkner, and Flannery O'Connor to Alice Walker, John Grisham, and Bobbie Ann Mason, among many others, generates the deep community cohesion that can fill all the chairs for an elderly woman's funeral.

And so, after a pause here for any who wish to straighten out their Christian groups vocabulary, we begin with hospitality, that southern and Christian virtue that is always both more and less than it seems.

SOME DEFINITIONS TO GET STARTED

A brief guide to terms used freely in this book and in other writing about religion in America may be helpful at this point:

Evangelicals are Protestant Christians who believe in the importance of sharing the gospel with others, because they believe in the centrality of Jesus Christ as Lord and Savior and the Bible as the ultimate authority for revealed truth to human beings.

Fundamentalists are evangelicals who insist that to be a Christian one must accept certain fundamental articles of faith, often including the virgin birth of Jesus, the inerrancy of the Bible, the bodily resurrection and physical return of Christ, and the substitutionary atonement of Christ on the cross for man's sin.

Pentecostals are evangelical Christians who emphasize direct personal experience of God through baptism of the Holy Spirit, just as happened to early Christians in the second chapter of the New Testament book of Acts. Pentecostals practice personal holiness and believe in the continued availability of healing, speaking in tongues, and other gifts of the spirit. When Catholics practice this same spirit-oriented piety they are called "charismatics," based on the Greek word for gift.

Mainline Protestants belong to one of the few national bodies like the United Methodist and Episcopal Church, all of which have evangelical congregations and members (especially in the South) alongside more progressive congregations and members. Southern Baptists are not mainline, but they comprise the largest denomination in the South.

Historically black denominations such as the African Methodist Episcopal (AME), AME Zion, National Baptist, Inc., and Church of God in Christ (COGIC) are strong in the South, both as bodies that make common cause with mainline Protestant denominations on justice issues and in their own right, alongside dozens of smaller black church bodies and independent congregations.

Black congregations are to found in each of the evangelical, fundamentalist, Pentecostal, and nondenominational categories, in addition to the mainline and historically black denominations.

Nondenominational churches are invariably Protestant, practicing as they do the Reformation principles of *Sola Scriptura* and *Sola Fides* (denoting that the only infallible authority is Scripture and that salvation comes only by faith). They may, nevertheless, deny having descended from the movement begun by Martin Luther. These congregations may be evangelical or Pentecostal, but the claim to be nondenominational is at base a rejection of the American denominational system that was strong for two centuries in favor of an autonomous model of the first-century church. These contemporary churches are following a well-worn path established by restorationist movements of the nineteenth century, such as the Disciples of Christ, the Churches of Christ, and the Landmark Baptist movements, all of which in their own ways sought to restore the Christianity to its primitive first-century origins.

PART
ONE

ROCK OF AGES CLEFT FOR ME

Southern Traditions Revised

1

I WAS HUNGRY, AND YOU
GAVE ME SOMETHING TO EAT

Hospitality, Scarcity, and Fear in Southern Christianity

The first I was aware that southern Christianity was different from the midwestern varieties I knew was on summer vacations in my grandparents' small town in Appalachia. Depending on which week we visited there would be a white revival tent outside the Baptist church, behind the Methodist church, or up the street from the Evangelical United Brethren church. If none of these were having a revival, then it was a good bet the Wesleyans were up on the ridge out of town or the Freewill Baptists were farther west on Route 141. I, knowing that surprises were inside tents, asked if we could go. My minister father, who had enough of revivals as a youth and especially knew better than to start going early in his vacation week, was firm in saying, "No." For many people revivalism is the essence of southern Christianity, and historically they have a great deal of evidence on their side. In the first years of the twenty-first century, when nearly every place in the South is air-conditioned, more and more people live in or near cities, and the revival tents are not so ubiquitous as in the 1950s and 1960s, we must search for less obvious signs of regional distinction if the case is to be made for a continuing form of southern Christianity. Since this book is descriptive and analytical in nature, recounting the many ways that Christianity is lived and expressed in the contemporary American South, it would cut against our purpose to argue too strongly that there is an essential southern form of Christianity. We will, after all, encounter people who, though they are in the South and all claim to be Christian, have a hard time accepting those claims from one another. This chapter, therefore, tries to get outside today's fights and ask: Is there anything in the way southern Christianity is usually practiced by all its claimants that would be owned by them as true and, moreover, even seem distinctively true to a neutral observer, say, from San Francisco, California, or Perth, Australia? I know what southerners would like to claim—their hospitality. And in a related vein, I know what most nonsoutherners find most striking—the food in terms of its kind, its flavors, and its abundance.

HOSPITALITY: SHARING AT THE TABLE OF PLENTY

We did not go to any revivals in those summers, but I received several other memorable tastes of southern Christianity. One of them had to do with hospitality expressed through food. The first was that when we arrived, one of my grandmother's neighbors had made a pineapple upside-down cake for our first night's dessert. I remember asking somewhat shyly, "When is Mrs. Morton coming over to eat it with us?" and being surprised to be told that no, she had just made it as a gift to celebrate my father's family's homecoming with his parents. This gift of food to eat with your loved ones without the giver present (a selfless gift, if you will) is one I have run into repeatedly since, but it works by a code with which I was theretofore unfamiliar.

Hospitality is key to the identity of southerners, whether it is expressed at a barbecue, a fish fry, or in dinner on the grounds—one of the most time-honored practices of rural churches. Christians in the South make of hospitality a central virtue, which they again express overwhelmingly through food. There are dishes brought in person to the homes of the sick and bereaved. There are meals made for families that have just had a new child, so the family's cook, presumably the mother, will not have to worry about putting a meal on the table for a time. And charity toward less fortunate members of the community is also expressed through food—in full meals made on particular nights for mass feedings, in support for soup kitchens and drop-in ministries, and sometimes in other kinds of hospitality like a warm place to spend the night on a cot in the church fellowship hall.

Practices of sharing and the rules for how, when, and why a people share or withhold forms of hospitality are as ancient as civilization. The Bible itself is rich with examples of hospitality, and these are some but not all the sources of southern Christian practice. In understanding what characterizes southern Christian practice, the other important place to start is with the meaning and importance of community. In their introduction to southern culture, John Beck, Wendy Frandsen, and Aaron Randall stress the long, isolated importance of the agrarian family (backed by the church) in shaping southern ways of life. They write that in "modern post-industrial societies, a host of institutions—schools and colleges, families, the mass media, government agencies, churches, groups like the Boy Scouts and the Kiwanis—define and transmit the culture. In the agrarian society that was the South for so long, it was the family that did this with little competition from any other institution save the church. Until the twentieth century, the South was mostly rural with few cities, and many southerners lived on farms."[1] Of course the same could be said about large portions of the Midwest, too, but for their similarities those communities are not southern in character. David Hackett Fischer has argued convincingly that the borderlands Scots-Irish and southern English settlers who predominated in southern white settlement account for much of the region's attitude toward the land, self-reliance, and violence.[2] Add to these immigrants the forced African migrants of the slave trade, and most of the ancestors of the southern populace down to late in the twentieth century are accounted for. Even when southerners began to express themselves in groups larger than the family, the analogy of the family remained powerful. People talk about their "church families," about the "Davidson family" or the "Spelman family" (about colleges) and from old mill and brick towns of the last century to privately held corporations like Chick-fil-A today, the model of owner as patriarch prevails. Chick-fil-A's Truett Cathy was famous for doing business only six days a week, saying, "It's a silent witness to the Lord when people go into shopping malls, and everyone is bustling, and you see that Chick-fil-A is closed."[3] Southern Christians tend to admire that witness, even as they go find another place open to eat on Sundays. Dan Cathy, the founder's son, took the father-knows-best moralism further by spending millions of dollars to stop same-sex marriage from becoming law and voicing his belief that, "as it relates to society in general, I think we are inviting God's judgment on our nation when we shake our fist at him and say, 'We know better than you as to what constitutes a marriage.'"[4] Community means belonging, and belonging begets standards for belonging, the genesis of southern Christian culture's much-remarked moralistic quality. So because you belong, you will get a meal when you are sick, and you will get told how to live your life. It is all a package.

Dan Cathy's vision of God-centered society sounds a lot like the historian John Boles's memories of growing up in the rural South the 1950s:

> I took absolutely for granted the cultural primacy of religion (meaning, of course, evangelical Protestantism). Every person I was taught to respect was a church member. School opened each morning with prayer, football games and the summer rodeo began with prayer, and gatherings from a family reunion to a Rotary Club lunch could not begin without prayer. Church services were held Sunday morning and evening, with Wednesday night prayer services. Every summer there was a scheduled week-long revival, with services each night. Every sermon I heard was structured to come to an emotional climax pressing sinners to convert, and we all waited—with the choir singing softly—as the preacher offered the altar call.[5]

Sixty years later, the South has grown and diversified, but religion is still not a solely private matter but one freely shared with neighbors, including non-believers and people of other faiths. The Rotary Club in nearly every city of any size will include members of the Jewish faith, but that does not stop the weekly invocation from usually ending "in Jesus' name, Amen." Publicly enacted religion at football games or at crowded restaurants are ubiquitous in the South. The contemporary South encompasses nearly eight million people, two time zones, and at least a dozen states, but kinship as a model of social relations continues to be strong, particularly within denominational families. And some denominational families are stronger in the South than others. The region contains, by the Pew Forum's count, just 37 percent of the nation's population but 49 percent of its evangelicals and 62 percent of its historically black affiliated Christians, while still containing 37 percent of the country's mainline Protestants.[6] Those who move from another region and perceive that religion is stronger in the South and decidedly Christian are on to something. With Christian community being built on the model of extended family, when we moved to Atlanta in 1993, I had to adjust to the southern branch of Presbyterianism and its unfamiliar, oft-repeated question, "Who are your people?" with its multiple valences. I quickly learned that its purpose is to figure out how the questioner and the questioned might be related—by blood, by school, by having gone to the same church at different times, by knowing someone, anyone, in common. Moreover, the newcomer who finds a bridge is no longer a stranger but a kind of kin. The person asking the question is proffering a deep kind of enduring hospitality—conditionally. The Yankee who finds the question strange will never quite fit in. This networking also works in the third person: "Tell me who she is." "Well, she is the widow of a minister from up north [where does not matter] but her first husband was the pastor of First Church, Little Rock, and you probably know her daughter Sarah Jane, who teaches nursery school here weekdays, even though she goes to Edgefield Methodist Church." (If the entire world were southern church people, Facebook would have been unnecessary.)

In addition to the strong sense of quasi-rural interdependence on close kinship networks, one does not spend much time in southern churches—high church, low church, black church, white church, Episcopal, Pentecostal, Baptist—before one picks up the joy of fellowship associated with food. There is joy in the feast itself, of there being new and more kinds of foods than one has at home. There is joy in the abundance of food, and one encounters a kind of guilt-free food zone. Church food has no calorie labeling but often plenty of sugar, salt, and fat. The culinary instructor and cookbook author Kendra Bailey Morris featured "An Ode to My Southern Baptist Food Roots" on her cooking blog in 2010 in which she fondly remembered her dad as a deacon in the church and her mom as a Sunday school teacher, which meant that Sunday was an all-day affair with lots of church on Sunday, casseroles, sweet tea, and kale cooked in fatback at midday, and then back for more church until well after eight o'clock Wednesday evening brought an institution familiar to countless southerners, then and now: "Later in the week there was Wednesday night church, which was prefaced by Wednesday night supper, an evening where the church ladies took over the kitchen, whipping up every comfort food imaginable. From fried chicken with white gravy and biscuits to meat sauce doused spaghetti, the hardworking ladies of our church created an array of decadent concoctions that culminated with a spread of homemade cakes and pies divine enough to make the angels weep."[7]

If that sounds like it might be too much of a good thing, particularly on a regular basis, it was—given how many of the "salads" were actually desserts in disguise, with marshmallows, coconut, Jell-O, maraschino cherries, and Cool Whip figuring prominently as common ingredients. But as Morris explains, "As true Southern Baptists, there isn't a whole lot we're allowed to do. Booze is off limits as is smoking, fornicating, non-secular music, even dancing in some instances, but there's one action that is completely acceptable—eating, and we do a heck of a lot of it, often in large, self-indulgent quantities."[8] Morris has her tongue planted in her cheek as she offers this explanation (she proceeds to give a "Church Lady" recipe herself). Nevertheless, there is truth in the idea that food gets a pass where so many other behaviors stand to strict scrutiny or disapprobation in southern church culture. This, too, may be changing.

In the fall 2016 issue of *SBC Life, the Journal of the Southern Baptist Convention*, Wendy Ashley took up the issue of "obesity in the body of Christ." While commenting that "you could walk into almost any Southern Baptist church in America and enjoy doughnuts and coffee before Sunday School" and potlucks and ice cream socials at other times, she noted ruefully that Purdue University researchers had found that churchgoers were more overweight than the general population and that Baptists had "the distinction of being the most overweight religious group in the study." Ashley attacked the problem as one of sin—that of gluttony, revealing a failure to walk in the light of God, poor stewardship of the body, and destruction of the temple of God.[9] So much for guilt-free church food indulgence. Yet perhaps there are even more factors at play than even those Ashley enumerates.

Kentucky-born southern journalist John Egerton was one of the founders of the Southern Foodways Alliance. In 1999, he convened a two-day meeting of fifty individuals to begin a nonprofit dedicated to documenting, celebrating, and exploring the diverse food cultures of the American South. In his letter calling people to the founding meeting, Egerton wrote: "The time has come for all of us—traditional and nouvelle cooks and diners, upscale and down-home devotees, meat-eaters and vegetarians, drinkers and abstainers, growers and processors, scholars and foodlorists, gourmands and the health-conscious, women and men, blacks and whites and other identity groups, one and all—to sit down and break bread together around one great Southern table."[10] Soon legendary southern food preservationists and advocates were involved with the organization—Edna Lewis, Scott Peacock, Jeanne Voltz—and a complex mission began to evolve. The alliance studies the history and variants of southern cuisine and promotes fresh food use, but it also has an activist dimension working against hunger and poor nutrition. This should not be surprising. Egerton himself believed that southern cuisine had been developed largely by people who were unlettered and "desperate to tease flavor from substandard meat and other ingredients." In his own writing about cooking, he advised using "recipes as guides, not instructions, adjusting proportions to their own tastes."[11] Long before Egerton even learned as an adult to cook the dishes he loved from his wife, however, he was interested in racial and economic justice. His most famous book, *Speak Now against the Day*, is an account of the brave souls in the generation before the civil rights movement who resisted segregation in the 1930s and 1940s.[12] One of the outcomes of his racial justice research, was his awareness that southerners across the lines of race and position cooked, ate, and loved the same food. He began writing more about southern food and the stories surrounding the cuisine.[13] Today the Southern Foodways Alliance is based in Mississippi, and each year it issues an award in Egerton's name, honoring activists who promote social justice in the food industry.

The scarcity that Egerton thought propelled southern cooking has additional consequences, however. It produces a long cultural memory of a time when there was not enough to eat; it is a memory that remains in the experience of too many living southerners. Some of these consequences are as follows. First, although southerners will give to those they know, they hate being forced to help others, especially those beyond their gaze. This explains why income taxes and property taxes are unpopular in the South, while regulation and unionization are seen as measures of coercion, and not acts of community self-government. Second, the theory that minimal government will promote the activity of charitable neighbors doing the right thing is often exaggerated. People who suffer, it is believed, down deep, have brought it on themselves in some way, through sloth, criminality, or lust, which Christian people just do not do. On the other hand, there is the possibility of decent people experiencing genuine misfortune, and for them, the deserving unfortunates, it is believed that charity exists. And third, as southern states have become more populous and diverse, the social horizons of Christians have not extended as far as their state's social realities extend.

Of course, the gap between a confidence in Christian charity and hospitality and the real needs of society is not twenty-first-century news. Race and class divisions even among people of ostensibly the same denominational brands of Christianity is an old story. And so, keeping the emphasis on food, shelter, and hospitality, we examine what some contemporary southern Christians are doing under conditions of insufficiency.

SCARCITY: THE ENDURING SOUTHERN PROBLEMATIC

Food is also important to the moral compass of southern Christians who are overwhelmingly more biblical than ritual in their theological orientation. Many even commonly call themselves Matthew 25 Christians, which means that—Protestant or Catholic—they would like to be judged before the throne of glory based on whether they fulfilled Jesus' command to care for the hungry, the homeless, the prisoner, the sick, and the naked:

> When the Son of Man comes in his glory, and all the angels with him, then he will sit on the throne of his glory. All the nations will be gathered before him, and he will separate people one from another as a shepherd separates the sheep from the goats, and he will put the sheep at his right hand and the goats at the left. Then the king will say to those at his right hand, "Come, you that are blessed by my Father, inherit the kingdom prepared for you from the foundation of the world; for I was hungry and you gave me food, I was thirsty and you gave me something to drink, I was a stranger and you welcomed me, I was naked and you gave me clothing, I was sick and you took care of me, I was in prison and you visited me." (Matt. 25: 31–36, NSRV)

It may be surprising, then, with all of the emphasis on church food and on expressing love through food, that the South—America's most Christian region, where 76 percent are churched in Christian houses of worship and 62 percent tell the Pew Forum on Religion and Public Life that religion is very important in their lives—is also the region where people experience the greatest levels of food insecurity.[14]

According to Feeding America, a nationwide network of member food banks, forty-eight million people in America are food insecure, as defined by using the U.S. Department of Agriculture's measures of lack of access, at times, to enough food for an active, healthy life for all household members and times of uncertain availability of nutritionally adequate food. The map that Feeding America generates using 2014 income data and self-reported food shortage data shows a preponderance of the nation's food insecurity in rural areas, with all rural portions of the southern states and Appalachian regions demonstrating food insecurity. The Mississippi Delta's large second congressional district took the prize for having the greatest food insecurity in the nation in 2014, with 29.9 percent of its population living below the Department of Agriculture's SNAP (Supplemental Nutrition Assistance Program) threshold of 130 percent above the poverty line. Some congressional districts in North Carolina, Georgia, Tennessee, and South Carolina trail closely behind in this dubious distinction.[15] The issue is not rural life, however: the overwhelmingly rural state of North Dakota has the least food insecurity. No, other things make southern hunger worse, most of them indices of poverty—lack of health care, poor educational outcomes, and low wages.

The quality of the South's prevailing cultural Christianity as a moral stance is revealed when it will at one moment push to put "In God We Trust" on license plates and in the next deem the expansion of Medicaid as an assault on the God-given system of free enterprise.[16] The downside of an emphasis on personal morality borrowed from the 1950s is that it continues to support a southern social Christianity that can be personally generous while being politically conservative and deeply suspicious of all systemic solutions for social ills. The irony could not be stronger: the region with the highest proportion of Christians in the United States, where more people personally feel obligated to visit prisons as a religious duty, is also the region with the highest rate of incarceration and use of the death penalty.[17] Nor does this high incarceration rate and use of the death penalty act as a moral object lesson deterrent: the states from Virginia to Florida to Texas and Louisiana also feature the highest murder rates in the country. "Vengeance is mine," says the Lord in the Bible (Deut. 32:35) that people carry to church on Sundays. Yet on weekdays they and their elected representatives—who are themselves overwhelmingly Christian—have created a vengeful system that begets further violence and vengeance. The sick may easily be offered a hot dish, but Medicaid was not expanded under the terms of the Affordable Care Act (Obamacare) in this region, and even the temporary housing of homeless people on church property can be problematic.[18]

At the beginning of the Donald Trump presidency in the winter of 2017, twenty-nine states had higher minimum wages than the federal minimum wage. Five southern states had no minimum wage: Alabama, Louisiana, Mississippi, South Carolina, and Tennessee. Georgia's state minimum wage, $5.15 per hour, was lower than the federal minimum wage. Only Florida, with its $8.10 minimum wage, Arkansas ($8.50), and West Virginia ($8.75), exceeded the federal minimum wage.[19] These lower-than-federal minimum wages are paid in select employment situations that do not fall under federal wage and hour guidelines, but the absence of minimum wages in Deep South states also reflects a mind-set that only the person paying the wage is in a position to determine how little or much an employee's work is worth. No wonder that so many working poor find themselves resorting to food banks in the South. The results of such a weak safety net are predictable, but some southern Christians hope for something more. They distinguish themselves across an ideological and theological spectrum of advocates grappling with human want in Jesus' name. These activists and caretakers distinguish the contemporary Christianity of the South as much as do the Wednesday night suppers that still feature more strongly in the Bible Belt than anywhere else in America.

Hospitality is a virtue that reflects well on the Christian decency of the giver. Yet it scales up poorly as an answer to systemic ills of societies and even of local communities. Although it is virtuous to give, those in need cannot compel hospitality from others. Moreover, assistance is most often extended to those in need who are most like the giver; thus my sister-in-law with cancer gets dinner for her family for three months from my church more readily than does the hungry family in the projects whom I do not know. This is not to denigrate the charity that Christians display—particularly to those within their circles of daily life. It is, however, to point out the easy fallacy that so often plagues southern lawmakers who believe that what works at their churches is the answer to what's wrong in their states. If people cannot get medical care, why not a free church health clinic? If they are hungry, why not go to a faith-based food bank?[20]

Hunger has motivated some of the most creative Christian activism in the South, a place that is constantly rediscovering its agrarian roots, it seems. One of the more established groups, the Society of St. Andrew, is a gleaning ministry that began in the late 1970s and early 1980s when three United Methodist ministers and their families, concerned about hunger and simplicity, felt called to live a simple life and help others do something about hunger. Sometime later, after a farmer asked them asked about the food waste they had described in a presentation at a local church, the ministry struck a partnership with food producers that led to one of its longest lasting practices—gleaning sweet potatoes. In June 1983 the first tractor-trailer load of salvaged sweet potatoes was delivered to the Central Virginia Food Bank in Richmond. Since then the practice of gleaning all kinds of food good enough to eat—but not pretty enough to sell—has spread as a Christian ecumenical practice beyond the Methodist fold in Virginia. The Society of St. Andrew has regional offices coordinating gleaning in Alabama, Arkansas, Florida, Georgia, Mississippi, North Carolina, South Carolina, Tennessee, and Virginia. The amount of fruit and vegetables gleaned now exceeds seven hundred million pounds. My back and my wife's van have been donated on occasion to get eight hundred pounds of fresh food into smaller bags and into urban food deserts where they can do the most good. As you might expect

for an organization begun by preachers, however, it is the Christian education in food justice and sharing our God-given abundance that is especially
salient to the mission. The society runs a summer camp for youth to get the
message across and offers the Harvest of Hope, an ecumenical study, worship, and mission retreat program for all ages, to the same effect.[21]

If the Society of St. Andrew has a decidedly mainline cast to its mission,
Feed America First feels more patriotic—even though it, too, is a faith-based
organization. Based out of Murfreesboro, Tennessee, it describes its mission
as simply "to provide food to those who feed the hungry." The organization
does not take food out of fields so much as off the hands of manufacturers,
retailers, and distributors. With the help of hundreds of volunteers every
month, these large-scale food donations are divided and send out to about
two hundred partner agencies (mostly food pantries and shelters) throughout Tennessee, Alabama, Mississippi, and Kentucky. The Murfreesboro area
is home to shipping and logistics, and Feed America First has turned these
resources to the service of their ministry. Feed America First's website is
red, white, and blue, and its fundraisers—Dancing with the Nashville Stars
and Drive Out Hunger—are favorites with the country music crowd. The
appeal goes deeper than the color scheme, for the organization founded by
Tom Henry and the late Don Herbert in 2000 was aimed squarely at allevi-
ating hunger in rural America. How, they wondered, "in the US, the rich-
est country in world history, how could we have neighbors (and their kids)
going without food?" Henry's focus is on the geographical areas where other
agencies are less strong:

> We at Feed America First focus upon our neighbors in need who
> live in small towns and rural areas, that portion of the 38,000,000
> Americans at risk of missing meals while they pay for rent, utilities,
> or medicine. Our partner agencies are the citizens who want to help
> their neighbors by operating church pantries, children's homes, and
> shelters for the abused, homeless, or recovering. They know their
> neighbors, and if Feed America First provides them more food, they
> touch more lives. After all, as I have been told, a loaf of bread given
> with love by a neighbor has a powerful accountability attached.[22]

The evangelical heart at the center of Feed America First is evident from its
monthly newsletters, which share news of generous gifts, but always lead
with testimony from people whose lives have been affected by the food
shared in one of the partner agencies. It is a constant reminder of how many

children know hunger to read of one exclaiming, "Oh, we'll have food to-night!" at a shelter. Likewise, the personal accounts of elderly and disabled people trying to live on extremely limited incomes put a face on the query "Who is my neighbor?"[23] Lay exhortation is alive and well as a form of religious communication.

The South as a region is to home to a remarkable array of domestic not-for-profits and international human service nongovernmental organizations. CARE, Habitat for Humanity, and the Carter Center are based in Atlanta, and Heifer International makes its home in Little Rock. Giving to big charities is part of what it means to be Christian for many, but equally constitutive of the hospitality of caring is what you do personally for others who are sick (bring food yourself) or lack clothing or shoes (make donations) or are homeless (build a Habitat for Humanity house) or in prison (participate in prison ministries and, more recently, reentry ministries). As Jesus said, "I was hungry and you gave me food. . . . I was in prison and you visited me" (Matt. 25:35–37, NSRV). Southern Christians like direct charity, but to this day there is a gulf between visiting prisoners and questioning the incarceration industrial complex.

LOVE AND RESISTANCE

If hospitality is traditional to southern Christianity, some people take it even farther than others in the Now South. Here we will examine where the line between hospitality and social activism gets set and transgressed, where the courage of some people's Christian convictions causes them to go a second mile either in self-sacrifice or in shaming their neighbors and leaders to do a little more. It is here that we find a creative tension between charity and justice that some want to explore with their lives. Being a Matthew 25 Christian has motivated hunger activists and medical personnel to take up new missions to change social realities in their neighborhoods and beyond. We also encounter southern Christian activists who are not content to stay within the circumscribed polite boundaries of hospitality when their interpretation of Matthew 25 seems to call for something more radical.

When I arrived in Nashville, Tennessee, in the year 2000 and began traveling among churches, I kept encountering the claim, "We participate in Room In The Inn," at churches of all sorts—Catholic, Methodist, Churches of Christ, Baptist, Presbyterian, Nazarene, Episcopal, Disciples of Christ, Adventist, African Methodist Episcopal, Lutheran. In 1985, Father Charles

Strobel, pastor of Holy Name Catholic Church, noticed people asleep in their cars in the church parking lot as he looked out from his bedroom window. It was below freezing, and he felt compelled to do something. "I went down and invited everyone to spend the night in the cafeteria." He did not think long about it because he knew deep down that if he did, he would find a way to talk himself out of it. There were consequences to such a decision, because the choice was never going to be about just one night. "What would the parishioners say? Or the bishop? Or the neighbors?" As Charlie tells the story now, "Like Scarlett O'Hara, I found myself saying, 'I'll worry about that tomorrow.'" He invited them to spend the night, and they stayed the winter. Within a week people were moved to pitch in and help with cots and food, and the next year a shelter named—you guessed it—Matthew 25 was born. The shelter was geared toward helping end homelessness, but hundreds were still left out in the cold, and that's where other churches have come in. From four congregations in December 1986 to thirty-one congregations by the end of that winter to more than 190 congregations today, Room In The Inn has grown as a program that insists on some basic commitments. Congregations provide volunteers to pick up twelve to fifteen homeless men, women, or families, provide a meal, and a warm, safe place to spend the night in comfort. The congregations and their volunteers understand that they are neither trying to convert people nor on their way to building a great shelter downtown; rather, they are committing to a relationship of hospitality for an evening. The gulf between people experiencing homelessness and those with ordinary American lives can seem vast when viewed through moving car windows. It can even remain so across a serving table. But when church hosts and their evening guests sit down at the same table for a meal, experiences of common humanity are available to all.[24]

Out of nearly thirty-one years of the enduring practice of this lifesaving winter hospitality, the financial and staffing basis for a more transformative approach to improving the lives of homeless individuals in finding paths out of homelessness, mental illness, and addiction was developed in another Strobel invention, the Campus for Human Development. The campus is headquarters for connecting with community partners and a platform for the more than three thousand classes equaling more than forty-four thousand instructional hours annually that Room In The Inn offers, covering subjects ranging from spirituality to GED preparation.[25] As for Room In The Inn, much like other good news, the story has traveled to other cities, inspiring churches in Clarksville, Murfreesboro, Memphis, and Chattanooga,

Tennessee, and Charlotte, North Carolina, to adopt the program in their communities.

Pete Gathje is an activist who earns his living as a Christian ethics professor at Memphis Theological Seminary and is one of the founding leaders of an entirely volunteer Christianity community of solidarity called Manna House in the Madison Heights neighborhood of midtown Memphis. It is a place of welcome for homeless persons and others in need. The community provides hospitality to these neighbors, and you can think of Manna as a living room for people from the streets.

When I sat down with him in 2014 to talk about his work at Manna House, Gathje had been back in the South, this time in Memphis, for sixteen years. Gathje described himself as "really happy to be back in the South." He said he loved Atlanta and loved Memphis and would never want to move out of the South. I asked him why. He said, "Part of the reason is the Bible. The South is a place where people still take the Bible seriously, even if it gets wackily interpreted sometimes. Or oftentimes. But still it's a book with authority that we can organize conversations around, and that was not the case in Kalamazoo, Michigan." (After attending Emory University, Gathje was a faculty member teaching ethics at Kalamazoo College.) In the South people take religion seriously enough that it is disputed, rather than being part of the landscape, Gathje finds. This is unlike the Midwest of his Rochester, Minnesota, upbringing, where religion was part of the uncontested nice background to the culture. Instead, in the South religion is involved with meaningful disputes. We talked about a live example where the Bible was changing facts on the ground. When I visited Gathje, Room In The Inn was expanding in Memphis. Trinity United Methodist wanted to join the program and offer winter evening meals and shelter to homeless people. A Shelby County ordinance, however, mandated that churches wishing to host overnight guests had to sit on at least five acres of property—much more than Trinity possessed. The church decided to go ahead. "We are going to offer hospitality to people from the streets. We don't care what the code is," Gathje reported. "It has been this really fascinating discussion that has erupted [as a result] about the relationship between church and state, property values, and hospitality for the poor, and people are claiming biblical justification on one side or the other. That's not the kind of argument you would get in the North." And for Gathje, there was something more: "There's the strong passion that we are being Christian disciples by offering hospitality.

It's not just a nice humanitarian gesture. I like that."[26] (And others did as well—Room In The Inn Memphis grew to twenty-five participating congregations in the 2016–17 season.)[27]

Gathje got converted, if you will, to this way of doing the Christian life during his graduate school days at the Open Door Community in Atlanta, an ecumenical Protestant community that was founded on the principles of Dorothy Day's Catholic Worker movement's radical solidarity with the poor. One difference between what Gathje had previously experienced, or even read about was the Reverend Ed Loring's fiery preaching that the mostly lay community then tried to live out through voluntary poverty, feeding the homeless, sheltering the mentally ill as neighbors, ministering to death-row prisoners, and advocating the end of the death penalty. It was not that Gathje was new to Christianity or communal life. He had been a Benedictine monk for three years previously. Yet, as he said, "I had never been in religious services that were emotional; it had always been a very head religion, a very rational Christianity." At the Open Door the passion for living the Good News was total. He remembers, "Here was a group that was really living [voluntary] poverty and simplicity of life. The monastery was sedate compared to that." Gathje got to see race and class in the South up close at the Open Door. He saw how the African American churches were opening themselves up for the Butler Street Breakfast for three hundred men, while white affluent churches were supportive at a distance. Across all of it, black or white, the Christians and churches connected to one another through the Open Door were all more committed to the authority of the Bible and more enthusiastic and emotive about their religious faith.

Reflecting on southern Christianity and its possibilities for transformation, Gathje said, "I love the passion around the Bible. I love the emotional involvement of the heart, though I wish it would be more thoughtful and self-reflective sometimes, but I do love that the Spirit moves in southern Christianity, that it is enlivening and is dangerous in the way that people's lives actually can get changed." I asked whether he saw any downsides. What was the worst part of southern religion? He answered quickly and forcefully, "I hate blood atonement. It is the justification for the death penalty and for all sorts of violence, and I think it is a ridiculous way to think about God and about the work and life and death and resurrection of Jesus." Then Gathje said something that chilled my spine. "I've been involved with work against the death penalty," he began. "And anytime I'm engaged with conservative Christians, blood atonement comes in as well as people say, 'If it is good enough for Jesus, it should be good enough for that S.O.B.'" The problem is that instead of being the death to end all deaths, Christ's sacrifice justifies more death. People keep saying that somebody always must pay the price.

There are a number of so-called union and refuge missions throughout the South built on other models than solidarity, where the food and shelter is given as an incentive for one's conversion. If you are poor, an addict, or living on the street, it is because you have not accepted Jesus Christ as your Lord and Savior, and there is a simple plan to remedy that. Accept Christ and your world will change; but with no Christ, you will have no peace. I asked Gathje what the Manna House theology is. "God stands with, identifies with, and even becomes those who are suffering and vulnerable on the streets," he said. "So we take Matthew 25:31 and follow it pretty literally—Jesus wasn't kidding. We aren't there to save people; it is our salvation that is at stake in our greeting and offering of hospitality to them." Not all southern contemporary Christianity, therefore, is premised on the sawdust trail to conversion. Manna House aims at something more communal and more eschatological. The volunteers are, in Gathje's words, "representing in some respects the reign of God where people of all sorts of different backgrounds are gathered around a common space, a common table, and we share our lives together in a way that is mutually beneficial." If that sounds like a vision of the ideal church, that is what they aim for, insofar as it is an expression of church and they have buried people and (more rarely) married people. But it is not like many other churches in appearance or membership.

Manna House itself is a low-slung red-brick house on a large lot. It is of perfectly vernacular architecture for Memphis of somewhat shabby, postwar construction, though with a newer black roof. Inside is what makes for the difference. When guests (and homeless people are always referred to as "guests," that is where the hospitality begins) enter and come up for a cup of coffee they are handed a cup of coffee in a real ceramic mug. By a person who greets them. That matters. The Styrofoam cups of coffee set out on trays, so common in refuge missions, are nowhere to be found. Treating people as guests is intrinsic to everything that goes on at Manna House. That also means that there is a lot of laundry that Gathje and other volunteers do to help their guests get clean—not only their bodies on shower days (Mondays and Thursdays for men, Tuesdays for women) but also other care for their persons. Shoes need to be replaced, because shoes are transportation for the homeless women and men who visit Manna. Clothes are cleaned or replaced when worn beyond use. There is no glamour in this form of community, but there is fulfillment. And for a number of guests there is a way out of a street life that isn't working. It comes through love and patience. Yet Manna is not by its own lights a social service agency but a community that opens and closes with prayers, offers time for reflection and fellowship. Its model even on the third Thursday foot clinic is none other than the community of Jesus' disciples who had their own feet attended to.[28]

Manna House is just one respite community of hospitality in a southern city, but it exemplifies a pattern of creative resistance to forms of death dealing found elsewhere in society, even replicated in some faith-based ministries. Where society keeps homeless people relentlessly on the move, Manna invites guests to rest and relate. Manna also sometimes inspires the agents of the powers that be to disobey their orders in favor of their own Christian consciences. Manna's reputation as a community that cares for lost souls is such that when the word went out that local police were about to conduct a sweep to pick up disorderly and disturbing persons (disturbing to the larger community), some police brought such persons to Manna instead of the police station out of their own compassion and the conviction that jail was not in these homeless individuals' best interests. One ventures to believe that those these police, too, are part of the passionate argument that is Christianity in the contemporary South.

The holy dissatisfaction with "things as they are" has long driven faithful people to do impressive acts of service. Taking care of the homeless, the sick, the orphaned, and the hungry is such a clear gospel mandate that one does not have to look far in the South to see people starting ministries. Even before the Great Depression there were free clinics for the poor run out of churches with physician members volunteering their services.[29] The Nashville metropolitan area of 1.8 million people has no fewer than seven large faith-based medical clinics serving adults among the working poor who have no insurance even after passage of the Affordable Care Act and those who cannot afford their copays and deductibles. Others work with immigrants—documented and undocumented—and feature a wide range of volunteer translators, and dental clinics provide a place for Christian dentists to volunteer their services to poor and indigent patients. Of the seven faith-based clinics, only Mercy Children's Clinic in Franklin has received significant reimbursement from governmental sources because their patient base of children is assisted by CHIP (Children's Health Insurance Program), which was expanded separately from the Medicaid expansion the Tennessee state government took a pass on. Still, the faithful determination to better the plight of the poor and uninsured by healthcare professionals, and by other people of faith to support their efforts, stands in stark contrast to the policies that perpetuate the problem of lack of access to affordable care.[30] These kinds of collaborations exist throughout the South, such as in the Midlands area of South Carolina (Columbia, Chapin, and even over to Edisto Island on the coast), where the Good Samaritan Clinic is supported by mainline Protestant churches, Catholics, black, white, and Hispanic Baptists, and health care organizations, all to reach underserved and uninsured persons in a culturally competent manner. Services include a wide range of medical, dental, and health education services that do not dance around HIV/AIDS, diabetes, obesity, hypertension, and heart disease. The Good Samaritan Clinic's motto is "Showing God's love by providing help and healing to those in need." The list of services provided, the explicit emphasis on helping Hispanic patients, and even the recently added classes for those seeking to become citizens demonstrate the clinic's targeted outreach. Like many other faith-based clinics, the Good Samaritan Clinic is running an alternative program to what South Carolinians have managed to conceive and support in the state and private sectors.[31]

For the better part of twenty-five years, the residents of Nashville have delighted in their city's growth and prosperity. And then between themselves they quietly confide, "As long as it doesn't become another Atlanta," by which they mean to denote Atlanta's legendary traffic problems. There are other problems they could be thinking about. Raleigh, Charlotte, and Greensboro, North Carolina, and piedmont and coastal South Carolina have all experienced rapid growth in recent decades. In places like Nashville where urban core rebuilding is especially strong, the displacement of poor people's housing and the criminalization of homeless people's coping techniques have been especially pronounced (much as was, and is, the case in Atlanta from the run-up to the 1996 Olympics onward). In Nashville, the alternative to cheap urban housing for many, especially homeless couples and people with pets, before the catastrophic flood of 2010, was a tent city near downtown along the banks of the Cumberland River. I first became interested in the plight of these residents when students in my divinity school began to collect warm winter clothes and dog and cat food for these refugees of the building boom.

Students and their passions come and go, but Lindsey and Andrew Krinks and their colleague in the work, Ingrid McIntyre, became even more deeply committed. Andrew went on to help found and edit the *Contributor*, a newspaper that gives homeless persons both a voice and a means to earn income through sales of its issues. Lindsey and Ingrid founded Open Table, a support and advocacy ministry that has in mind ending homelessness in Nashville. Both women are ordained ministers, with Ingrid functioning as the executive director and networker with all the powers and principalities in the city that care about solving homelessness and those that should. After being educated at Boston University's School of Theology, she worked in the United Methodist hierarchy in Nashville to develop both piety and patience for her work. Lindsey for her part works in homeless outreach, housing advocacy, community organizing, street chaplaincy, and education; she describes herself as dedicated to "journeying with those who are marginalized, both on and off the streets." Ingrid and Lindsey explain how they got into this work: "At its prime, just before the flood in May 2010, about 140 people (along with over a dozen cats and dogs) called Tent City home. When the flood hit, we evacuated the residents and their pets to the Red Cross Shelter at Lipscomb University and promised them that we would not abandon them. In the midst of the post-flood chaos, we didn't grasp the gravity of that promise nor did we foresee the ways it would change our lives."[32] When the immediate crisis was over, the city did not come through with housing, so it was back to tents on 124 acres donated by an automobile dealer. Then the city caved to pressure from the tent-dwellers' new neighbors, saying—literally—not in my backyard. A church pitched in the use of its parsonage as housing for some. And the volunteers kept going. They took enough time off from their eighty-hour workweeks to found a 501(c)(3) in June 2011. McIntyre explains the name. "When people ask about the name 'Open Table,'" says McIntyre, "they ask if it's about a 'food thing.' I tell them that we're all motivated by our faith and that to us, Open Table means a place where everyone is welcome. The table is never too full."[33]

And what does it mean to be a street chaplain? Krinks writes in her spiritual blog, Dry Bones Rattling, "I'm a street chaplain and homeless outreach worker with Open Table Nashville (OTN). When I'm out on the streets, I carry my medic bag along with housing applications, anointing oil, blankets, gloves, and socks. At OTN, we tend wounds, share burdens, help people access housing, build community, and listen for hope. But all these things are not enough—we also work to disrupt cycles of poverty and oppression." Then she quotes one of her favorite Christian theologians, Dietrich Bonhoeffer: "We are not to simply bandage the wounds of victims beneath the wheels of injustice. We are to drive a spoke into the wheel itself."[34]

Open Table Nashville ministers to the homeless in sickness and in health and is working to bring solutions to the problem, including a village of "tiny houses," affordable microhouses that provide the community of the old Tent City, but with healthy conditions and the city's blessing. In the meantime, they can be fierce opponents of officialdom when developers and politicians regard their people as problems. Underneath the good that is done for others, Open Table is radically looking to change the world. In a talk given at First Unitarian Universalist's "MLK Day: State of the Dream" event in 2016, Krinks explained why she stopped, in her words, serving the poor:

> I stopped serving the poor because what is needed is not service but solidarity. What is needed is not charity, it's change. Concrete, systemic change. I stopped serving the poor because "the poor" are not projects to manage or problems to solve . . . they are brothers and sisters—siblings—to love and journey with and struggle alongside. They are my friends and coliberators.
>
> In his last speech to the Southern Leadership Council in 1967, Martin Luther King said that models of service were simply not enough. He said that we have to ask bigger questions about the whole society. "We are called upon to help the discouraged beggars in life's marketplace," said King. "But one day we must come to see that an edifice which produces beggars needs restructuring."[35]

Hospitality is alive and well in contemporary Christianity in the American South. Nevertheless, its practice runs a wide gamut from the merely cordial welcome of good manners to forceful resistance to all those who would turn away those who bear Christ's likeness. Some people take their religion very seriously here in the South.

THE REGION WITH THE SOUL OF A CHURCH

In a 1922 essay entitled "What Is America?," G. K. Chesterton wrote about being irritated and then amused by the questions he was asked when he applied for admission to the United States. His memorable conclusion was that "America is the only nation in the world that is founded on a creed. That creed is set forth with dogmatic and even theological lucidity in The Declaration of Independence," and its ascription of all rights and equality to nature's God the Creator pleased Chesterton the British believer very much. He called America a "nation with the soul of a church."[36] In 1967, the American religious historian

Southern Traditions Revised

Sidney E. Mead picked up the phrase and after exploring the possible meanings of the religion of the Republic at last concluded: "I would argue that the one most constant strand in its theology has been the assertion of the primacy of God over all human institutions."[37] Now, sixty years later, I would argue that the binding glue of the religion of the Republic does not hold together nearly as much as it did when either Chesterton or Mead wrote—except in the American South. Here God's primacy is so uncontested that state chapters of the American Civil Liberties Union often have difficulty finding plaintiffs to try to enforce the separation of church and state in instances where local schools are still sponsoring prayer in rural district classrooms.

Though the number of "nothing in particular" religious adherents is growing in southern cities, the sense that God stands watch over all human institutions is still strong throughout the South.[38] But if this is the region with the soul of a church, there is considerable diversity of opinion as to what *kind of church* is implied by that shared identity. To oversimplify the options just a bit, the question comes down to whether the church at the center of southern Christian culture is a magisterial church, a gathered church, or a refuge. This makes considerable difference for how the region's majority Christians differently approach their shared commitment to hospitality. People with magisterial conceptions of church have a sense that their church is both a "y'all come" church and a moral institution that bears responsibility for all souls in society. It is no wonder, then, that Father Charles Strobel and Pete Gathje, as Catholics, and Ingrid McIntyre, as a United Methodist, come from traditions that conceive of the church having no real parish boundaries; hospitality must be extended to one and all. Welcoming everyone to the table is, for them, no metaphor but the literal command of Christ.

People with a gathered conception of church see its work to be among those who answer Christ's call. Hospitality is therefore extended to those inside the blessed community and to those who might accept the invitation to turn their lives around and accept Jesus' invitation to follow him. This is the view of church that is operationalized in Jackson, Mississippi's Gateway Rescue Mission. It puts its doctrinal statement on its webpage for all to see, and it is clear about its rules, among them: three nights per month in its homeless shelter for men, max. The real work of the mission is not about meeting the homeless where they are; it is about seeing that every man is given a proper chance to turn his life around. This is part of what Gateway's executive director Rex Baker describes as "Proper Charity" in a blunt statement of Gateway's philosophy on its blog. It reads in part:

At Gateway Rescue Mission, we strive to work with two groups of people; those who are willing to help themselves and those who are unable to help themselves. Some people need temporary assistance and a gentle push to get back on their feet. Some need long term help breaking an addiction. If they are willing to help themselves, we are here to help them.

Others simply are not able to help themselves. Due to physical or mental limitations, or both, our work with them is a ministry of mercy. We see people everyday who depend on a meal from our kitchen for proper nutrition, and we are here for them also.

But we try to draw the line with those who are able, but unwilling to help themselves.[39]

People in the gathered church position cannot understand what people like Pete Gathje or Lindsey Krinks—who accept people off the streets without trying to change them—are all about. The reverse, of course, is also true.

Last, there is the refuge. The refuge conception of church is perhaps less familiar, but it can be found anywhere there are Christians who belong to oppressed minority groups. The refuge is the place where people can be received with hospitality among their own kind without prejudice. Because of the problems faced in the outside world, refuge churches orient their hospitality to "the community," which in the South often perforce means the black community or the Hispanic community. One can search a long time before one finds a general "y'all come" homeless ministry like Manna House sponsored by a refuge church, but health and education ministries tied to the refuge's own communities such as the South Carolina health ministries discussed above are frequent.

In the complexity of the contemporary South, actual ecclesiastical identifications do not indicate everything that one might like to know about how these ecclesiologies—theories of the church—are operationalized. Thus, Lindsey and Andrew Krinks came out of the gathered Church of Christ but are living their lives inspired by the big-picture magisterial ideas of Lutheran Dietrich Bonhoeffer and National Baptist Martin Luther King Jr. Many mainline Protestant churches, meanwhile, may think of themselves as open to everyone and sponsor ministries of hospitality to the "less fortunate" but actually extend little personal Christian hospitality beyond their own race and class circles. The ways that the term "hospitality" are used and practiced by various Christians and groups in the South today reveal the complexity of the culture and its religious forms.

Despite the intricacy of the Christianities at play, there are some commonalities, some little notes of grace that tie these various expressions together. What makes a culture cohere—even with a simmering argument under way about what it means to be Christian and practice hospitality—are the agreed forms, norms, and folkways that allow its people who think of themselves as Christians in the South to communicate. We have already mentioned the love of food, and Gathje referenced the way that the Bible serves as a common text. To these we would add a certain emotional register in which things religious are spoken, mourned, and celebrated. And to lighten it all, there is a humor that the religious sometimes employ to make the holy bearable. All of these grace notes help keep the different Christianities from completely breaking down from one another, but the strains can be huge.

DIVIDED BY FEAR

Throughout the year I spent interviewing pastors and scholars and ordinary people about religion in the contemporary South, I always made certain to ask one question of each interviewee: "How do you know when you're in the South, religiously speaking?" One person helped me put my finger on both the gratifying aspects of southern Christianity and its deeply fraught characteristics. Willie Jennings is a distinguished theologian who was then teaching at Duke. Like me, he grew up in Michigan, but unlike me he grew up in the black church. "When I say the words 'southern Christianity,'" I asked Jennings, "what pops into your head?" Jennings answered,

> Well, for me it would have to be my parents because I, growing up in
> Michigan, considered them still very much southern Christians. And
> what that means is that there is a certain set of habits that die hard
> no matter where you are. When I came here [to North Carolina]
> in 1987 to do doctoral work, what struck me immediately was that I
> had never lived here but it was like coming home. Everybody here
> acted like my mom and dad. And what I mean by everybody is all
> those people who shared what Walker Percy called that part of the
> world that is haunted by the Holy Ghost—the South. That has been
> so much the reality of life here that there are folk you can tell have

been shaped by the church, and then there are those who are yet being shaped by the church. And by shaping I don't mean it always in a positive way, but just the reality of it. So, the way I would put it is that southern religion for me has several kinds of tested and powerful elements. There is the reality of habit and rote. That people go to church on Sunday morning.

Jennings contrasted this to his earlier experience from graduate school in California, where church was optional, only for those who found it "meaningful." But in the South, he pointed out, "Even in contexts where the church and the pastor are not that edifying, not that life giving, people yet get up and go to church."[40]

For all the things that unite southern Christians and make them more like their neighbors within the region than like people of the same denominational families outside the South, the contemporary South is a region divided. Local and state politics, churches, and even families are riven by racial wounds, by fear of immigrants, and by a determination to resist (or embrace) the direction in which the broader American culture is moving when it comes to matters of gender and sexuality. In our conversation Willie Jennings depicted the depths of division in light of statewide Republican control in North Carolina for the first time since Reconstruction:

Since the strong turn to the right politically and socially you have had that utter distinction between black and white get heightened in very palpable ways, especially in North Carolina. Primarily because, you know, white southern religion has in many ways here been absolutely coopted by the political right, by the Republican Party, and wrapped itself so tightly inside those sensibilities that increasing numbers of southern whites in North Carolina and South Carolina, too, I would say, can't make a distinction—and they won't make a distinction—between what it means to love Jesus and what it means to follow the Republican Party's platform.

Meanwhile, among African American Christians (and a minority of white Carolina Christians), intense piety and intense love of Jesus leads to totally opposite conclusions. This, Jennings said, is ironic. "I was at a [white] church," he said, "and I was talking about how is it possible that people cook alike, enjoy the same kind of food, know the difference between a poorly cooked piece of corn bread and a well-cooked piece of corn bread,

Southern Traditions Revised

understand how you are actually supposed to make grits as opposed to folks *trying* to make grits?" Everybody was laughing at what he was saying, then came the clincher. "How is it that we are so racially divided? And the room got absolutely quiet, but they knew what I was talking about."

One answer to Jennings's question is that for multiple reasons southern Christians continue to worship in largely racially separate congregations. Long-lasting multiracial congregations are the exception to the rule, but increasing rates of interracial marriage and biracial identity account for what progress we can count.[41] The other thing I have discovered is that when bishops or others have merged churches with the idea that they will start out half and half, they do not stay that way for very long, unless there is a pastor who's got just the DNA for that and stays a long time, or unless there are equal biracial pastoral power-sharing arrangements in place from the start.[42]

Even Pentecostal churches like the Church of God (Cleveland, Tennessee) find themselves at a crossroads as to whether to be loyal first to the eight hundred thousand or so mostly southern Republican white members who pay the bills but who are on the numerical decline or to go where the growth is, in the Hispanic part of the church in the nation and internationally.[43] Part of the southern Christian problem is that people have been thinking in terms of the black-white binary for so long that the rapid influx of Hispanic immigrants has caught them mentally unprepared. Some Christians have reacted with open arms and others with fear. But perhaps it is most telling that the less powerful churches (in the South) seem to have done best in welcoming Spanish-speaking Christians to their ranks. The Catholic Church is one such example. Another is a tiny, decidedly southern denomination, the International Pentecostal Holiness Church (IPHC) started largely in North Carolina, which was overwhelmingly white. In the past twenty years, it has deliberately targeted Latino Pentecostal growth. Now upwards of 30 percent of its membership is Latino, and almost all the new church plants in the IPHC are oriented to Hispanics.[44] This is, however, not a universal integration, a church for all peoples, nations, and races; that model is still quite rare and successful in only a few eastern metropolitan centers.[45] The refuge model of church exists for a reason, and that reason is that racism in society and in its churches. Hospitality is hard work.

Finally, the Christian South is a region still divided over how much it wants to embrace or resist the gender and sexuality mores of the rest of the nation. Inside churches, women have fewer official roles of ordained leadership than elsewhere in the country, even though they are the backbone of every congregation in every tradition. Even more telling, perhaps, is the reaction to advances in gay rights, which were greeted with dismay by a majority of Christians in the South but celebrated by more than many observers might have expected a decade ago. The changes in the national legal climate have led to more resistance under the cover of law than during any time since the days of school desegregation, and this time religion and the "right to conscience" of public officials not to participate in parts of the marriage process they find religiously objectionable are in the forefront of the conflict. In Alabama, for instance, despite a federal court order finding a legal right for same-sex couples to marry in February 2015, as of March 4, 2015, none of the sixty-seven counties would issue such couples a marriage license, in part because the state's Supreme Court chief justice told probate judges that they were not subject to the ruling. A month after the U.S. Supreme Court found a right to marry in the Constitution applying to all people in the *Obergefell* decision on June 26, 2015, noncompliance was still being practiced in Alabama via the old-fashioned strategy of bureaucratic obstruction.[46] Even by the end of July, 2015, nine Alabama counties were issuing no marriage licenses at all, and three counties had the full courage of their convictions, standing firm in the courthouse door and not issuing marriage licenses to same-sex couples.[47] In my state of Tennessee a legislator issued his own directives to county clerks not to issue same-sex marriage licenses and sought the impeachment of the state's governor and attorney general for not demanding a rehearing of *Obergefell* within the twenty-five-day rehearing period.[48] North Carolina legislators enacted a law over the veto of their governor that allowed state court officials to refuse to perform a marriage if they have a "sincerely held religious objection," a measure aimed at curtailing same-sex unions.[49]

The most famous case of Christian conscience resisters was, perhaps, that of Kim Davis, the Rowan County, Kentucky, clerk who went to jail for contempt after refusing a federal judge's order to issue marriage licenses. She claimed that to do so was to violate her conscience as an Apostolic Christian, and she was freed only after agreeing not to interfere with her deputies performing the same task. For going to jail, she drew national attention, with some comparing her to Rosa Parks and others to George Wallace.[50] Two Baptist presidential contenders, Mike Huckabee of Arkansas and Ted Cruz of Texas, fought for the honor of escorting her from jail and proclaiming her cause as their own.[51] This might be good electoral politics—particularly for attention-starved Tea Party Republicans in the first summer of Donald Trump—but the most remarkable aspect of the southern region's response

Southern Traditions Revised

to the ruling permitting same-sex marriage was how much voluntary compliance and even joyful celebration ensued. Hospitality again. No southern legislative body ever seriously entertained same-sex unions, let alone marriages. Yet as of this writing, one of the hot-mess questions in the more moderate churches is whether to host such marriages in their sanctuaries. The Bible, family, hospitality, honor, ideas about the meaning of sin, forgiveness, and the nature of the church itself as a community—it could not be a more classic southern problem.

A nation, country, or body of people is known by its common practices, beliefs, tastes, modes of expression, and even fights that repeatedly vex it. Christians in the contemporary South possess all the makings of distinct peoplehood. They take the Bible seriously, then fight over what it means. They celebrate hospitality, then divide on to whom it should be extended. They are clearly the products of their collective past and of their unifying and fractious present. What remains, and what makes their present story compelling, are the several ways that they continue the deep themes of a long collective identity and the ways that they are breaking new ground in the new century.

THE RELIGION OF THE
LOST CAUSE, RELOADED

Twenty years ago the former pastor of historic Scots Presbyterian Church in Charleston asked me if I knew why people from Charleston liked to go to China so much. I should have known that it was a setup for a joke, but knowing that he had just been to China, I said, No, I didn't, and asked him why. He laughed as he said, "Because it's the only other place on earth where they worship their ancestors!" I was to discover that Charleston does have an especially strong reverence for its old families (and one's reverence is likely to be considerably enhanced by actually being one of their descendants). Yet Charleston is not alone in maintaining a worshipful stance toward the people and institutions of the past. The Old South, military service, and sacrifice in the Civil War maintain a grip on people's imaginations in the South in a way that no 150-year-old event holds purchase in the North or West. William Faulkner's line from *Requiem for a Nun*, "The past is never dead. It's not even past," is quoted so often in the South because 150 years after the end of the Civil War debates about the meaning of the conflict, the legacy of slavery, and the question of Confederate honor are very much alive.[1]

Rippavilla Plantation is located on the outskirts of Spring Hill, Tennessee. Today Spring Hill is known first and foremost for a massive General Motors automotive plant, but before the Civil War it was the northernmost community in Maury County, a rich agricultural area at the northeastern extent of the Natchez Trace, an early national wagon-wheel superhighway leading from western Nashville, Franklin, and Columbia, Tennessee, to Natchez, Mississippi, and from there by the River Road along the Mississippi River itself down to New Orleans. The many period plantations in this area were begun in the opening decades of the nineteenth century by enterprising men and women and their families, always with the labor of enslaved persons, or, as our Texas-born guide at Rippavilla Plantation is always careful to say, "servants." It might seem a small thing to notice, but the preferred term in use to refer to those owned by others in the condition of slavery at most contemporary historical sites like Thomas Jefferson's home, Monticello, is now "enslaved person," because to call people "slaves" is to assent to their status of being different and inferior ontologically to their masters and mistresses. Say "slave" too much and you rob people of their humanity in memory, just as they were robbed of it before while alive. The term "servant" used at Rippavilla does explain the function certain black bodies played in the house before and after slavery, but it elides the differences between being an owned person and someone paid for one's work and free to leave it behind. The plantation house itself, like most others in the region, preserves multiple histories at one time, but it is not the first house in which the principal family owning the land lived and where enslaved persons served. Indeed, the first house that John and Susan Cheairs lived in was not near the main road between Columbia and Franklin but close to the center of the eleven thousand acres they worked, closer to the slave quarter and to their fields in every direction. Middle-aged prosperity allowed the Cheairs to erect a grand home with twelve-foot, nine-inch ceilings on the first floor and fourteen-foot ceilings on the second floor, with walls made entirely of red brick, and to start the project over not once but twice, to make sure that the walls would stand for a century—a goal they easily fulfilled.

Though Nathaniel Cheairs (1818–1914), who built this house, had an exciting role in the Civil War, returned to his home, and is represented by photographs and furniture throughout the home donated by his descendants, the many portraits hanging throughout are actually not of the Cheairs family but of their cousins the McKissicks, who lived across the street. The McKissick home subsequently burned, but the oil portraits that once hung in their ancestral home now grace Rippavilla. Another "family" we can think of as remembered and celebrated at Rippavilla plantation is the brotherhood of Confederate generals who made the dining room of the plantation their headquarters. General John B. Hood and his general officers met in the dining room and held their war council breakfast on the morning of November 30, 1864, feted by a breakfast of ham biscuits and coffee provided by the lady of the house, Susan Cheairs. Hood was none too pleased, having discovered that Union general John Schofield (coincidentally his West Point roommate) had been following Hood ever since the Battle of Atlanta, an annoyance that Hood hoped to end before Schofield could reinforce the Union stronghold of Nashville.[2] Instead, Schofield had snuck right by him during the night of November 29, 1864, and Hood angrily ordered his generals to lead their troops to catch up and attack.[3] Badly wounded himself, with one arm in a sling and a leg amputated with a peg for a prosthesis, he urged his officers to "prove their bravery." Before the day was out six Confederate States of America (CSA) generals were dead and another eight wounded in the Battle of Franklin, one of the bloodiest single engagements of the war for either side.[4] Upstairs at the plantation there is Civil War detritus, weaponry, and signifiers of valor in the War between the States.

It is also upstairs at Rippavilla where our guide points out the doorway through which "house servants" came and went to their quarters (note again, "servants," never "enslaved servants"). Then it is pointed out that on the property after the war stood a schoolhouse where the Freedmen's Bureau taught house servants and field hands how to read and write, but "the government messed that up," we are told, as the story segues to Reconstruction. "You've heard that story, give them forty acres and a mule?" our guide continues, "We all know how that worked out."[5] In fact, although there is little factual basis for this account of the Freedmen's Bureau's work, northern carpetbaggers did impose taxes that had to be paid off or the property was to be forfeited to new debt factors. (Nathaniel Cheairs did manage to pay off the debt to get his house back.) Finally, it is in this last room of the house, where family articles begin to include more informal photographs, in which we find Sam Bond's portrait and effects, together with those of Emma Burns, both of whom are black. Sam Bond served William, the second-generation Cheairs son, as plantation overseer and is pictured in a number of playful,

Southern Traditions Revised

informal scenes with white children from the big house, with other equally well-dressed African Americans. Emma Burns, meanwhile, is pictured as a young woman in a headcloth and a big smile on the grounds of the plantation and in a mid-twentieth-century studio portrait taken at some expense. The story is that she moved with William Cheairs to Nashville when he left Rippavilla. Clearly, the stories that wealthy white southerners tell of black servants and retainers being so close so as to be "like members of the family" are not just stories. But when we move out into the slave quarter and see archaic, substandard housing that was clearly still in use even after electrification in the twentieth century, and the further contrast between well-marked family graves and a separate slave cemetery of perhaps five times the size but without a single individual marker, we are struck by just how far the category of family does not extend.

Leaving the mansion, we move toward a structure now marked "Slave House" and see that twelve houses originally occupied this area several football fields away from the plantation house. Each such house offered one main room with a fireplace and a loft area. It is evident that this remaining house was used for a long time into the twentieth century. There was rudimentary electricity with knob-and-tube wiring and a single bare bulb hanging from the ceiling. Unfortunately, there are windows haphazardly repaired with corrugated steel instead of glass. The postslavery conditions of voluntary servitude are difficult to contemplate. It is not just Rippavilla that poses these hard questions about history and memory, about how things should be remembered. Plantations, battlefields, cotton fields, and slave quarters, and untended cemeteries are physical reminders throughout the South that a war was fought and people died over how to live and who could be free and then continued to suffer in those same places after the war was declared at end.

Leaving Rippavilla I stop for gas between Spring Hill and Columbia, and at the counter I notice there is a copy of something called the *Hard Times News* available for a dollar. It contains arrest records of meth addicts, sex offenders, and more. I ask the checkout clerk whether it's local. He replies, "It's just the four counties right around here, a kind of police blotter." He adds a personal opinion, "It's pretty humorous." I buy a copy. Humorous or not, it is a sign of the times in this part of the rural South that what used to be some of the wealthiest country in the nation, dotted with plantations and with the homes of generals from the Revolutionary and Civil Wars and presidents of the nineteenth century, is now covered with the signs of the misery of addiction and rural poverty. Before going on to our next stop we seek out a café

Figure 1. "Slave Cabin," Rippavilla Plantation, Spring Hill, Tennessee.
(Author's photograph)

on Columbia's historic square. Columbia is Maury County's seat, and there is enough business to keep the place going better than most southern small towns, but as we turn the corner to return to our car, we run almost headlong into an emaciated twenty-something girl with one tooth in her mouth and an older relative trying to calm her down about her upcoming meeting with her lawyer. Meth may be keeping the downtown courts and law offices busy, but I see no humor in the hard times on evident display. We proceed back to the country and to the remembrance of the nineteenth century.

THE SONS OF CONFEDERATE VETERANS

Since moving from a one-man operation in Jackson, Mississippi, in 1996, to Columbia, Tennessee, the Sons of Confederate Veterans (SCV) has more than doubled its membership to more than thirty thousand members. This number may not sound like a lot in the age of signing yourself up for affinity groups on the Internet, but the SCV is no mere casual sign-yourself-up group; not everyone can join. The SCV is a heritage group, where applicants pay to prove that they have an ancestor who served honorably in the army or navy of the Confederate States of America. Once one is a member, one can belong to one of over seventeen hundred camps arrayed in every state and many foreign countries across the world. Why would someone belong to such a group 150 years after the Civil War? And, moreover, what does it mean that the number of men who want to be counted as sons has grown in recent years? Today the sacred battle for collective memory about a war, its "real purposes," the atrocities committed on southern soil, and the honor of those who fought and died for their homeland and kin, is perhaps stronger than at any time in the twentieth century.

The SCV grew out of the United Confederate Veterans (UCV), an association formed in New Orleans on June 10, 1889, by veterans of the Confederate States Army and Navy. Although there had been numerous local veterans' associations in the South, this was the first attempt to organize centrally. The UCV grew rapidly throughout the 1890s, culminating with 1,555 camps represented at their 1898 reunion. The next few years marked the zenith of UCV membership, lasting until 1903 or 1904, when veterans were starting to die off, and the organization went into a gradual decline. It was at the 1906 UCV reunion that Lieutenant General Stephen Dill Lee, UCV Commander General, charged the men of the next generation to carry on their fathers' cause: "To you, Sons of Confederate Veterans, we will commit the vindication of the cause for which we fought. To your strength will be given the defense of the Confederate soldier's good name, the guardianship of his history, the emulation of his virtues, the perpetuation of those principles which he loved and which you love also, and those ideals which made him glorious and which you also cherish."[6]

For early Confederate veterans and even more for Confederate widows and orphans, the fact of real defeat at the hands of the Union (or, as southern partisans still prefer to call them, "federal troops") stung in a way that improved memory, rather than obscured it. When I was a child in Michigan, long before Vietnam came to a crashing halt, the boys on the playground would take time out from playing Army to proudly say to each other, "We're the one country that's never lost a war!" Suffice it to say, once I learned about the Civil War and about the concept of country, I wondered how playground talk went south of the Mason-Dixon Line. Later I came to understand (at camp) that if northern twelve-year-olds might be able to name William Tecumseh Sherman and Ulysses S. Grant as Union generals and place Grant and Robert E. Lee and at Appomattox Courthouse, southern twelve-year-olds could name another dozen general officers of the CSA and debate their merits. What those southern twelve-year-olds of the 1960s knew and did not know did not just come out of books, much less textbooks. It grew from the sad experience of the defeated region and the determination to turn it into something like victory in the same way Christ turns death into triumph. This, then, was the long cultural shadow of what historian Charles Reagan Wilson has called the "religion of the lost cause."

The cause of which Wilson wrote in 1980 was the same as the Sons of Confederate Veterans were charged with vindicating by Commander Lee in 1906. The term "Lost Cause" was actually coined early after defeat by a Richmond, Virginia, editor named Edward A. Pollard, who published a book entitled *The Lost Cause* in 1866.[7] In doing so he created a postwar myth that extended the antebellum southern belief in the South's moral superiority to that of the commercial, "atheistic" North. Wilson tracks how this became a southern civil religion, preached from pulpits across the region to a grieving and wounded white populace who wondered how, if God really favored their cause, he had seemed to desert them so entirely at the hands of father Abraham and his troops. As Wilson notes, "The South faced problems after the Civil War which were cultural but also religious—the problems of providing meaning to life in society amid the baffling failure of fundamental beliefs, of extending comfort to those suffering poverty and disillusionment,

Southern Traditions Revised

and of encouraging a sense of belonging in the shattered southern community."[8] The answer to this disorder was the creation of a new order that depended on the valor and dignity of certain Confederate heroes that, even if dead or defeated, served as models of southern Christian virtue.

Even though not every southern minister was a celebrant of the religion of the Lost Cause (and it was Exodus being celebrated in the newly independent southern black churches), those who were in the late nineteenth to early twentieth centuries effectively managed to garb their Christian witness in southern pride and patriotism. As Wilson says, "They used the Lost Cause to warn Southerners of their decline from past virtue, to promote moral reform, to encourage conversion to Christianity, and to educate the young in Southern traditions; in the fullness of time, they related it to American values."[9] Because it blended with American patriotism, especially after the Spanish-American War, the Lost Cause civil religion and the work the myth performed culturally were never contested on a national scale until the civil rights era. Nonetheless, the Lost Cause myth's effects on shaping white southern sensibilities of successive generations were profound. For instance, Robert E. Lee's birthday, January 19, became a holiday throughout the South and schoolchildren were led to reverence his image, thanks to the promotion efforts of the United Daughters of the Confederacy.[10] Father Abram Ryan (1838–1886), the Catholic poet-priest of the Confederacy, wrote some of the very poems that schoolchildren were required to memorize to learn of Confederate bravery. Still, he must have been surprised when he saw his young niece looking at a painting depicting the death of Christ and, asking her if she knew who killed him, she replied without hesitation, "Oh, yes, I know. The Yankees."[11]

For the Sons of Confederate Veterans today, more than a century after they accepted their charge to vindicate the cause, their efforts revolve less around Pollard's 1866 vision of promoting an alternative vision of what America (or even the South) is and can be than in setting the record straight about their version of the Civil War, their ancestors, and their organization. Here are the big three things they want others to understand:

First, SCV members want to promote a "correct" reading of the causes of the war between the states—as they see it. They despise the interpretation offered at most national battlefields, and in Ken Burns's famous documentary, which makes the Civil War about slavery and thus about race. (Their account, truthfully, notes that few northerners in antebellum America had done anything to end slavery and that most southerners who fought for the cause of the gray were too poor to own slaves. But it conveniently overlooks that most southern states' secession statements, which cited their legislatures' causes for leaving the Union, explicitly cited the protection of slaveholding as a way of life.)[12]

Second, these men know that their great (great) grandfathers did not own slaves and did not benefit directly from slavery (unlike Yankee benefactors on Wall Street in New York, or the "pious shipping barons that founded Brown University," we were told). Their ancestors fought for their homeland; they behaved honorably, so it is a culture of honor that defends them and their memory against such charges, which leads to the third main message of the organization.

Third, the curious new note in latter-day Confederate soldier remembrance is the celebration of black Confederate soldiers, the active recruitment of black, Native American, and Hispanic soldier descendants. Their purported factual reality is used as a basis for securing the claim that "it wasn't about slavery, or these slaves wouldn't have served and then been paid Confederate pensions in later years for their services." Quite apart from whether that is an ironclad chain of reasoning, it demonstrates that the SCV itself like, much of the rest of the South, has gone multicultural. Not only does the group not exclude African Americans out of a segregation principle, but it has come to seek out actively every Cherokee, Choctaw, Chickasaw, African American, and Mexican Texan descendent it can find as a part of the rainbow story of who the southern Confederate veterans were. Indeed, one of the most touching moments to us as visitors was the SCV staff members' pride in describing how they helped an elderly actual daughter of a free black Confederate soldier prove her credentials and be accepted by the United Daughters of the Confederacy. The presence of enslaved and free blacks in the CSA camps during war is incontestable. Their willingness to be there and the work that is imputed to that willingness in the here and now has inspired pitched historiographical battles.[13]

My wife had asked me before we toured Elm Springs, an antebellum mansion and the international headquarters of the SCV, what this visit would have to do with the theme of my book on contemporary southern Christianities. I replied, "Just watch," and no sooner than we were admitted to the gift shop, we saw two items that illustrate the way religion runs through the SCV. The first was a calendar of contemporary artist Mort Künstler's depictions of Civil War scenes. Künstler works in a realist romantic style that can be compared to both Norman Rockwell (though without the humor) and the early twentieth-century illustrator J. C. Leyendecker. The particular image of Künstler's that caught my eye was a painting of Stonewall Jackson standing with his horse by a river. The calendar month is for October 2013, but the image refers to Stonewall Jackson's last words, for not only does Thomas "Stonewall" Jackson possess a legendary military reputation as Robert E. Lee's best general, but he also retains something of a Christian saint's legend as well. When he was accidentally but mortally wounded by friendly fire at the Battle of Chancellorsville, Jackson voiced his wish that if he was being called home, he hoped he would die on the Lord's Day. Sure enough, this Presbyterian deacon, Sunday school teacher, and teetotaler died on Sunday afternoon on May 23, 1863.[14] His final words were a request that could be literally and symbolically interpreted, "Let us cross over the river and rest under the shade of the trees."[15]

On a calendar today, Jackson engages both the Christian piety of the Confederacy that invoked God in its constitution (unlike the U.S. Constitution then or now) and Christ through its flags and ensigns that embrace the St. Andrew's cross, and the military religion of great old generals as virtual saints. Stonewall Jackson and his peers, then, remain models of Christian manhood under duress—the continuation and personalization of the religion of the Lost Cause that Charles Reagan Wilson wrote about. Yet as long as their example is remembered and emulated, they impart a kind of gentlemanly Christian chivalry that can never be defeated by death or defeat in war. Baylor University professor Thomas Kidd remembers that this was imparted to him when he was a boy growing up in Atlanta. Writing in 2013 at the 150th anniversary of Jackson's death, Kidd recalls, "It is hard to say how many southern boys today share a childhood like Don Williams's, who sang in 'Good Ole Boys Like Me' about growing up 'with a picture of Stonewall Jackson above' his bed. But for many boys (mostly white boys, I assume?) of my generation, male relatives and friends still spoke of Stonewall as one of our heroes, whenever the topic of 'The War' came up."[16] With Stonewall, as Kidd points out, you get slavery, but he remains one of the most popular Civil War generals, whether immortalized in stone on Stone Mountain in Georgia or in oil paintings and calendar art by Mort Künstler.

The other item in that gift shop that I found fascinating was the SCV *Chaplain's Handbook*.[17] On asking whether this was a merely historical item reflecting usage in the Civil War among Confederate chaplains or was meant for contemporary usage, I learned that it was a guide for today's chaplains in each camp to suggest correct usage so they "don't just go off with their own ideas." I bought a copy and took it home. What one finds inside the *Hand-book* is not unlike older editions of the Episcopal *Book of Common Prayer* and the Presbyterian *Book of Common Worship*; indeed, some of the content appears to be drawn straight from those sources, along with the short books of prayers, hymns, and devotions printed by Methodists and Baptists for soldiers to carry into their service.[18] Much of the material is from the years of war, 1861–65. There are period wedding and funeral services, prayers, hymns, and more. There are articles on being a southern gentleman, pieces on praying in public, and prayers for public use. The volume is bound in gray cloth, bears the SCV symbol, and resembles books of the Confederate era. The *Handbook*'s author/editor, then the SCV chaplain-in-chief, is H. Rondel Rumburg, a Baptist minister and prolific author of books with historical and religious themes who also edits the "Chaplains' Corps Chronicles of the Sons of Confederate Veterans," an online periodical for chaplains of SCV camps. The current chaplain-in-chief is Ray L. Parker, and in the June 2015 issue of the "Chaplains' Corps Chronicle" his article performs some of the very work that Charles Reagan Wilson saw postwar southern clergy doing, working in the minister's idiom of Christian meaning-making while advancing the SCV's contemporary purpose of setting the purposes of the war record straight in the here and now. A small excerpt of Parker's article takes you into the heart of the chaplain's perspective:

> In the Old Testament the Lord instructed Moses, "Proclaim liberty throughout all the land unto all the inhabitants thereof" (Leviticus 25:10). The message of Moses was a message of liberty. The Lord spoke to the Prophet Jeremiah, "And ye . . . had done right in my sight, in proclaiming liberty every man to his neighbor" (Jeremiah 34:15). The Apostle Paul wrote to the church at Corinth, "Where the Spirit of the Lord is, there is liberty" (II Corinthians 3:17). Liberty is a good thing. Liberty is right.
>
> The Southern States desired a good thing in seeking freedom and liberty. They were right in the desire for a government of the people, by the people, and for the people. Their anticipation was not the destruction of the North, but rather peaceful co-existence between the people of the Confederate States and the people of the United States. The Southern States had no plans to amass a great military force and march to Washington. Their desire was to live in peace, enjoying freedom and liberty. This was good. This was right.[19]

Just as happened a century ago, the honor of the southern states is being upheld on Christian grounds. Yet, if that backward-looking defense of honor and heritage begs all kinds of questions about what would have happened to slavery on both sides of the Union-Confederacy divide, those are not the historical questions that drive these men.

How Christianity fits into the contemporary relevance of the Civil War has a range of positions, of which Chaplain Parker's might be called an antiquarian defensive position. Still, there are other men associated with the symbols of the Confederacy who employ those symbols and Christianity in other ways. Neo-Confederates, mostly outside the SCV in other organizations like the League of the South, led by Michael Hill, tend by contrast to theologize the Civil War (as southern Presbyterian theologians themselves did during the war) as a heretical and unorthodox attack on Christian civilization.[20] Here claims about history are made so as to reclaim the banner of a Christian culture for the South today in resistance to what the League of the South calls the federal "Empire" from without.

The reenactor community of chaplains represents yet another position, in which re-enacting the Civil War is cool masculine weekend behavior, no matter which uniform you wear, but just as in the camps of the war itself, Christianity's place is in redeeming the individual. That is how it looks to Chaplain Alan Farley, who started out playing a Confederate soldier, then felt called as a devout Christian to add chaplaincy to his role. For more than thirty years now he has engaged in ministering full-time to the Civil War reenacting community through the organization he leads, the Re-Enactor's Missions for Jesus Christ.[21] He works collaboratively with men depicting CSA, U.S., and Christian Commission chaplains, but their objective is not only to do what chaplains did 150 years ago but also to make conversions in the camps of today where reenactors of the twenty-first century can dedicate their lives to their savior, Jesus Christ.

Before we leave Elm Springs we are invited to come to a three-day sesquicentennial event in memory and honor of Sam Davis, the "Boy Hero of the Confederacy," to be held in November 2013 at his parent's home in Smyrna, Tennessee. My ears perk up because I have heard the name before, and a quick check of the trusty iPhone reminds me why. When we had just moved to Tennessee from Georgia in the year 2000, our daughter came home from a trip to the state capitol in connection with learning Tennessee history, which by law is taught to every fourth grader in the state. She came home most impressed by the story she was told of Sam Davis, the good boy who was hung as a spy because he would not reveal his commanding officer who, unbeknown to their Union captors, was in the cell with him. Davis's strength of character in jail and on the gallows, and the slippery way he was tried and executed, left a lasting impression on those who met him in his last two days. My daughter told us the tale with amazing attention to accuracy, the way children can relate every detail of a favorite movie. She even gave a reasonable facsimile of Sam Davis's last words to his mother from a letter he wrote:

> Dear Mother; O how painful it is to write to you! I have got to die tomorrow—to be hanged by the Federals. Mother, do not grieve for me. I must bid you good-bye for evermore. Mother I do not fear to die. Give my love to all.
> Your dear son.
> Mother: Tell the children all to be good. I wish I could see all of you once more, but I never will anymore.
> *Sam Davis*[22]

When the weekend of November 22–24, 2013, rolls around, I find myself attending a three-day event to commemorate the capture, trial, and execution of Sam Davis hosted by the Sons of Confederate Veterans Camp #33, Murfreesboro, Tennessee, hosted at the Sam Davis home. Though the home itself is still next to a cotton field, it is right down the road from a giant Nissan auto plant. In fact, the street signs on the way there—Nissan Drive, Lee Victory Parkway, Nissan Parkway, Sam Davis Road—demonstrate that the new and old South occupy the same space. The event includes a Friday night seminar, lectures, tours, military demonstrations, and a Sunday memorial service. I make it a point to talk to as many people as possible over meals and at gatherings. They have come from as far away as Mississippi, Florida, Ohio, and South Carolina for the event. On Friday night three papers are given: a serious historical account of Coleman's Scouts, the unit Davis was a part of, a dramatization of the trial itself, and a paper contesting the legality of the execution on the basis of President Abraham Lincoln's standing order prohibiting executions without his further approval. The barbecue was good, but the SCV members and their wives were eating up the history. Moreover, I discover that the claims at headquarters that the SCV welcomes members of color is true. There are indeed such members present, and they are treated with respect. On Saturday I tour the Davis home, which does a more balanced job of representing the lives of both family members and enslaved persons during the war and after than did Rippavilla. I notice that the church working the concessions on Saturday is a multiracial Baptist church. This Civil War remembrance business makes for less clear lines of representation than one might think. I also learn that the reenactors are friendly across blue and gray lines with one another and interested in the fine details of one another's uniforms, units, and equipment.

All in all, the SCV's claim to be about heritage, not hate, was well sustained throughout the weekend. Talking with men and women about their heritage of soldier's service made me think about my own. I went home each day to a front room full of wedding furniture that had belonged to my grandfather's grandfather and his wife. Nathan Wilson Mills of Springfield, Ohio, had been badly wounded, losing the use of an arm and both legs in the Battle of Chickamauga. The story goes that my great-great grandmother Maria brought him back from Nashville in a wagon to recover. The very idea of a war between the states and on familiar ground draws you up short and causes you to pause, but so, too, should the specter of an entire nation (and I mean first and foremost the United States) with slavery in its DNA. It is a war that affects us all to this day, more than most choose to acknowledge.

Not surprisingly, the Sons of Confederate Veterans' emblem is the Confederate Battle flag, but that flag is also used by hate groups as a symbol to convey the belief that people of African descent are inferior in the here and now. That is a problem for the group. Attempts to purge the organization of all white supremacists in the 1980s and again in the mid-1990s in a national leadership contest led to some backlash but also to a greater assertion that the flag did not belong to such hate groups.[23] The most recent such disavowal, adopted in 2010, is forceful. In the "whereas" section it mentions the Ku Klux Klan repeatedly (negatively) and decries "Confederate extremist political groups and individuals who seek to clothe themselves in respectability by misappropriating the banner under which our southern ancestors fought for a Just Cause which is as noble as much latter day is ignoble." In effect it says, You racists do not have a just cause, and your cause it not ours. The statement concludes with these words:

LET IT BE FURTHER RESOLVED, that the Sons of Confederate
Veterans in General Convention assembled, does hereby condemn
in the strongest terms possible the inappropriate use of the
Confederate Battle Flag or any other flag, seal, title or name bearing
any relationship whatsoever to the Confederate States of America

or the armed forces of that Government of the Confederate States of America by individuals or groups of individuals, organized or unorganized, who espouse political extremism or racial superiority.[24]

Those who want to see the Confederate Battle flag as a symbol of sacred honor in a long-ago cause and deny the image to hate groups and individuals saw their cause get even harder in June 2015, when it was again appropriated in ways that indelibly spelled racist hatred and murderous rage.

CAN A FLAG KILL?

On Wednesday, June 17, 2015, Dylann Storm Roof, age twenty-one, attended a Bible study in Charleston's Emanuel African Methodist Episcopal Church, Mother Emanuel to members of the AME, one of the oldest AME churches in the country and the oldest in the South.[25] Though he stayed for the entire hour-long Bible study with a dozen other people, all of them African American except for himself, and sat quietly next to the pastor, the Reverend Clementa C. Pinckney, the purpose of his visit was not spiritual. Just as the meeting broke up, he killed nine individuals with a .45 caliber automatic pistol, reloading often with fresh magazines in order to shoot each victim multiple times. He left one woman alive to tell others what he had done and why he had done it (two others feigned death). The elderly woman later reported what happened through Sylvia Johnson, a relative of the deceased pastor. One of the victims, Johnson said, tried "to talk him out of doing the act of killing people." Roof then replied, she recalled, "'I have to do it.' He said, 'You rape our women, and you're taking over our country. And you have to go.'" Earlier Roof began his violence with these words, "You all are taking over our country. Y'all want something to pray about? I'll give you something to pray about."[26] Within hours of the shooting, Roof was identified as a troubled young man who had self-radicalized in the wake of the Trayvon Martin killing after concluding that George Zimmerman was the real victim. By his own account, "[I] entered the words 'black on White [sic] crime' into Google, and I have never been the same since that day." He also learned about the website of the Council of Conservative Citizens, a southern white supremacy organization left over from the Jim Crow era whose leaders advocate an Anglo-Celtic theocratic separatist government for today.[27] Soon Roof was identifying himself as the Last Rhodesian, and flaunting the Confederate Battle flag in tens of photos on his website and other social media that were filled with white supremacist hatred expressed toward blacks and Hispanics.

Southern Traditions Revised

Though Roof failed in touching off the race war he sought to start in Denmark Vesey's historic church, and Charleston embraced the victims' families with an extra measure of its characteristic southern grace, it was the family members themselves who surprised the nation in their Christlike response to their victimization at the hands of Roof. Christians being Christian at the point of their execution, and family members saying, "You have hurt me and my entire family, but I forgive you," to Roof at his bond-setting appearance changed the conversation in South Carolina and beyond. The meaning of this forgiveness, directed primarily at cutting the poisonous root of bitterness for victims, was lost on most white observers. Meanwhile, some black activists outside the church context rejected the optics of forgiveness because it looked a lot like participating in one's own racial victimization.

The focus quickly shifted to the Confederate Battle flag. What role did this symbol of heritage for soldiers' sons and daughters have in twenty-first-century America, particularly since in South Carolina's case it was resurrected to fly at the state capitol only in 1962 as a symbol of massive white segregationist resistance to federal attempts to enforce integration of schools and public accommodations? The weaker politicians tried to duck the issue and say that the flag is important to people—without seriously examining who all it might be important to and for what reasons. The more courageous politicians, including the forty-year veteran mayor of mostly white Charleston, Joseph P. Riley Jr., said it's time to put the flag where it belongs, in a museum. If that were to happen, then only Mississippi would still have the Confederate Battle flag as a part of its state flag, or flying on its grounds, where it could not even be reduced to half-staff for the nine-day mourning period for Roof's victims of racial hatred. That little aspect of the South Carolina state law that kept the Confederate Battle flag flying high while the American and state flags were flown at half-staff had people rankled and made this flag a totem, an object of religious devotion that seemed utterly obscene, even to Republican senators and the governor, Nikki Haley, who had tacitly supported its continued presence in past flag fights.

The ridiculousness of waiting prompted two North Carolina activists, Bree Newsome, a pastor's daughter, and Jimmy Tyson, to come and take the flag down themselves without waiting for the South Carolina House of Representatives to get around to acting. "We removed the flag today because we can't wait any longer," Newsome said in a prepared statement. "We can't continue like this another day. It's time for a new chapter where we are sincere about dismantling white supremacy and building toward true racial justice and equality." Newsome also quoted from Scripture.[28] Both Newsome and Tyson were arrested, and the state police returned the flag to its pole for a few more weeks. For her symbolic and actual courage in the face of national dismay and political inaction, Newsome became a folk hero and a nationally sought-out campus speaker.

So why all the fuss on the news shows, and in blogs and newspapers about the Confederate Battle flag? Did the flag kill nine people in Charleston? Or, to put it another way, if the flag had come down in Columbia and been relegated to history like the Rhodesian flag and the apartheid era South African flag, would that have prevented racialized hate from entering Dylann Roof's troubled mind? Probably not, but at this point in our national history it became clear that just talking about mental illness without a word about the lethality of firearms and the racial motivations of the killer would not do. And that is where the flag returned to the conversation. For most Sons of Confederate Veterans, and for most Civil War reenactors, the flag is foremost a family heritage symbol, and for many whites in the South it has been, as Brad Paisley said in his "Accidental Racist" duet with LL Cool J, a nearly thoughtless southern pride identifier:

> To the man that waited on me at the Starbucks
> > down on Main, I hope you understand
> When I put on that t-shirt, the only thing I
> > meant to say is I'm a Skynyrd fan

But Paisley, the songwriter and collaborator with Cool J, is not so naive as that, as later he sings:

> Our generation didn't start this nation
> And we're still paying for the mistakes
> That a bunch of folks made long before we came
> And caught somewhere between southern pride and southern blame

But as historically enlightened as that point of view might be, LL Cool J necessarily raps about what he sees:

> So when I see that white cowboy hat, I'm thinkin' it's not all good
> I guess we're both guilty of judgin' the cover not the book
> I'd love to buy you a beer, conversate and clear the air
> But I see that red flag and I think you wish I wasn't here[29]

In point of fact, the Paisley–Cool J duet had some other, lamer lyrics that led to its reception as an effort in antiracism being about as successful as the subsequent Starbucks offer to each customer to have a conversation about race as baristas and customers took up the admonition to "Race Together," written on each cup.[30] The point remains, the wounds of slavery and the meaning of the Civil War remain deeply fraught more than 150 years after Juneteenth, that day on June 19, 1865, when Union soldiers, led by Major General Gordon Granger, landed at Galveston, Texas, with news that the war had ended and that the enslaved were now free—*two and a half years* after President Lincoln's Emancipation Proclamation and nine weeks after the cessation of all hostilities.[31] Then, some people did not want other people to be free or even to know that they were free. Today, a suspicion hangs in the air that some people perhaps have not come very far from that perspective.

The Charleston killings gave southern white politicians and opinion makers the opportunity to declare that they, too, saw what African Americans saw when they saw the Confederate Battle flag. One of the more surprising—at least at first—was the Reverend Russell Moore, head of the Southern Baptist Convention's Ethics and Religious Liberty Commission. He typed up what he thought on his blog, and given the topic, it went viral. In it he wrote, "The flag of my home state of Mississippi contains the Confederate battle flag as part of it, and I'm deeply conflicted about that. The flag represents home for me. I love Christ, church, and family more than Mississippi, but that's about it. Even so, that battle flag makes me wince—even though I'm the descendant of Confederate veterans." Moore then went on to make a powerful Christian argument that everybody has mixed history to be proud of and live down, but he ended his blog with a more powerful appeal to not put self before others: "White Christians, let's listen to our African American brothers and sisters. Let's care not just about our own history, but also about our shared history with them. In Christ, we were slaves in Egypt—and as part of the Body of Christ we were all slaves too in Mississippi. Let's watch our hearts, pray for wisdom, work for justice, love our neighbors. Let's take down that flag."[32] Moore's moral clarity sent the signal to other leaders—college presidents, governors, legislators—that even in Mississippi things needed to change and there was safety in doing the right thing for a change. As it turned out, Moore's conversion on the battle flag had come earlier, when a decaying Mississippi flag, pulled from the wreckage of Moore's Biloxi hometown in the wake of Hurricane Katrina, caught his eye. He was planning to have some African American friends over when he saw that flag, with its Confederate cross in the upper left corner, through the eyes of his guests as if for the first time. Rather than explain it away, he pulled it away from the wall, and it fell into pieces on the floor. And thus began his change of heart.

The last days of June 2015 featured a lot of Confederate Battle flag re-movals, as politicians followed South Carolina's lead in relegating the flag to museums and dustbins. Walmart pulled the flags and battle flag–themed apparel from their stores and announced that the company would no longer sell these items. Target, Amazon, and eBay quickly followed suit. It was as though dominant-culture America had just woken up to the semiotics of hate that the flag represented to people of color and to the people who did not want black and brown people around. But like any good Christian con-version story, feeling really low and becoming determined to do something about it is just the beginning.

A week into the crisis I heard an interview with Bryan Stevenson, an Alabama attorney who heads the Equal Justice Initiative. He is a well-known advocate who has helped death-row prisoners have wrongful convictions overturned and has argued successfully before the Supreme Court against life sentences for children under seventeen years of age. Having thought a lot about guilt and innocence in this country, he demonstrated again why he is already the recipient of a MacArthur Foundation "Genius Grant." Stevenson acknowledged that the symbols needed to come down, understanding that this was just the beginning, because the wounds they exacerbated had been unattended for so long. "Everybody in this country has inherited a burden," Stevenson said, "We've all been infected with a legacy of racial inequality. A narrative of racial difference was created in slavery and rather than confront it, we have tolerated it. And in the South we have celebrated it." That's where the flags, monuments, and mottos like "Heart of Dixie" come in for Steven-son. "These images and symbols have created some very real problems," he said, "including the presumption of dangerousness and guilt that gets as-signed to people of color." He contrasted the United States with its terrible past with Germany, South Africa, and Rwanda, countries that had or were trying to get through what was shameful in their history so that they could move forward: "We don't talk about this history. We haven't learned to man-age the shame and the guilt. We haven't dealt with it, so we just deny it."[33]

People say that you cannot undo history because, after all, it happened in the past. But the history that matters comes from the stories about the past that we keep telling. Right now those stories collectively lead us to perpetu-ate white over black construals of who matters in America. The years 2014,

2015, and 2016 were ones when the "presumption of dangerousness and guilt that gets assigned to people of color" led again and again to dead black bodies in the street and to the cri de coeur protest "Black Lives Matter," which was too often met with its clueless seminegation, "Of course. All lives matter." After the Charleston Nine died, my Vanderbilt colleague Amy Steele drew the parallel between these victims of Dylann Roof's sick understanding of racial history and the dead urban black victims of the past two years. Steele is also a minister, so she closes her reflections with a prayer, an answer, if you will, as to how to begin the process that Stevenson says we need to deal with our guilt and shame: "My prayer is that in fighting back, pastors, imams, priests, rabbis, bishops, and the faithful everywhere take on the urgent challenge now to inspire communities to tell the truth about our country's racial and ethnocentric past and present. If we are worth our salt and its flavor, we will not back down from the challenge. For before reconciliation must come truth."[34] At the time of the last funeral for the Charleston Nine, that of the Reverend Clementa C. Pinckney, Americans, but particularly white southerners, seemed to be at a moment of crisis. African Americans waited apprehensively. Would new truths be exchanged for old falsehoods in the name of creating a new joint history? The racially divided society had missed opportunities before—at Reconstruction, at *Brown v. Board of Education*, at a funeral for four young girls killed in a Birmingham church bombing, at the death of Martin Luther King, and so many other times—but these were new historical actors: how would they play their parts?

Two years later after the terrible events in Charleston, the evidence is decidedly mixed. Dylann Roof was condemned to death in a federal hate crimes trial and demonstrated that he had learned nothing. Some victims' families at the sentencing offered forgiveness even as they grieved his acts, but others agreed with Gayle Jackson, the niece of Roof's victim Susie Jackson, who prayed for Roof's mother but, after watching his lack of repentance, said, "I want your soul to burn in hell."[35] Some glorifications of the Civil War and slavery have come down, but opponents have tied up further removals in layers of bureaucracy and law. Mississippi's leading artists, actors, and writers—Morgan Freeman, John Grisham, Greg Iles, Kathryn Stockett, Archie Manning, Jimmy Buffett, and more—led an appeal to remove the battle flag from the corner of the state flag in August 2015, but the flag still flies.[36] Heritage, with its veneration of the past, is a religion nearly as powerful as the Christian tradition that formally dominates the region. Too often in the second decade of the twenty-first century, the price of letting past ways control present actions in the South is that its churches do less to break down the barriers of race, class, and clan than they do to bury the dead and comfort the bereaved when hatred and misunderstanding have done their worst.

RATTLESNAKES, HOLINESS,
AND THE NEARNESS OF
THE HOLY SPIRIT

When people found out I was writing a book about religion in the South, I was surprised how often I was asked, "Are you going to be talking about serpent-handling Pentecostals?" The question came from my devout Catholic next-door neighbor, Joe, from other professors, from people I had just interviewed in distant cities, and indeed from a striking number and array of people. In response I often explained that the emphasis of the book was on contemporary Christian practices in the South, and while the mountains of eastern Tennessee and Kentucky and western Virginia and North Carolina were part of the South and Pentecostals were a big part of what makes for southern Christianity today, not all Pentecostals took up serpents by a long shot. In fact, out of tens of thousands of Pentecostal churches and at least three million believers in the South, only about forty churches with roughly one thousand total adherents pick up snakes. That usually appeased my questioners, until one gave me the missing clue I needed to understand the frequency of the question by responding in turn, "I just wondered because of the National Geographic Channel series *Snake Salvation*, and I wondered what you thought about that."

Snake Salvation, a fourteen-part program produced by the National Geographic Channel filmed mostly in 2012 and aired beginning in the fall of 2013, features modern snake-handlers. The show specifically features the lives of Jamie Coots, pastor of the Full Gospel Tabernacle in Jesus Name in Middlesboro, Kentucky, and Andrew Hamblin, pastor of the Tabernacle Church of God in LaFollette, Tennessee. So far as I can see, the series was inspired by a much better 1995 book by Dennis Covington, *Salvation on Sand Mountain*.[1] As it turned out, I talked a lot more than I initially wanted to about rattlesnakes, copperheads, and cottonmouths in 2013 and 2014, especially with journalists after the central figures in the National Geographic series were arrested. First, Jamie Coots was held for illegal possession and transportation of venomous snakes when three rattlesnakes and two copperheads were discovered in his vehicle during a vehicle search. The incident became central to the plot of episode 3 in the series, as seemed appropriate: run-ins with the authorities come with the territory for the Coots family. Back in 2008, seventy-three illegal vipers were recovered from the home of Jamie Coots's father, Pastor Gregory James Coots, in a Kentucky governmental sting operation cleverly codenamed Twice Shy. Later in the fall broadcast season, a similar fate befell Coots's young Tennessean counterpart, twenty-two-year-old Andrew Hamblin. But early Christianity–style Christians wear state opposition to their faith practices like a martyr's crown, and the courtrooms became like the apostle Paul's Mars Hill in Rome—a great place to share the faith.

Shortly after the serpent-handling pastors' stories went national and mainstream because they could be seen on cable television, National Public Radio aired a story that approached the subject with NPR's signature brand of studied respect tempered with skepticism about all things religious or supernatural. The radio story heard from those who claimed that the practice of taking up serpents is apostolic and directly follows Jesus' own last words in the Gospel according to Mark: "And these signs shall follow them that believe; In my name shall they cast out devils; they shall speak with new tongues; They shall take up serpents; and if they drink any deadly thing, it shall not hurt them; they shall lay hands on the sick, and they shall recover" (Mark 16:17–18, KJV). The NPR report's listeners also heard from herpetologists, who were asked the obvious question: "Why don't these Pentecostal preachers get bitten much by poisonous snakes, and when they do get bitten, why do they survive?" The herpetologists and wildlife experts noted that snakes, when fed an inadequate diet of mice and rats and water, become sluggish and begin to lack the capacity to defend themselves. Public Radio's follow-up on the story included a subsequent piece involving Hamblin's arrest for mistreatment of reptiles and an astounding number of letters, calls, and emails from listeners on the Thursday *All Things Considered* segment, in which listeners respond to stories. Without exception, the responses featured on the broadcast took the position of the serpents versus those who would use them for religious purposes.

As the national stories died away somewhat, regional interest along the Blue Ridge Mountains continued for some weeks. After Andrew Hamblin was arrested other believers got upset with him for exposing their practices in the first place through bringing the glare of publicity and the air of sensationalism to their faith practices. Hamblin meanwhile justified himself by saying that he was trying to draw attention to a "declining way of life." The serpent handlers who had their practices declared illegal in the 1940s took their case all the way to the U.S. Supreme Court on religious grounds, asserting that serpent handling was necessary to salvation. Contemporary handlers do not go that far. Now Hamblin had gone one step further in taking religious snake handling down to the level of diminishing folkways, like the hammered dulcimer or clogging, that needed to be preserved as a link to our past. This changed somewhat after lawyers became involved, and in television coverage of his preliminary hearing on December 17, 2013, by Knoxville's WATE-TV, Hamblin was again asserting a religious-liberty claim to free exercise under the First Amendment. When on January 8, 2014, a grand jury in Hamblin's home county failed to indict him for failure to possess a venomous snake permit for his church's fifty-three snakes, the pastor rejoiced, "Today was a major victory, not only for serpent-handling people, but for Christians everywhere."[2] The snakes themselves did not fare so well: those that did not die of weakness shortly after their seizure had to be destroyed because of parasites they contained that precluded their return to the wild or placement in a zoo.[3]

The phone call I received about the whole rattlesnakes affair that sticks with me most was from a perceptive journalist from the *Chattanooga Times Free Press*, Kevin Hardy, who asked me a version of this question: "If it's in the Bible, and the Bible is so important for Protestants in the South (and we know it is because they're always telling us so) why don't all—*or more*—Christians take up serpents than just the thousand plus practitioners in the forty churches in Appalachia we know about?" I think that is a very good question about the Bible, the South, Pentecostals, rattlesnakes, cottonmouths, copperheads, and just how far advocates of the Full Gospel are prepared to go.

So why do some Christians take up serpents? And to start with Kevin's question, why do so many other Christians "pass" on that part of the Bible?

For mainline college-educated Protestants the answer might come down to the fact that the earliest known versions of the Bible do not contain that last chapter of the Gospel of Mark. It was clearly added during the second century, and the only place Jesus says anything about taking up serpents or drinking poison without harm is in this one disputed passage. That said, most southern Christians are more biblically literally minded than that, and another way to read what is being said is that this "gift" may be construed as more apostolic than some of the other charisms of the early church. That is, the gift of handling serpents could be given to be a sign for the early growth of the church rather than for the edification of the continuing church, such as healing and speaking in tongues might be. That is the line that other Pentecostals and charismatics have taken along with their evangelical sisters and brothers. This interpretive line does reveal that, for all their apparent claims to literalism, southern conservatives and fundamentalists do not actually cut their sinning hands off, pluck their eyes out, drink poison, or pick up serpents, just because Jesus says so in the Bible. Even fundamentalists can tell when Jesus is using a metaphor—at least when it is in their interest to do so.

This leaves us with another question, one about the people who do handle snakes and drink strychnine: How did nineteen centuries go by before some Appalachian Christians took up serpents and placed them at the center of their worship? The answer, I think, lies in the fact that for the earliest readers, this second-century addition to Mark was in keeping with Jewish, and by then Christian, great signs and wonders for God's people in God's time. (For comparison's sake, read Isaiah's vision of the peaceable kingdom: "The sucking child shall play over the hole of the asp, and the weaned child shall put his hand on the adder's den" [Isa. 11:8, RSV].) Those early Christians would have recognized snakes as a real danger and the promise of overcoming them as something very special indeed, but not something that they should, as we say now, "try at home." Detached from its original setting in life, Mark 16:18 took on new life in the context of the late nineteenth and early twentieth centuries, when holiness and Pentecostal revivals first taught that the Apostolic Age had not ended, as the evangelical and Catholic traditions had thought, and that speaking in tongues and healing and other gifts of the Spirit were still available. Add to this a region (the southern Appalachians) in which poisonous snakes were plentiful, antidotes were as yet undiscovered, and children and adults alike died of accidental poisoning and snake bite with regularity, and the words of Jesus became—it seemed—another text for their times to some Christian believers in the mountains. If most Christians do not want to pick up serpents out of an abundance of caution, and because they remember Jesus' words in Matthew 4:7, "Thou shalt not tempt the Lord thy God" (KJV), we can at least understand how some early Pentecostals, reading the Scriptures for themselves in rattlesnake country read Mark 16:18 as especially relevant to their lives.[4]

For Pastor Andrew Hamblin, snake handling with the protection of God's Holy Spirit is nothing less than an experience of being in the presence of the signs of God's presence. Before his legal troubles began, he told a *Tennessean* video crew, "It's an out of the world experience to feel that; to feel God in such a way that you are holding death right in your hand. There is an old saying amongst our people, 'There is death in that box' and there is. There's a many people laying on a hillside from a serpent bite. But when that perfect and only comes from God out of heaven on high, that covers you and protects you, there is peace."[5] Far from being angst-filled about being bitten, these Pentecostals are, they believe, in the ecstatic presence of the Spirit of God.

A psychologist of religion named Ralph W. Hood spent a good part of his career tramping through the Appalachian Mountains and becoming close to Christians who engaged in taking up serpents as part of their ecstatic worship. His conclusion after decades of study is that "serpent handling likely emerged independently in many regions of Appalachia. All that is required for the practice to emerge is an environment in which there are plenty of serpents and a community of believers who accept and believe the plain meaning of Mark 16:18." He also observed that the practice of handling emerged out of geographical contexts where people were already handling poisonous snakes as a common folk practice.[6] Though the practice is small in contemporary terms, its link to the South and its place in early intra-Pentecostal theological disputes is the source of ongoing scholarly fascination.[7]

Most southerners and certainly most Pentecostal Christians in the South would like not to be associated with the infinitesimally small number of serpent handlers. On the other hand, the unwillingness of juries to convict snake-handling faith leaders in the Appalachian South is a testament to people's ability to tolerate unusual Christian practices, especially when the law is ready to intervene. Tolerate is perhaps too small a word for what is going on, for to a remarkable degree the judgments reflect a communal acceptance that the Holy Spirit is alive and well and active in the world, even if the snakes are repugnant and their handlers misguided. In the early twenty-first-century South, the basic premises of Pentecostalism are more strongly shared than in any earlier time; alongside evangelicalism, Pentecostalism is the strongest contemporary force in southern religion. How did this happen?

PENTECOSTALISM AS THE OTHER SOUTHERN PROTESTANTISM

Charles Darwin, the great evolutionary biologist, noted that those engaged in his profession fell into two basic types: "Those who make many species are the 'splitters,' and those who make a few are the 'lumpers.'"[8] It has subsequently been observed in nearly every field of scholarship that people discover things about the phenomena they are studying by grouping different items together to show how they are more alike than one might have believed or by dividing the same people, phenomena, cells, or practices that seem to be alike to demonstrate their distinctive characteristics. Many earlier treatments of southern religion stressed the overwhelmingly evangelical Protestant character of church membership of the southern states. By this measure, Baptists, Methodists, and Presbyterians (in that order) and white and black Protestants (in that order) constituted a "southern way of doing religion." Obviously, this style of analysis belongs to the lumper school of scholarship. Foremost among its practitioners are Sam Hill, Kenneth Cauthen, and John Lee Eighmy, all of whom worked on contemporary southern Christianity in the 1960s, 1970s, and 1980s.[9] Other historians of southern religion advanced the understanding of what characterized religion in the South. Among these stand out Donald Mathews for his re-creation of religion in the Old South, Bertram Wyatt-Brown for his analysis of how codes of honor and chivalry shaped Christian morality as much as the other way around in the Old South, and more recently Christine Leigh Heyrman, who has seen the roots of today's Christian conservatism in the nineteenth century's conversionist revival-stoked faith.[10] All three of these lumpers serve as examples of scholars who have seen things that unite their subjects in history and have helped shape a very clear view about what constitutes southern religion. Heyrman writes: "Evangelicalism's complex beginnings in the early South would probably claim the curiosity of only a small circle of historians were it not for the fact that this legacy now shapes the character of conservative Protestant churches in every region of the United States."[11] So the lumper school of explanation in southern American religious history does have a lot to offer us by way of an understanding of some of the commonalities that one finds in southern churches, culture, and politics. In fact, if you confine yourself to worshiping in a Baptist church, at a Church of Christ congregation, or in many Methodist and even Presbyterian churches, all of the aforementioned books would help you as a congregation member new to your church and community understand it as an example of "southern religion." But were you to venture away from downtown churches into the country, or even into a southern town's back streets, you would encounter a large number of congregations with names that are not part of that evangelical Protestant common front that early nineteenth-century settlement wrought. Just opening up my online Yellow Pages for Nashville and environs, I see the following church names under a listing of Home > Nashville, TN > Pentecostal Churches:

Christ Church
Full Gospel Mission Church
True Christian Pentecostal Witnesses
New Life Apostolic Church
Friendship Pentecostal Church
First United Pentecostal Church
East Nashville United Pentecostal
Living Word International Church
Emmanuel Church of Christ
Greater Christ
East Nashville Point of Mercy
Jerusalem Pentecostal Church
Church of God Sanctified
First Apostolic Church
Greater Harvest Church of God
True Way Church of Our Lord Jesus Christ
Grace Apostolic Church
The Original Church of God
Redemptive Way Assembly of God
Cathedral of Praise Inc.
Spanish Pentecostal Church of God
Hendersonville Pentecostal Church
Goodlettsville Pentecostal Church
Pentecostal Assembly Church
The Turning Point
Original Christ Temple Church
Bethel House of God
Cornerstone Church
Emmanuel Apostolic Temple

Rattlesnakes, Holiness, and the Nearness of the Holy Spirit

The first thing we see in this list is some of the ways that the names carry claims of originality, including apostolic gifts; of truth, including the true way toward Christ; and, above all, of being places where the sanctified assemblies encounter the living God in Spirit and in person. My favorite has to be Bethel House of God, which, like New York, New York, underlines the main point in its name: Bethel is, after all, Hebrew for "house of God."

What we also see from the list is an imposing category of churches that do not fit into the grand narrative of evangelical, Baptist-dominated southern Protestantism: Pentecostal Holiness churches and nondenominational churches. This is where the splitter tradition of analysis can help us understand what else was and going on in the South in the nineteenth century that gave rise to the plethora of churches that dot the southern landscape today. This is because it turns out that splitting was not just a scholar's exercise but also an important exercise of religious freedom and innovation on the part of southern Christians in pursuit of true faith as the Holy Spirit led them (and still leads them, they say) to experience it. As of this writing, the American South is home to fifty-seven Pentecostal denominations.[12]

THE ORDINARY ROOTS OF EXTRAORDINARY FAITH

Pentecostalism as we know it now is one of the South's great exports that came back early from its world premiere in California's Azusa Street revivals beginning in 1906, and it is still changing Christianity in the South. If you go looking for its roots, you find yourself moving farther and farther back in time. Some would say all the way back to A.D. 33, but for our purposes, let us just go back to the original American restorationists, the Presbyterians who gathered in 1801 in Cane Ridge, Kentucky, for a revival meeting and emerged as nothing fancier than "Christian" after experiencing the Holy Spirit at the revival.[13] They came out determined to have no creed but Christ and no church but a restoration of the New Testament church in all its purity. From this impulse for restoration comes the Churches of Christ, the Disciples of Christ, and a strong ahistorical movement in Baptist circles in the South called Landmarkism, which taught that Baptist churches rather than Catholic churches *were* the original Christian churches dating from the Acts of the Apostles.[14] So any time you see an older southern church with a cornerstone that reads A.D. 33 on it, now you know what that is about. It is a church thinks it came, not out of the Protestant Reformation, but straight from Jesus and Jerusalem and the birth of the church on Pentecost.

Added to the Pentecostal family tree is a whole other line of holiness faith from the Methodist-Wesleyan side of the Protestant family. While John Calvin (1509–1564) had influenced most of the Protestant family to believe that sanctification (becoming holy) was a lifelong and incomplete process in this life after one was made right with God (called justification or salvation), John Wesley taught a more hopeful doctrine.[15] Wesley (1703–1791) believed that one could attain what he called complete perfection in holiness over one's lifetime if one opened one's life up to the help of the Holy Spirit.[16] What was a minor emphasis in Wesley's work became a major enthusiasm in nineteenth-century America as holiness societies within Methodist and other Wesleyan circles began to work at helping the already saved to achieve perfection in this life. These societies emphasized prayer, temperance, and refraining from gambling, dancing, card playing, and other frivolous entertainments. Even reading popular novels was banned in favor of gospel tracts and inspirational literature. Bible reading, regular attendance at exhortations and prayer meetings, and singing spiritual songs became the culture of holiness. A morphology of receiving the second blessing of entire sanctification—as it was also called—grew up, so just as knowing when you were saved was of great consequence to eighteenth-century Calvinist evangelicals, it was especially important to have an experience of one's second blessing and to know you had experienced it. Perhaps this movement's greatest systematizer was Phoebe Palmer of New York, who described Christian perfection less as a process and more as a definite crisis, and as a "second blessing." Palmer also originated another teaching: that God's altar sanctified the sacrifices placed on it. In her scheme every human sacrifice made before God was made holy, and when the individual lived up to the conditions of entire consecration, he or she could "claim the blessing" of the sacrifice put before the Lord on God's altar. From Palmer's energetic teachings on holiness as a second blessing and on claiming the blessings of holiness from God's altar would come, in time, a vast array of holiness, Pentecostal, and prosperity gospel practices in the twentieth century. First, however, these ideas percolated in and even divided the Methodist churches, especially in the South.[17] The enthusiasm for holiness was fueled by summer encampments and local holiness fellowships, and especially by newspapers dedicated to testimonies of how others had experienced their second blessing (and by extension modeling for anxious readers how they might experience their own entire sanctification).[18] Over time different answers about the path to holiness generated competing churches. This interest in the means of grace and the methodology of being saved and blessed and blessed again has remained a constant unto this day in Pentecostal circles. But before we introduce the third source of modern Pentecostalism, let us pause for a brief taxonomy intermission.

MANY NAMES

Sometimes a person from outside the Pentecostal fold will marvel at all the names for churches and denominations that hint at differences but will not be able to understand why these are important enough to call out on the church's sign. To take just four of dozens of such possibilities, What is the difference between Church of God (Cleveland, Tennessee) and Church of God in Christ? And what is the difference between the International Pentecostal Holiness Church and the United Pentecostal Church International? What I tell my students and people wanting to learn more is to think about these names and the churches they represent in terms of both history and the stakes of salvation. The churches began in such localized circumstances that many carry similar nomenclature, but the names they employ are meant to signal ways to salvation. To devotees, a lot is at stake about getting the understanding and the practice right. In fact, because eternity is at stake, questions about whether God is worshiped in a triune form (Father, Son, and Holy Spirit) or in Oneness (in Jesus' name alone) has split Pentecostalism deeply from the beginning. And yet people in the Pentecostal world recognize one another. What were once enclaves that did not mix are heritages that blend into identities. In thirty-five years in theological education I have heard students (and professors) speaking in code to one another: "My mom was Jesus Only, and Dad was Church of God, Anderson, but I grew up in Portland going Four Square and when I went to college I got involved in a Vineyard Church, so that was a big change." From that I understand (after years of listening, friendship, and translation) that the speaker's mother was from a non-Trinitarian Pentecostal body, her father was from an old-time holiness church, and she grew up in a charismatic church that believed that all the gifts of the Spirit are available now, tongues and healing included, but starting in college she joined an evangelical fellowship that for all its vibrancy was neither Pentecostal nor holiness in its orientation. In the many varieties of holiness and Pentecostal churches we find in the South today, we encounter both moral and aesthetic choices in addition to regional and racial origins. Understanding ultimate moral choices in religion seems easy enough: believe this, and do this (and do and believe only these things),

Southern Traditions Revised

and you will have eternal life. So much of southern Christianity appears to be premised on morally exclusivist grounds: the preacher may not actually say, but will at least strongly imply, that if you are not a good and true believer in this particular church, then you are going to spend eternity in Hell. However, it turns out that Christianity in the South is (practically speaking) an ecumenical affair when it comes to where we think people are going to spend eternity; few of us are sure that our church alone shelters all the saints. Most of us know enough rascals in our midst to hold out hope for some of the sinners, too. Considered that way, the neighboring church might have something that can be said for it. And on the other hand, where to go to church to praise God, to get saved, to be blessed by the baptism of the Holy Spirit, and maybe even the gifts of the Spirit: that decision has aesthetic and social dimensions. Our church, our worship, is a more beautiful way to be with God (we think), but it is clearly not the only way. Most Christians in the South will clearly enunciate their preferences, but they will be loath to tell someone else what they may not believe, pray, or do in their own church. Christian liberty is not to be found in the Constitution, but it is a right in which southerners are well versed from way back.

TO CALIFORNIA AND BACK AGAIN

In the early 1900s various preachers and teachers, notably Charles Parham in Topeka, Kansas, had earlier advocated the idea that the original gifts of the Spirit at Pentecost just fifty days after Christ's resurrection at Easter were still available to true believers. Yet it was on Asuza Street, in a broken-down building in Los Angeles, that a Louisiana-born son of former slave parents, William J. Seymour, who had learned this doctrine in just five weeks of listening to Parham's teaching in Houston, brought about the revival that is credited as the birth of modern Pentecostalism. Seymour had been asked to guest preach for a month in Los Angeles. It turned into a much longer engagement. For days and nights, for weeks on end in the spring of 1906, preaching, prayer, unaccompanied singing, glossolalia, and strange bodily seizures among the racially mixed congregation attracted a crowd of gawkers. The *Los Angeles Times* made the Asuza Street Revival front-page news but described the services in a disdainful tone:

> Breathing strange utterances and mouthing a creed which it would seem no sane mortal could understand, the newest religious sect has started in Los Angeles. Meetings are held in a tumble-down shack

on Azusa Street, near San Pedro Street, and the devotees of the weird doctrine practice the most fanatical rites, preach the wildest theories, and work themselves into a state of mad excitement in their particular zeal.

"Yoo-oo-oo gou-lou-oo come under the bloo-oo-oo boo-loo," shouts an old colored "mammy" in a frenzy of religious zeal. Swinging her arms wildly about her she continues with the strangest harangue ever uttered. Few of her words are intelligible, and for the most part, her testimony contains the most outrageous jumble of syllables, which are listened to with awe by the company.[19]

But what the *Los Angeles Times* clearly mocked it also publicized, and the phenomenon grew. Part of what we see the reporters already noticing was the increased presence of black southerners. Southern black migration accounted for nearly all of the tripling of California's black population from 1900 to 1910.[20] And in California, even while Jim Crow ruled the South, William Seymour's Apostolic Faith Mission was an interracial movement, just like the original Christian Pentecost. The headline for September 3, 1906, showed that Pentecostalism was stretching even the West's more relaxed gender and race norms: "Women with Men Embrace: Whites and Blacks Mix in a Religious Frenzy."[21] From the very beginning, therefore, in Pentecostal circles women have led more than in evangelical ones, and even in the South the color line has never been on such prominent display as in other churches. Eschewing the marks of social respectability in the name of Christ is a point of pride in humility that perhaps accounts for why Pentecostalism is the fastest-growing form of Christianity globally.

The same trains that made African American migration from the South to southern California possible also enabled southern holiness leaders to travel to 312 Asuza Street and experience the new Pentecost for themselves, and so they did; black and white they came. The white evangelist Gaston Barnabas Cashwell and the black minister Charles Harrison Mason both made the journey in search of Holy Ghost baptism, and finding it they began new churches back south. For other southern leaders, just hearing about the new doctrines put into practice and learning about amazing events from Christian periodicals led them to transform their holiness fellowships in a clearly Pentecostal direction. The first general overseer of the Church of God (Cleveland, Tennessee), A. J. Tomlinson, saw it as flames of the Spirit consuming Tennessee, Georgia, and Alabama: "The Fire is spreading for miles and miles in every direction."[22]

To understand why Pentecostalism grew so quickly in the South we have only to review the preceding history the way a farmer reviews how a field has been prepared for planting. First came the restorationist ground, shared by a large number of evangelical southerners, to live and worship as Christians with the New Testament faith of the early church. Then came the Wesleyan and Holiness emphasis on two works of grace—salvation and sanctification—that created a kind of hothouse of ongoing Christian experience. Now Pentecostalism brought the process full circle by actually living the Pentecost experience of nineteen hundred years earlier in the eternal present, courtesy of the Holy Ghost. One Pentecostal newspaper made the case plainly: "Many are being saved, sanctified, filled with the Holy Ghost, and speaking in tongues."[23] Why would one settle for less than the full gospel? Finally, what one learned in an early 1900s Pentecostal service was that the gifts of tongues and apostolic healing in this age were for a purpose. The end was near: Jesus was coming, and soon.

Did Pentecostalism catch on? Based on the figures gathered by the Bureau of the Census in the Religious Census of 1916, 81 percent of Americans associated with the fledgling Pentecostal denominations lived in southern states.[24] Part of that amazing growth was due to the wholesale conversion of entire southern Holiness denominations, such as the Church of God (Cleveland, Tennessee) and the Church of God in Christ, to Pentecostalism. It is important to recognize that these churches were in the Holiness movement well before they embraced Pentecostal teachings and practices. Still, Pentecostalism continued throughout the twentieth century to grow disproportionally in the South. For its success in that century and in our own, we must look to its two great emphases and the way they have fit the southern context. Pentecostalism is pessimistic about the world, and Jesus is coming soon to save us from this world, not to make it better, as more liberal Christians might think. Therefore, there is in many Pentecostal circles interest in the end times, premillennialism, and discouragement about this world and its imperfectability (even the idea that the United Nations or other efforts might represent signs of the coming Battle of Armageddon). These are perennial concerns for some southerners and something that the Pentecostal family offered more generally to the southern worldview. One only has to tune into Pat Robertson's Trinity Broadcasting Network for a healthy dose of these signs that the end may be near.

Paradoxically for a worldview in which darkness and evil loom so near, Pentecostalism may be the most hopeful Christianity there is, for the Holy Spirit is even nearer than any evil and is empowering God's faithful so that they can do all things through Christ, who gives them strength (Phil. 4:13). Praying for the healing of disease, the repair of broken hearts and relationships, for new jobs, is not an appeal to the court of last resort the way that it can feel in other faiths, but just the way God works to bless God's children when they ask for what they need. They cannot, by their own action, keep the world from ending, but if God wants them to be happy and wealthy, who are they to argue? In this respect the early Pentecostals and the faithful of today stole an advance on the restorationists. The goal was never just living like New Testament Christians. Instead Pentecostal Christians want to experience the presence of God right now. Historian Grant Wacker calls this experiencing "heaven below." In the conclusion to his wonderful study of early Pentecostals he explains the successful spiritual and material well-being negotiation achieved in Pentecostalism: "Since God's Holy Spirit did everything, Holy Spirit–filled Christians did nothing. But since Holy Spirit–filled Christians did nothing, they were free to do everything. That conviction, as inspiring as it was ironic, gave Saints the two greatest goods that mortal existence had to offer: a life beyond in all its fullness, and the life at hand in all its richness. It was heaven below."[25]

Pentecostalism also proved to be a lasting fit with a southern background for other reasons as well. Southern moralism was already strong, and a sense that people needed to rely on the Holy Spirit to conquer their inner demons and other temptations was widely shared. Moreover, the Pentecostal and Holiness traditions "worked" in the sense that behaving in a holiness way between services made you a more sober, more employable, more respectable person before God and your neighbors, and even in your own estimation. Another clear advantage for fledgling Pentecostalism was that it was born in the same cultural moment and region as the blues, southern gospel, and jazz. Given Pentecostals' commitment to get up and move around and praise the Lord with one's whole being, the Pentecostal churches were destined perhaps to lose track of time but never to be boring.

CONTEMPORARY SOUTHERN PENTECOSTALISM

Two of the largest Pentecostal churches in the South are the Church of God (Cleveland, Tennessee) and the Church of God in Christ (COGIC).

Southern Traditions Revised

Spending time in their institutions provides a sense of how the Spirit-shaped life makes a difference in the day-to-day lives of contemporary southern Pentecostals. Although the Sunday services of the predominantly white Church of God (Cleveland, Tennessee) have come to be sometimes hard to distinguish from those of many Baptist churches, a trip to the church's Lee University demonstrates that a holiness approach to shaping lives remains distinctive. Likewise, a visit to Cathedral of Praise Church of God in Christ, a congregation associated with COGIC, demonstrates that when it comes to praise and preaching, the conviction in "heaven below" is alive and well.

Redemption from sin, turning one's life around, starts in most Christian theology by acknowledging the bad things you have done and the good you have left undone. Reconciliation comes after confession and the seeking of forgiveness, and it always involves others. A remarkable instance of what is supposed to happen when people commit sin in Christian community occurred on the campus of Lee University in Cleveland, Tennessee, in the winter of 2014. Lee began as a Bible institute sponsored by the Church of God (Cleveland, Tennessee). Interestingly, at Lee a profession of faith in Christ is not required for university admission. As faculty member David Roebuck explains, "That's intentional. The intentionality is we'll take you however you are. We'll pray and work for your conversion."[26] I explained to him that while I was preparing for our interview I learned that two sorority members at Lee had made a blackface rap YouTube video in poor taste, but I could not imagine a college or university on the secular side of things handling it better. My school and many others would have basically criminalized the students for hate speech, I allowed, whereas Lee had counseled them like a Christian family that this was not cool or funny but rather cruel and racially insensitive. Later, I observed, when a black reporter from a Chattanooga television station was trying to get African American students at Lee to say that the video was a terrible, horrible thing, the students interviewed instead put the incident in the context of their peers' lack of development and understanding; the reporter got both less and more than she hoped for. Of course, the video was racially offensive, but the black students who had every right to be offended had another language ready besides simple condemnation. As Christians, they made clear, they could expect their sisters to transform and their college—their community—to help make that happen.

David Roebuck confirms my impression that the Lee administration is very intentional and good about not just being reactive. Later in the afternoon I go on an admissions tour and ask a rising senior from Atlanta about the incident and other typical college issues—drinking, drugs, sex, loss of faith—and he explains how Lee surrounds students with mentors on their halls, in dorms, in chapels, and in the presence of faculty, all in the name of student development. My student guide's exact words about the ethos were: "It's still very family oriented in the sense that we're all here together, we're all learning, and we're going to learn from you. We're a family." In my own head I'm reflecting on how different this Christian university is from so many other colleges with honor codes that already assume that students know how to behave honorably. It is also very different from Liberty University in Virginia, where a system of strict demerits and penalties guides students back on the right track. At Lee, there is a sense that the university plays the role of a loving, faith-nurturing parent in a developmental sense. So reconciliation can be as sweet as learning the errors of one's ways or as bitter as the chastening rod.

Cathedral of Praise Church of God in Christ is on Clarksville Pike, an exurban rural route leading north out of Nashville. The Sunday I attend is November 12, 2016, the first Sunday after the election of Donald J. Trump to be the forty-fifth president of the United States. Though it is no surprise that Tennessee voters voted for Trump, this Sunday I choose not to go to my Presbyterian church, where the members are still in shock and grief that Hillary Clinton did not manage to pull off the election. On this Sunday, I am looking not for lamentations but for a word of faith and hope. Bishop Jerry Maynard and his congregation do not disappoint in this regard.

Like nearly all Pentecostal churches I know, and most contemporary evangelical ones for that matter, the service begins with praise music. Praise music is not intended to be like an organ prelude or a choral introit in a traditional worship setting—a time to collect one's thoughts. Instead, it marks the beginning of one's participation in raising praise to God. A good music leadership team can have the congregation crossing the line between singing along and praying in song. Cathedral of Praise's principal song leader this morning is a great worship music leader. Most of what we are led to sing is quite contemporary. We begin with Chris Tomlin's 2010 "Our God," a full-throated affirmation of the majesty of God that includes:

Our God is greater, our God is stronger
God You are higher than any other
Our God is Healer, awesome in power
Our God, Our God[27]

Next up is what is commonly called the Anthem, recorded first by the Planet-shakers and then by numerous gospel artists. It declares both Christ's victory and the believer's claim on the result:

> Hallelujah you have won it all for me
> Death could not hold you down
> You are the risen king
> Seated in majesty
> You are the risen king[28]

After each song, the band keeps a groove going in the background as the song leader raises spoken prayers of praise keyed into the congregation's situation and to the mood of the next song. Our third praise song is Hezekiah Walker's 2016 smash gospel hit "Better," which recognizes that even though your life may seem out of control, with people letting you down, that is not the last word:

> Whatever state I find myself in
> I learned how to be secure
> Knowing that God
> Will supply all my needs
> And He'll work things out for my good
> It will get better
> Better . . .
> [Repeated][29]

The music conveys a message of hope for all seasons: "It will get better, because God is in control." Whatever mood one brings to the Cathedral of Praise it will be lifted by the choruses of "Better" that repeatedly rise by half-steps. After three praise choruses affirming God's victory, we are all on our feet singing. Then comes the choir's modern showstopper—Richard Smallwood's 1996 "Total Praise." It is constitutionally difficult if not impossible to feel sorry for yourself, I think, after listening to "Total Praise." That is the affective logic of beginning with praise.

Bishop Maynard knows that the warm glow of praise choruses notwithstanding, this has been a bad week for the African American community, seeing President Obama's legacy rejected at the polls and a man deaf to black America raised up in his place. He asks, "Is anyone ready to give up?" He waits for a beat. "I'm so glad. I was going to change your mind if you were. Sometimes we need a change of mind. It's going to get better!" Maynard says, referencing the praise song we had just sung minutes earlier. After some regular life-of-the-church matters, including recognizing the mothers of the church in their eighties and nineties, Bishop Maynard gets down to the business of changing our outlook on life by appeal to the Scriptures in his sermon. His text for the day is from Exodus 14:13–15:

> 13. And Moses said unto the people, Fear ye not, stand still, and see the salvation of the Lord, which he will shew to you today: for the Egyptians whom ye have seen today, ye shall see them again no more forever.
>
> 14. The Lord shall fight for you, and ye shall hold your peace.
>
> 15. And the Lord said unto Moses, Wherefore criest thou unto me? speak unto the children of Israel, that they go forward. (KJV)

The theme of the sermon is "Go Forward." Like so many black church preachers before him, Bishop Maynard is comparing his flock to the ancient Israelites. He builds a bridge to the congregation, acknowledging that he, like they, knows that the community and the nation have experienced setbacks before. He recalls some of these to mind: "We have experienced reversals before—the recession, 9/11, Vietnam, Iraq, Afghanistan, Iran, North Korea." The election is one more of these setbacks, and he has come back this week from St. Louis, where he was supposed to be, because his sense is that his place is with his congregation, who have been brought low by the election results. As Pentecostal Christians, the victory is in God's hands, but it is easy to forget at moments like this. "We are moving onward," he says, but he also notes, "We like to live in the valley of complaint." The work for the faithful? "We need to rid ourselves of that posture," he declares. "Moses understood that when he said, 'Do not be afraid.'" But of course fear still exists, especially in moments like this, and so, Maynard says, "We do things that do not make a lot of sense because we are afraid."

Bishop Maynard finds his word of faith in the Good News that Moses conveyed to a people delivered by God who were still afraid of what came next. "Stand still and see the salvation of the Lord," says Moses. The larger theological and existential takeaway Maynard preaches is that "it is not so bad when we go *through* something and God is on our side." And then he does something clever with the text that I did not see coming. Moses says, "You will not see these Egyptians again." Maynard says that this means that you may see some other "Egyptians" (or problems), but you will not see that problem again. This is classic Pentecostal assurance that what God promises,

God delivers. In this context, it means that if God rids you of one problem, he will rid you of another problem. Maynard calls on his church members to stand by the strength of their faith, even now: "If God is in control of your house, why are you concerned about who is in control of the White House?" He adds, "When we complain and protest, what good does it do us?"

As for an alternative to moping and complaining? "It is time for us to protest where God is!" Maynard says, "Standing still does not mean being dumb. It does not mean I wait on you. It means waiting on the Lord!" This is a day for reminding the faithful that their faith covers all aspects of life. "Do not be worried about your job, house, business because the truth is in. God is faithful," Maynard affirms.

When things look bad, they have a way of distracting believers, but the Pentecostal way is to believe that the final victory is already certain. "Even the death on the cross was not a loss but a victory," Maynard reminds the church. And then there is the dimension of what believers need to do to co-operate with God's plan: "When your spirit is low you are going to sink. You are going to sink, but if your spirit rises you are going to rise." A good way into the message Maynard asks the question that might be on some of the more conservative members' minds, "Why are you talking about the election, Dr. Maynard?" Then he answers his own question, not with a political justification but by doubling down religiously: "Because I have to; because God will make a way. It is going to be all right. As a matter of fact, in your faith—it is already. 'Go forward,' God says." And then we are simultaneously the Hebrews and ourselves asking in fear, "What about the Red Sea—I know, I made it," Maynard supplies in a humorous retort for God. "God wants us to trust him," he says. Therefore, it might look bad, but with God all things are possible.

At the close of the sermon, Bishop Maynard drops his voice. "This is coming from me, not the Lord." (Bishop Maynard is clear to make plain that he is about to make a political point about the consequence of faith.) "If you are concerned about who is in the White House, do not fear to communicate with them. Look at them straight in the eye and tell them: Go forward!"

Pentecostalism's hope in the face of adversity is one of its most salient aspects. God entered history, proclaims Scripture, but God can do it again, because, as the saying goes, "He did it again today." Those words helped open Cathedral of Praise's service. They are not meant merely as metaphor. Before the offering Bishop Maynard offers a soft prosperity gospel pitch for generous giving. Bless the Lord in our giving and we will be blessed in our lives. Again, he employs humor to make the point: "Don't be going having no

Bentley plans if you're just a Yugo giver." There are laws of trust and proportionality at work here. Above all, in sickness and health, in good times and bad, God is near. "The Lord giveth and the Lord taketh away. Blessed be the name of the Lord" (Job 1:21).

A century after the world first heard of Pentecostal Christianity and American Christians were divided by the practice of "tongues speech," a 2006 Pew Forum report revealed that perhaps 40 percent of all Pentecostals never speak in tongues themselves, and only 25 percent of U.S. Pentecostals responding indicated that their churches usually feature someone speaking in tongues. "I think that the classic Pentecostal belief that speaking in tongues was the real evidence of the second baptism of the Holy Spirit is, at least in practice, not widely accepted around the world," said John Green, senior fellow at the Pew Forum. "I think these communities are defined more by other types of spiritual practices than by speaking in tongues."[30] Indeed, Pentecostalism in the contemporary South is not only practiced in particular Pentecostal congregations, many of which never feature glossolalia in their worship service, but has also spread into nondenominational and so-called Bapticostal churches. This second process, a kind of *pentecostalization* of southern Christianity, can been seen in the way that Pentecostalism's colorful, musical worship has in the past half-century gone from being viewed as the uncultured worship of a lower class to being widely emulated in churches in general. Think about all the borrowings that have been made from Pentecostal churches into evangelical and mainline houses of worship during recent years. First there were praise bands and praise choruses at the beginning of the church service with words on song sheets or screens, not hymnals. Add to that preachers coming out from behind the pulpit, telling great stories and showing emotion. And with these practices came others testified to in the book of Acts—women speaking in church, and a fellowship that was as interracial as we imagine the day of Pentecost itself being, or at least as close as we can imagine it from inside southern community. Evangelicals previously not interested much in premillennialist eschatology, a Pentecostal strength, began to speak about the rapture (not specifically mentioned in Scripture), an event when the Christian dead are to be resurrected and believers still alive are gathered up with them.

Measured by the number of adherents in Pentecostal and Holiness denominations in the South, roughly only 6 percent of the southern religious population are Pentecostals.[31] Measured by the way Pentecostal beliefs and modes of worship have infiltrated other Christian bodies in the South, the movement's impact is incalculable. Yet in the final analysis neither praise bands nor a greater cultural interest in the rapture are Pentecostalism's true legacy. Throughout a wide swath of southern Christianity Pentecostalism has succeeded in making God seem nearer than ever before. In churches in the South and beyond where people believe that the Spirit of God is as close as prayer and enters into the very beings of worshippers gathered for sincere and ecstatic praise, Azusa Street's fire is still burning and reshaping organized Christianity like a refiner's fire.

WASHED IN THE BLOOD
IN THE RED STATES

Religion and Politics

I know what you may be thinking when you read that title above: this must be a chapter about the Tea Party at prayer. At least that is the reaction I get during the twenty or so times a year when my commitments take me out of the South and into cities and states in other regions. My colleagues, friends, and even new acquaintances in Colorado, New York, Minnesota, and Pennsylvania can read the maps on election night and comment accordingly. What they see is that but for an occasional blip around a populous but geographically compact urban area, the map of congressional districts is strikingly red in the southern states, in much the same way as a map of the leading religious body for the same counties would be the color assigned for Baptists. (In the definitive *New Historical Atlas of Religion in America*, Baptists are shown in yellow, but I don't think it's a color they would have chosen for themselves.) So things look from a thousand miles away: right-wing religion backs right-wing politics. Yet that is not the whole story. Indeed, up close, the distinguishing factor of southern politics is that everything that is discussed in a political or public forum eventually gets turned into a moral issue. There are no simple technical policy issues (except maybe roads, which everyone is in favor of, unless the contract bidding process is corrupt, in which case it becomes a moral issue).

Contemporary religion and politics, as seen from inside the South, is complex, much more complex than national television pundits or outside observers might think. Even so, the religion and politics players tend to fall into three basic camps. First are the law-and-order Christian conservatives, whose politics tend toward legislating personal morality while business is given free rein to be guided only by "the unseen hand" Adam Smith thought was nearly the hand of God. The second camp is filled with heirs of the southern civil rights movement who prioritize progress on education, jobs, restorative justice, race relations, and voter rights ahead of limited government. Each of these two groups has noted activists, some of whom we will meet below. There is a third tradition of religion and politics in the South, and these are the people who believe that their religion teaches them how to be better people but that politics has no place being discussed from the pulpit or in church. They also have no use for preachers who appear in public forums telling citizens or lawmakers what God expects them to do. This quietist middle and the activist left and right sides of the southern faith and life story make religion and political life more of a contact sport today than at any time since the 1960s. Despite those red state maps, the state houses themselves and state supreme courts are full of religiously charged issues in the early twenty-first century: abortion, sex education, creationism and evolution in public schools and textbooks, voter suppression, racially inferior schooling, biased incarceration policies, capital punishment, marriage equality, outlawing homelessness, bathrooms for transgendered persons, and making it illegal to aid undocumented persons with transportation, medicine, or food. The states may look decidedly red on national political media maps, but in today's South the politics are red-hot.

When you print a set of mental images to go with the words "southern politics and religion," what do you picture? Is it a white-haired, white-skinned older male practicing demagoguery in the U.S. Senate? Or maybe is it someone like the late Robert Byrd holding forth about "our sacred traditions"? Or do you have a more modern image in mind? Perhaps you picture a middle-aged man or woman with too much hair and hairspray gloating about the solidly Republican South? Having lived in Georgia in the 1990s, I still picture Newt Gingrich, but Lindsey Graham or Nikki Haley will do just fine. For many observers, the category of southern politics and religion is all about conservative, some would say right-wing, politics. There is something to that, as we shall see, for in terms of who wins the most elections in the region, conservatives have held the upper hand forever, even when the solid South was solidly Democratic before 1964. Politics is more than winning elections, however. It is the contest over how people in a given area will live and govern themselves. Maybe, then, your image of the southern politician is John Lewis, Jimmy Carter, Julian Bond, Terry Sanford, or Andrew Young. By these standards there is a lot more to discuss about southern religion and politics than merely noting Republican dominance. Indeed, even in those red congressional districts there are always people who vote Democrat (even some who will vote Green Party), and many elections are about whether a candidate is blue or red enough by local standards to represent her or his constituents. Moreover, the real southern politics takes place at the local and state levels. It is at these levels that this chapter focuses to examine a distinctively southern political-religious conversation that has both progressive and traditionalist sides, which can differ dramatically according to the state that is having the "conversation." In Dixie as much as anywhere, all politics is local, but be the speaker liberal or conservative, the accent, cadence, and vocabulary will still sound a lot like church.

If your image of the southern politician is male, there may be a factual basis for your stereotype. Women are noticeably underrepresented in government in the southern states. While the national average percentage of legislators who are women in 2017 is 22.4 percent and states like Vermont (40 percent), Colorado (39 percent), and Arizona (38.9 percent) lead the nation, West Virginia (13.4 percent), South Carolina (13.5), Mississippi (13.8 percent), Alabama (14.3 percent), Louisiana (15.3 percent), Kentucky (16.7 percent), and Tennessee (16.7 percent) all figure among the bottom ten states for female legislative representation. At present, only one southern women serves as president of her senate, and only one is speaker of her state's house. Though most states have some women in their congressional delegations, Kentucky, South Carolina, Georgia, Arkansas, and Louisiana have none, joining Mississippi, which has never sent a woman to Congress. Shelley Moore Capito of West Virginia is the region's lone woman in the Senate.[1] Not all politics is electoral, as we shall see, but bear gender politics in mind as we encounter three stories of religion and politics, southern style.

In Alabama we will meet a distinctive voice in state Supreme Court chief justice Roy Moore, who engaged in the symbolic politics of Ten Commandments allegiance to the point of being stripped of his judicial office, only to win it back by popular demand (and to be stripped of office yet again). Also in Alabama we will meet four bishops who staked out a Christian politics of resistance to the nation's harshest law aimed against undocumented persons in the second decade of the twenty-first century. Last, we will meet the Reverend William Barber II, the North Carolina clergyman and NAACP (National Association for the Advancement of Colored People) leader who, under the banner of Moral Mondays, has organized perhaps the most successful religious-political movement in the South since the civil rights movement of the 1960s.

JUSTICE ROY MOORE AND THE BANNER OF CHRISTIAN LIBERTY

The chief justice of Alabama's Supreme Court, Roy Moore, is famous for his defiance in refusing to remove a five-thousand-pound granite rendering of the Ten Commandments from the rotunda of the state Supreme Court building, which he had placed there six months after his original election in 2000 to this judicial office. Through a series of court challenges and judicial ethics panel actions that led to his removal in 2003 he remained defiant, demonstrating a faithfulness that, for other Christians, was reminiscent of Shadrach, Meshach, and Abednego refusing to bow down before King Nebuchadnezzar in the book of Daniel. This time, however, it was a Christian judge, who believed that the American frame of government was Christian, refusing to bow down before secular neutrality, and more people in Alabama loved him for it than not. "There's nothing illegal in what I did," Moore argued in a 2012 interview after a campaign speech at a Birmingham country club, looking back on his adherence to God's law as the foundation of American law in the Ten Commandments case. "Our money says 'God' on it. Our Pledge of Allegiance says 'under God.' So tell me this," he asked, with a rhetorical flourish: "How can a chief justice not acknowledge the sovereignty of God?"[2] Shortly thereafter, in the election for chief justice, the people of Alabama decided that they liked the way he carried himself more than his Democratic opponent, a criminal defense attorney who had run for public office ten times before without a win to his name. Moore's high status as a jurist among conservative Christians is sometimes depicted by the media as out of the legal mainstream (and members of the Alabama bar as a whole hold him in low regard), but I think it is more accurate to recognize him as one of the most influential representatives of a type that one encounters in the Christian Legal Society, in David Barton's revisionist popular histories about the so-called Christian founding of America, and in the Republican Party throughout the South.[3] In sum, Moore is a paragon when it comes to belief that America was, is, and should remain a Christian nation.

Roy Moore's view of the nation as a Christian land under the sovereignty of God begins with his interpretation of the Declaration of Independence and its principal author, Thomas Jefferson, whom historian Joseph Ellis has aptly called the American Sphinx because Jefferson remains a riddle to even careful historians and curious Americans nearly two centuries after his death.[4] During the most active phase of legal activity on the issue of same-sex marriage, for instance, Moore gave a visitor a copy of a booklet entitled, "One Nation under God," which included the Declaration of Independence, the Constitution, and other framing documents so as to underline his judicial philosophy before any questioning about the issue of the moment began.[5] Again and again, this straight-arrow West Point graduate and Vietnam veteran wanted to make the point that in his view this is a Christian nation and that judges who say otherwise are just "people in black robes" abusing their authority.[6] Moore often turns to Jefferson as his authoritative founder to articulate this point. Thus, in a letter to Alabama governor Robert Bentley in January 2015 explaining why the state should not comply with a federal court ruling allowing same-sex marriage in Alabama, Moore quoted a fairly cranky, older Jefferson at length:

> On December 26, 1825, Thomas Jefferson wrote:
>
> I see as you do, and with the deepest affliction, the rapid strides with which the federal branch of our government is advancing towards the usurpation of all the rights reserved to the States, and the consolidation in itself of all powers foreign and domestic; and that too, by constructions which, if legitimate, leave no limits to their power. Take together the decisions of the federal court the doctrines of the President, and the misconstructions of the constitutional compact [U.S. Constitution] acted on by the legislature of the federal branch, and it is but too evident, that the three ruling branches of that department are in combination to strip their colleagues, the State authorities, of the powers reserved by them, and to exercise themselves, all functions foreign and domestic.
>
> Letter to William Branch Giles, December 26, 1825
>
> Jefferson's words precisely express my sentiments on this occasion.[7]

If you were to read the whole of Moore's letter, you would also see Mark 10:6–9 identified as Alabama's true definition of marriage (though if followed, it would also rule out divorce) and the rest of his case being made in terms of states' rights and the duty to resist tyranny, a line of thinking that Moore here traces to Jefferson. Other Christian conservatives love to talk about the "Doctrine of the Lesser Magistrates" and the legitimacy of "interposition," which says that lower officials have a duty to disobey unjust laws from higher officials and courts.[8] All of this following-the-higher-law-of-God talk is interesting, but starting with Moore's reading of the Declaration of Independence, you may want to interject, "But was not Jefferson a Deist?" Moore does not read him that way. Neither did the Moral Majority's Jerry Falwell see Jefferson that way. In the same office at Liberty University where he died in May 2007, Falwell maintained a massive bust of Jefferson on his conference room table. For Falwell, Jefferson was associated with religious freedom. Jefferson himself wanted to see himself that way, for he arranged to have his gravestone read:

Here was buried
Thomas Jefferson
Author of the Declaration of American Independence
of the Statute of Virginia for religious freedom
& Father of the University of Virginia[9]

Just what being the author of the "Statute of Virginia for religious freedom" means, however, is open to interpretation. Sixty-seven miles northeast of Lynchburg, in Charlottesville, the Thomas Jefferson Memorial Church—Unitarian Universalist, near the campus of the University of Virginia—is also named after Jefferson. Therefore, in one case Thomas Jefferson is the patron saint of religious freedom—the freedom to be aggressively evangelically Christian; in the other, Jefferson is the forefather of the freedom from evangelical Christianity: in short, a hard-to-decipher sphinx. Indeed, although I as a historian think that Patrick Henry is a better model for a Revolutionary Era defender of Christian America, the real point to absorb for understanding contemporary conservative southern Christianity is that people who share Roy Moore's belief that the founders set out to create a nation whose laws presuppose what the Declaration terms "the Laws of Nature and Nature's God" in Christian terms (that is, denoting *Laws of the Bible*, and the *Bible's God* in their reading of the phrase and not something French and philosophical) are numerous in the South. God, America, and the family are a package, and any threat to the package is an intolerable assault on law and faith equally. When these partisans talk about liberty, which they do frequently, it is not freedom to do anything one wants to do that they have in mind. Instead, when they hear and say "liberty" they have in mind a particular kind of liberty—the freedom to do the right thing, a God-given right to do right by God. Christians have been struggling with this paradox at least since the apostle Paul wrote the Letter to the Galatians: "For you were called to freedom, brothers and sisters; only do not use your freedom as an opportunity for self-indulgence, but through love become slaves to one another" (Gal. 5:13, NRSV). Ever since that time, and especially in heavily Baptist places like Alabama, Christians have been proclaiming their liberty and telling one another how good Christians should live.[10]

Eventually, on September 30, 2016, Roy Moore's actions in issuing the order stating that probate judges "have a ministerial duty not to issue" marriage licenses to same-sex couples caught up with him. That is when the state's Court of the Judiciary suspended him from the bench without pay for the remainder of his term, through the year 2019, when he would be too old to run again for office. Interestingly enough, some members of the court made it clear that they did not disagree with Moore on the morality of same-sex marriage; still, they came down hard on him for an order that was "incomplete, misleading, and manipulative" and wrote that the order's purpose was to direct probate judges "to stop complying with binding federal law."[11]

FOUR ALABAMA BISHOPS WELCOME THE
STRANGERS IN THEIR MIDST

If fear of breaking the family-America-law-God bond that assures victory in all things drives a rather punitive jurisprudence in much of the South, it is also the basis for draconian responses to undocumented persons. Alabama, which does not border Mexico, was nevertheless quick to jump on the bandwagon when it came to enacting legislation making the state inhospitable for what it called illegal aliens. Arizona had acted first, and even although many provisions of Arizona SB 1070 were under injunction from enforcement, Alabama upped the ante, with its own HB 56 crafted independently by Kansas secretary of state Kris Kobach and cosponsored by Alabama state representative Micky Hammon and Alabama state senator Scott Beason. Titled the Beason-Hammon Alabama Taxpayer and Citizen Protection Act, the law became the harshest anti-immigrant bill ever passed by a state legislature. It was signed into law on June 9, 2011, by the Republican governor of Alabama, Robert Bentley, himself a deacon and Sunday school teacher at First Baptist

Church in Tuscaloosa.[12] One of the most onerous aspects of the law was that it made rendering assistance to other human beings in the form of transportation, food, first aid, shelter (provided that those other human beings were undocumented citizens of other lands) felonious conduct. In this sense, the law went so far as to say that for Christians the answer to "Who is my neighbor?"—that is, who must I love as myself?—was not "Everyone is your neighbor," as generations of Sunday school children had been taught. Rather, Alabama legislators wanted Christian charity strictly limited by citizenship. This went too far, thought a number of Alabama religious leaders, and it certainly did not sound like Jesus. Thus was set a conflict between the law of the Heart of Dixie and the higher law of God, the law of the gospel. Soon after Governor Robert Bentley signed the bill into law, the U.S. Justice Department, civil rights groups, and four Alabama bishops filed lawsuits to prevent its enforcement.

The lawsuit, *Parsley v. Bentley*, filed by two Catholic prelates, Archbishop Thomas Rodi and Bishop Robert Baker, along with Episcopal bishop Henry Parsley Jr. and Methodist bishop William Willimon, constituted the first time that a group of bishops had filed suit to stop an anti-immigrant law at the state level.[13] The bishops argued that the sections of HB 56 that criminalized transporting or harboring an undocumented immigrant and prohibited any actions that "encourage or induce" undocumented immigrants to live in the state interfered with Alabama citizens' First Amendment right to freely express their Christian faith, especially the performance of the sacraments and church ministries that serve the poor. The bishops were forceful in their condemnation of HB 56, publicly calling it "the nation's most merciless anti-immigration legislation," a point that neither supporters not detractors of the act argued. Archbishop Rodi of the archdiocese of Mobile spoke in support of the unusual action of bishops suing the governor: "No law is just which prevents the proclamation of the Gospel, the baptizing of believers, or love shown to neighbor in need. I do not wish to stand before God and, when God asks me if I fed him when he was hungry or gave him to drink when he was thirsty, to reply: yes, Lord, as long as you had proper documents."[14] Bishop Willimon of the North Alabama Conference of the United Methodist Church called the bill an embarrassment (presumably to the state) and said that it was motivated by "intimidation and meanness." The law included a provision that made it illegal knowingly to hire or give a ride to an illegal immigrant. Thus a church volunteer who gave someone a ride to the doctor could be prosecuted, religious leaders feared. "One of the most nefarious aspects of this law is it appears to criminalize Alabamians in the act of being helpful and compassionate," Willimon said, calling the claim that an immigration crackdown would create jobs "particularly repugnant."[15]

Bishops saying things to their extended flocks from a moral point of view is not that unusual, even if Catholics, Episcopalians, and Methodists agreeing to speak with one voice is much more so. Yet the media bites, even the ones that compared their resistance to HB 56 to Martin Luther King Jr.'s rejection of the need for Christians to follow unjust laws in his famous "Letter from Birmingham Jail," paled in significance to the first-order religious speech they employed in addressing the court.[16] That is to say, unlike so many who have wanted to invoke King's mantle by quoting him in the midst of conflicts, the four bishops succeeded by doing what King had done almost half a century earlier—by invoking the Bible's claims on Christians to convince the court that said Christians could not follow the teachings of their faith within the strict bounds set by HB 56:

> The Anti-Immigration Law, No. 2011-535 of the 2011 Regular Session of the Alabama Legislature, violates the First Amendment rights of members of Alabama's faith community to freely exercise their requisite duty to practice the Gospel. Biblical teachings to extend hospitality to all people without reservation are obligatory to members of Alabama's Episcopal, Methodist and Roman Catholic religions as well as other faiths. These Bible-based instructions to feed the hungry, shelter the homeless and clothe the naked are in direct conflict with the Law's restrictions against assisting undocumented Alabama residents. Representative Micky Hammon, who sponsored the House Anti-Immigration Bill ("HB 56"), admitted that the intention is to ensure Alabamians are inhospitable to strangers. "This bill is designed to make it difficult for them to live here so they will deport themselves," Representative Hammon said.[17] In contrast, the Bible is replete with directions on how to selflessly welcome all people without reservation such as:[18]
>
> 1 John 3:17
>
> But if anyone has the world's goods and sees his brother in need, yet closes his heart against him, how does God's love abide in him?
>
> Matthew 25:35–40
>
> "For I was hungry and you gave me food, I was thirsty and you gave me drink, I was a stranger and you welcomed me, I was naked

and you clothed me, I was sick and you visited me, I was in prison and you came to me." Then the righteous will answer him, saying, "Lord, when did we see you hungry and feed you, or thirsty and give you drink? And when did we see you a stranger and welcome you, or naked and clothe you? And when did we see you sick or in prison and visit you?" And the King will answer them, "Truly, I say to you, as you did it to one of the least of these, my brothers, you did it to me."

Exodus 22:21

You shall not wrong or oppress a resident alien, for you were aliens in the land of Egypt.[19]

And so it went, in a crisply argued legal brief that used the Christian gospel in its simplest and least contested form, together with clear teachings from the Law and the Prophets in the Old Testament to argue that Alabama Christians, simply by following the essential teachings of their faith to love their neighbors, serve the poor, and welcome strangers would themselves become criminals. The bishops and their lawyers moved the frame of the discussion from undocumented persons to the rights of Alabama Christians to observe their faith in action:

> Members of Alabama's Episcopal, Methodist and Roman Catholic churches will perpetrate crimes by knowingly providing food, clothing, shelter and transportation to those in need without first ensuring compliance with the stipulations of the Anti-Immigration Law. Moreover, the ministry of the churches, by providing such services to known undocumented persons, is criminalized under this Law. To forbid members of Alabama's faith communities from providing these services is in violation of their sincere religious belief to help others without reservation. Members of Alabama's Episcopal, Methodist and Roman Catholic churches are so sincerely committed to welcoming strangers that they demonstrate their commitment by engaging in ministries throughout the state to provide meals, housing, transportation and educational services.[20]

The biblical and catechetical mandates to act on love of God and love of neighbor were strong for each of the represented traditions, and the religious leaders and their legal team made a case based on their religious traditions, to be sure. Yet, lest anyone think they were making a merely theoretical complaint about HB 56, the bishops' brief went on in the case of each of their churches to show the particular ministries in particular cities and counties and towns of Alabama where they were—as Christians and as churches of Christians—doing the work of welcoming aliens, binding up broken limbs and hearts, feeding the hungry, sheltering the homeless, and clothing the naked, with special emphasis on how those ministries were open to the very Hispanic immigrants the law was targeting for "self-deportation." A gauntlet was thrown down, in effect, by these princes of the churches: Under the U.S. Constitution we have the right to practice our faith, and our Christian faith requires that we welcome the stranger as a neighbor, an act of faith this law seeks to criminalize. Which law will give way, the First Amendment of the Constitution or HB 56?

The concerted action of the bishops had some of its intended effect. On September 28, 2011, U.S. District Judge Sharon Blackburn entered a preliminary injunction against several sections of the law, including section 13, which criminalized transporting or renting to an undocumented immigrant. These parts of the law never passed judicial review and remain blocked. Some of the harshest provisions of the law, including the requirement that Alabama schools check the immigration status of new enrolling students and their parents, however, were allowed to stand, even though they were repeatedly tested in other legal actions.

Though each of the four bishops spoke on behalf of the gospel, the Catholic bishop and archbishop had larger Hispanic constituencies in their churches and greater support from white Catholics to stand up for their coreligionists. Episcopal bishop Parsley took an early stand on the issue on constitutional grounds, a special passion for religious liberty for which he was known.[21] He had also served as the diocese's bishop since 1999 and had announced his intentions to retire before the crisis was at hand. Between his good service and Episcopalians' good manners, he came off relatively unscathed politically. United Methodist bishop Willimon was not so lucky, and he and his wife both received calls at the office and at home telling him what they thought of his political views on "illegals." Some of those callers were happy to add that they were United Methodists.[22] Although United Methodist bishops are powerful when it comes to making appointments of clergy, they get to hear about any and everything from the people in their conferences. Willimon was nevertheless determined not to be the kind of bishop that one of his predecessors had been, one of the eight recipients of the "Letter from Birmingham Jail," accused in it by Martin Luther King of counseling patience with genuine and obstinate evil.[23] Instead, Willimon was inclined to cite the theologian Karl Barth at times when the church had a choice of being popular with the state or being the church of Jesus Christ. In his autobiographical reflections on his time as the bishop of North Alabama, he quoted the 1934 Barmen Declaration, in which Barth had a guiding hand: "The church has to testify in the midst of a sinful world, with its message as with its order, that it is solely [Jesus Christ's] property, that it lives and wants to live solely from his comfort and his direction."[24] Willimon also was heard to lament on occasion, "We've created an ecclesiastical system whereby clergy are protected from ever having to take any risk whereby they might be hurt by Jesus!"[25] Suffice it to say, the angry calls about suing the governor over HB 56 were not welcome in the Willimon household, especially when they came from fellow United Methodists, but they were understood as the cost of discipleship.

It is easy to think that what happened in Alabama could not happen elsewhere, but throughout the South in the years that followed, various forms of helping the poor, the immigrant, the homeless, and the hungry were treated to various forms of criminalization and restriction via zoning. Sheltering even a few homeless people in a church during the bitter cold was held to be a zoning violation in Memphis.[26] Feeding the homeless was restricted by law in 2013–14 in these southern cities: Birmingham, Alabama; Jacksonville and Gainesville, Florida; Atlanta, Georgia; Covington, Kentucky; Charlotte, Raleigh, and Wilmington, North Carolina; Columbia and Myrtle Beach, South Carolina; and, Nashville, Tennessee.[27] In a region where political appeals are frequently made for cutting government assistance "because churches are better equipped to help the poor," it seems perverse to set limits on the very groups who seek to offer help in God's name. But then again, you have to think about the kind of people religion compels people of faith to feed and shelter, and that is bound to make some people squeamish, uncomfortable, and frightened.

WILLIAM BARBER II, MORAL MONDAYS, AND
THE POLITICS OF MASS PROTEST

Many times during my career in theological education I have heard some version of the question, "Where are the Martin Luther Kings of today?" The questioners were invariably looking to the civil rights movement as a golden age in living memory of moral leadership provided by religious leaders, and to King as the example of what clergy could do for society beyond narrow parish boundaries. The question remains problematic for me in at least two ways. First, it undervalues the work that priests, rabbis, ministers, and imams do in their daily work binding up the brokenhearted and forming the moral and religious sensibilities of people and communities. King and his Southern Christian Leadership Conference colleagues would not have had much to work with if generations of preachers and teachers had not formed consciences waiting to be troubled into supporting the right side of history during the civil rights era. The other problem with only remembering MLK when we ask where are the Martin Luther Kings of today is that we fail to see how many people were involved in the movement then or to realize that the size of King's reputation was made in no small measure because of the enormity of the evil and opposition he and Rosa Parks, James Lawson, John Lewis, Diane Nash, C. T. Vivian, Ralph David Abernathy, Fred Shuttlesworth, and so many others had the courage to face.

Despite my twin reservations about such questions, in the spring of 2013 I began hearing more and more about a remarkable religious leader in North Carolina whom everyone, it seemed, was comparing to Martin Luther King Jr. The man's name was William J. Barber II. The Reverend Dr. Barber had been the pastor of the Greenleaf Christian Church, Disciples of Christ, in Goldsboro, North Carolina, since 1993 and the statewide executive director of the North Carolina NAACP since 2006. In 2007, he had formed a coalition of progressive groups in the state called Historic Thousands on Jones Street (HKonJ) People's Assembly Coalition, composed of ninety-three North Carolina advocacy groups, all the while building the North Carolina NAACP into the largest chapter in the nation. People in the North Carolina "movement" knew William Barber, and his professors from Duke Divinity School, where he went to seminary, knew him as one of their finest graduates, but the rest of the country was about to hear from him because things were changing so rapidly in North Carolina that Barber was soon to be called to a bigger pulpit, so to speak. Events create their own appointment with destiny, just as in words that one of King's earliest biographers once applied to him, "When the man and the hour were met."[28] Once again, there was a zeitgeist of incipient protest and a preacher in the right place to center it in faith.

On Monday, April 29, 2013, Barber stood before nine hundred assembled protesters gathered on Jones Street in front of North Carolina's capitol building in Raleigh and read a prepared statement spoken on behalf of the nine hundred North Carolinians who proclaimed their choice of "Nonviolent Civil Disobedience in the Face of an Avalanche of Extremist Policies That Threaten Healthcare, Education, Voting Rights, Especially the Poor, African-Americans, Latinos, Women, Seniors and Students." The statement opened as civil rights statements of half a century earlier had, with an invocation of the civic religion (in this case from the North Carolina Constitution's Declaration of Rights) and then an invocation of the law of God (in this instance from the prophet Micah), and found the current state leaders wanting:

> We hold it to be self-evident that all persons are created equal; that they are endowed by their Creator with certain inalienable rights; that among these are life, liberty, the enjoyment of the fruits of their own labor, and the pursuit of happiness.
>
> All political power is vested in and derived from the people; all government of right originates from the people, is founded upon their will only, and is instituted solely for the good of the whole.
>
> The people of this State have the inherent, sole, and exclusive right of regulating the internal government and police thereof, and of altering or abolishing their Constitution and form of government whenever it may be necessary to their safety and happiness; but every such right shall be exercised in pursuance of law and consistently with the Constitution of the United States.
>
> The book of Micah asks us, "What does the Lord require of you? But to do justice, love mercy and walk humbly with God." It is in a spirit of openness to the prophet's question that we gather here as people of faith and citizens of North Carolina.[29]

Then Barber launched into a litany of the actions that Governor Pat McCrory and the legislature had taken to undermine voting rights, civil rights, and economic equity since taking office. Anticipating that some would deplore his group's protest tactics, he said later in his speech: "So we have no other choice but to assemble in the people's house where these bills are being presented, argued, and voted upon, in hopes that God will move in the hearts of our legislators, as he moved in the heart of Pharaoh to let His people go. Some ask the question, why don't they be quiet? Well, I must remind you, that it has been our collective silence that has quietly opened the city gates to these undemocratic violators of our rights."[30] Seventeen protesters were arrested that day, and a movement to frustrate

Figure 2. The Reverend William J. Barber II addresses supporters at
Moral Monday 11, July 15, 2013. (Photograph by Phil Fonville)

and reverse the Republican agenda in North Carolina and other southern
states was born.

The Moral Mondays protests never might have occurred as weekly
events if not for the stunning reversals in North Carolina electoral politics in
the first dozen years of the new millennium. In 2008, North Carolina, a state
that often split between Democrats and Republicans but had not given its
Electoral College votes to a Democrat since Jimmy Carter in 1976, narrowly
voted to give them to Barack Obama. This, plus the Tea Party conservative
movement starting in 2009, pushed Republicans to ensure that never happened again. The elections of 2010 led to Republican control of both houses
of the North Carolina General Assembly for the first time since the end of
Reconstruction in 1896. In 2012, Republicans retained control of the legislature and voters elected a Republican, Pat McCrory, as governor. The stage
was set for implementation of a right-wing wish list of policies: lawmakers rejected seven hundred million dollars in federal unemployment benefits and
passed up federal funds to expand Medicaid for half a million people; voted
to raise taxes on nine hundred thousand poor and working-class people;
slashed funding for preschool and kindergarten; and pursued the truly wild
idea of letting legislators receive gifts from lobbyists. Later sessions would
see a preference for vouchers and homeschooling over public education. To

Southern Traditions Revised

make certain that Republicans cemented their electoral base, voter ID bills aiming at disenfranchising nearly half a million older, browner voters without government-issued identification were passed. Measures were also taken to curtail early voting, same-day registration, and Sunday voting.[31]

The community had seen enough. What followed was a textbook example of how grassroots organizing can and should work. The coalition of progressive groups, HKonJ, saw many of their dearest causes—health, education, civil rights, economic equality, environmental justice—under threat. The Republicans, for their part, lost no time in trying to turn back the progress of the civil rights movement, and the pace of the changes they sought caught North Carolinians up short. Suddenly people who thought that they lived in an exceptional southern state, that is, a state in the South that did not engage (anymore) in a racialized politics more reminiscent of Alabama or Mississippi, learned overnight how wrong they were. These were the kinds of people who surprised themselves by joining Moral Mondays, becoming part of a movement affiliated with the NAACP. One of them, Courtney Ritter, a mother of three from Pittsboro, was arrested for the first time in her life in June 2013 and made it a point to keep coming back as a supporter. Journalist Ari Berman reported, "She wore pearls and a cardigan for her arrest, 'to look as conservative as possible.'" As much as she was determined to convey her respectability as seriousness for the cause, Ritter also felt the connection to what had gone before: "I felt a moral obligation to all of those people in the civil rights movement who had put their lives and jobs on the line. I wanted them to know that what they did mattered." Perhaps most tragically, North Carolina in the present seemed too much like what she had read about Alabama in the days of segregation. "I made a choice to leave Alabama, and my husband and I deliberately chose North Carolina," Ritter said. "We chose it because it was southern and familiar, but it was a lot more progressive than Alabama. . . . What's happening in North Carolina almost felt personally offensive to me. I thought, 'Wow, I could've stayed in Alabama.'"[32]

Of course, the black population of North Carolina had never been convinced that the state had rejected its Jim Crow past and turned into a smart and genteel version of the Research Triangle, Charlotte, and the Triad, writ large. This is where the Reverend Barber came in, for he was prepared with a deep analysis, a set of progressive allies, and something else rarely seen in public—a willingness to use the ordinary stuff of biblical exegesis, moral argumentation, and old-fashioned preaching in public to make a Christian case for why what the governor and legislature were doing was wrong. More remarkably for the twenty-first century, Barber somehow managed to do it in a way that did not offend his allies of other faiths and of secular dispositions. A colleague of mine told me poignantly of seeing a woman at a protest with a sign indicating that she was a "Jewish agnostic for Moral Mondays" listening to Barber with a big smile on her face. Did the fact that he is basically preaching a Christian sermon bother you, talking about Jesus even, my friend asked her. "No," she replied, "I just never thought I would live to see the day when Christians down here would stand up for other people like this."[33]

So every Monday while the North Carolina legislature is in session for three years and running, the Moral Mondays–Forward Together coalition of the North Carolina NAACP and HKonJ has been protesting, singing, and worshiping by the thousands, and getting arrested by the tens and hundreds. The Forward Together part of the name is an addition to signal that they do not simply react but are about promoting a forward-looking set of social priorities. It comes from an old civil rights call and response where the leader shouts, "Forward together," and the marchers shout back, "Not one step back." The Moral Mondays–Forward Together leaders have taken the movement to other cities in North Carolina and inspired similar movements in Georgia and South Carolina.

Barber also knows how to make memorable protest theater to dramatize what is at stake. In September 2013, back in Raleigh for the eighteenth Moral Monday, with a back-to-school youth-oriented protest, more than two hundred demonstrators carried three empty coffins making a long, silent procession to the executive mansion. The silence of the marchers was punctuated by periodic singing of the civil rights protest hymn "We Shall Overcome." The coffins themselves represented another "children's crusade," the 1963 Birmingham phase of the voting rights movement that included the bombing of the Sixteenth Avenue Baptist Church in which four young girls were killed. Stopping at the governor's mansion, Barber referenced their deaths as martyrs to the movement in his remarks: "That blood [of the martyrs] says to us, 'We were martyred . . . for equality and equal protection under the law. Don't you dare go backwards. Don't you let our dying be in vain.'" Barber continued, "We say to the current leadership of North Carolina, 'If you stay with this extreme agenda, we love you but we will fight you, covered in the blood of the martyrs.'"[34]

Barber is a powerful speaker, but his greatest power is persuading others that they must rise up and speak and protest and stand for others' rights. Yale theology professor Willie Jennings, formerly of Duke, sometimes substitute

Southern Traditions Revised

preached at Barber's church so that Barber could be elsewhere leading the movement, but Jennings himself was led to break a vow of sorts to his parents to avoid (as a black man) ever getting arrested. He wrote about "Why I Got Arrested in North Carolina" in an essay in the journal *Religion Dispatches* that went viral. NPR's *Weekend All Things Considered* host Jacki Lyden asked him, "What made you change your mind?" Jennings's answer spoke to the crux of the faith dilemma the Moral Mondays movement put before people like him:

> A black man in this country knows that it's very easy to step on the path that leads to incarceration. And so my dear dad, one of the things that he impressed upon me very early is that we're going to do everything possible, Willie, to make sure your entire life you never see the inside of a jail cell or prison cell.
>
> So it was a psychological battle for me to do this because I knew that in some ways, I was breaking a sacred promise to my dad. But there was another promise that I had also made to him, and that I would try to embody the teachings and the life of Jesus. And concern for the poor, oppressed, vulnerable is at the heart of that.[35]

Then what of the comparison to Martin Luther King? In every instance I can find of William Barber's media appearances where such a question is likely to be raised, as in his sermons and public addresses, Barber is always quick to point out King's later messages about neglect of the poor of any race, the pursuit of war over education, and the things that make for peace. A typical example of Barber's rhetoric of prophetic inclusion reads as follows:

> Martin Luther King, Jr. said 46 years ago in one of his last sermons that if you ignore the poor, one day the whole system will collapse and implode. The costs are too high if we don't address systemic racism and poverty. It costs us our soul as a nation. Every time we fail to educate a child on the front side of life, it costs us on the back side—financially and morally.
>
> Every time we deny living wages, leaving whole communities impoverished, it costs us on the back side. Every time we fail to provide health care on the front side of life, it costs us on the back side. Every time we attempt to suppress the right to vote, it tears at the heart of our democracy and the necessary foundations to establish justice.

The greatest myth of our time is the notion that extreme policies harm only a small subset of people, such as people of color. These extreme policies harm us all.[36]

This particular text comes from an online issue of *Sojourners*, an evangelical progressive publication, but like all of Barber's efforts, it has a scriptural basis ("We must remind those who make decisions regarding public policy what the prophet Isaiah said: 'Woe unto those who legislate evil . . . rob the poor of their rights . . . make children and women their prey.' Isaiah 10: 1–2"). His *Soujourner's* article also contains his central conviction about transformative politics in the South, that a fusion of progressive whites and people of color, who cared out of faith about their brothers and sisters, and out of a general commitment to simple justice might be the basis of a much needed "Third Reconstruction." Only when people set aside race and class to promote justice, as they did in 1865–98 and in the civil rights years, has the South, Barber argues, ever moved forward.[37] How wide is the prophetic agenda the Moral Mondays–Forward Together movement proclaims? This is the list recited at most gatherings:

1. Pro-labor, anti-poverty policies that create economic sustainability by fighting for employment, living wages, the alleviation of disparate unemployment, a green economy, labor rights, affordable housing, targeted empowerment zones, strong safety net services for the poor, fair policies for immigrants, infrastructure development, and fair tax reform;
2. Educational equality by ensuring every child receives a high quality, well-funded, constitutional, diverse public education as well as access to community colleges and universities and by securing equitable funding for minority colleges and universities;
3. Health care for all by ensuring access to the Affordable Care Act, Medicare and Medicaid, Social Security and by providing environmental protection;
4. Fairness in the criminal justice system by addressing the continuing inequalities in the system and providing equal protection under the law for black, brown, and poor white people;
5. Protecting and expanding voting rights, women's rights, LGBT rights, immigrant rights, and the fundamental principle of equal protection under the law.[38]

With all of these causes, rights, and interests being pursued under a common banner, it is no wonder that Barber has found groups who see their interests represented in the movement. Indeed, the coalition is said to number more than two million adherents in all affiliated groups in North Carolina. The real wonder, however, is that in a region where many of the above issues and people and religion do not normally mix, it is precisely under a banner of prophetic justice inspired by the Hebrew and Christian Scriptures that the coalition collectively pursues peace and justice for the variously defined "least of these."[39] On May 11, 2017, Barber announced at a press conference that he would be stepping down after twelve years as North Carolina's NAACP president to form a twenty-five-state poor people's organizing campaign. He would be broadening the parish once again, even as he continued to serve as pastor of Greenleaf Christian Church in Goldsboro.[40]

VALUES VOTERS ONE AND ALL

Throughout this chapter three kinds of political power are on display, none of them conventional lawmaking, judicial review, or the other basic stuff taught in high school civics classes. Judge Roy Moore was a public official, to be sure, but he will be remembered for his demonstration of his Christian faith behind his judicial robes. The Alabama bishops demonstrated the politics of a higher law, of obeying Christian conscience instead of an anti-immigrant state law. They probably achieved as much as they did because neither the First Amendment of the Constitution nor Matthew 25 contains exceptions pertaining to undocumented persons, and the Alabama state house cannot change a word of either document. Sometimes good people in positions of power reminding others of their pledged duties still have real power in the South. Last, William Barber demonstrated yet another form of political power, that of alternative values–based mass protest, where the goal is to call de jure government leaders and their policies into constant question and to delegitimize their role whenever possible while building a support base for formal legal challenge in the courts and at the ballot box. Barber has inspired a few lawsuits in North Carolina, too, as well as citizens' movements in other states, all of which have brought more people into the public affairs of those states than at any time in the past forty-five years.

The essential political divides in the South in all of these issues are, at first glance, formal and symbolic: Do we or do we not recognize trusting in

God and God's commands as the foundation of all laws in society (including prayer in school and at the beginning of city and town council meetings)? That is just the surface, however, the kind of story the nightly news loves to cover because it has two vociferous sides. The more fundamental grounds of the religion and politics argument are as ancient (and philosophical) as the question Cain asked God in Genesis: "Am I my brother's keeper?" (Gen. 4:9, KJV). In the Christianity-saturated politics of the South, the first answer to that moral question is always, "Yes," but that yes means different things depending on the rest of one's ideological commitments. For southern evangelicals, fundamentalists, and Catholics in the 2014 general election, being my brother's keeper often meant voting for a constitutional amendment in several states to "protect the unborn." For mainline Protestants and black church Christians, and some Catholics, among others, it often meant expanding Medicaid under the terms of the Affordable Care Act so as to cover more poor and vulnerable brothers and sisters. In the South, the overwhelming majority of politically active people see themselves as values voters, but not everyone comfortable with that terminology votes the way the label would predict.

PART TWO

GULF COAST DISASTER

Religion Is Only as Good as What It Does

5

OUR CHURCH IS CLEANING
UP AFTER KATRINA

Most Americans who were alive in the waning days of August 2005 have vivid, media-framed memories of the nightmare that was Hurricane Katrina for New Orleans, southern Louisiana parishes, and coastal Mississippi. Bodies on the street—black bodies, apparently dead, abandoned outside the New Orleans Convention Center. Crowds of poor people deserted by the buses that were supposed to be their escape route, finding the only high ground on a giant interstate overpass. Citizens using small boats to save people off the roofs of their bungalows. Homes in the Lower Ninth Ward with a spray-paint code to indicate that dead bodies had been found. Hundreds of miles north, convoys of trucks filled with ice, unable to approach the affected areas due to traffic snarls. And, in an ominous sign of things to come from the Federal Emergency Management Agency, FEMA trucks stuck in the same traffic.

In addition to these enduring images of helplessness and occasional re-sourcefulness, stories and phrases stick in our memories. The story of the St. Bernard Parish nursing home residents drowned in place in their beds needs no pictures to be terrifying. Likewise, the terrible choice clinicians faced when their life-support-dependent patients at Memorial Medical Center in New Orleans could not be evacuated or provided the necessary emergency power still haunts a more than decade later. Nowhere else in modern America have doctors and nurses euthanized their patients en masse or in the absence of informed consent. At Memorial, when the power went out and the indoor temperatures climbed above 100 degrees, seventeen patients dependent on artificial means for life support were injected with drugs, hastening the end of their lives.[1] And with all of this misery—seen, heard, and retold—another phrase will also stick to Katrina: "Brownie, you're doing a heck of a job," uttered by President George W. Bush to his FEMA director, Michael Brown, became shortened to "heckuva job," a two-word signification of government failure and cronyism.[2]

When it comes to Hurricane Katrina, everyone remembers New Orleans and the vicinity, but people in Mississippi claim that they were forgotten by the media, and there is clearly something to that assertion. No one who has seen pictures of the gigantic storm surge towering over cars, buildings, and even the ocean itself in Biloxi, Waveland, Pass Christian, Bay St. Louis, or any of the other hurricane-ravaged coastal Mississippi communities is likely to forget those images, but the New Orleans story did take up more media attention. Why? Because it was a story of human and government failure of epic proportions, leaving people to blame. For weeks and months to come, whether in Louisiana or Mississippi, the basic narrative of hubris, avarice, incompetence, racism, and neglect on the part of governmental entities and insurance companies was fed with additional material. Hurricane Katrina was an American tragedy, but this chapter explores a less familiar dimension of the Hurricane Katrina story, that of the religious response to natural disaster and human calamity.

I think my favorite early media memory from Hurricane Katrina came after the storm had passed over New Orleans and vicinity on Monday, August 29, but before the levees broke. There was already extensive damage to homes, and the electricity was out. A television reporter on assignment eager to report something visual on the big storm saw a white man outside a low-slung red-brick Baptist church setting out long white folding tables. The reporter asked what he was doing, and the man replied, "People are without electricity and they've got to eat. We are a church, it's something we're good at—feeding people. So I came down and we're getting ready to feed the hungry." As I recall, the reporter then asked, "Are you doing this for your church members?" The Baptist man gave the reporter a long look like she was not from around here, and then responded, "No, this is for anybody who is hungry and needs food. It's what we do as a church. We feed people." I watched the television with a smile as the message of the Gospel

Religion Is Only as Good as What It Does

according to Matthew 25 went out live on CNN. "I was hungry and you gave me something to eat." This chapter is about how Christian groups, among others, demonstrated their character through the last decade of cleanup from Hurricanes Katrina (August 2005) and Rita (September 2005). Their assistance went well beyond food to shelter, to speaking out against powers and principalities, advocating for prisoners, and rebuilding churches, homes, and communities.

The night before that television interview in Louisiana, ninety miles to the east in Biloxi, Mississippi, the remarkable seventy-four-year-old pastor of Main Street Missionary Baptist Church, the Reverend Kenneth Haynes, was on his knees praying to the Lord that his two-story brick church building two and a half blocks from the Gulf of Mexico would survive the storm. Earlier, knowing what was coming, he had opened the church's second-story fellowship hall to members and neighbors from the surrounding mostly one-story and frame houses nearby. He even sent out his deacons, younger men, to compel and assist neighbors to make the journey through the gathering tropical storm winds. Already, as he prayed, nine feet of water was filling the ground level and coming up the stairs to the second story, where more than 120 people were gathered. Haynes's prayers did not go unanswered, and his courage became a rock the next day as his members and neighbors went forth to assess the damage, including finding people dead who had stayed behind in their homes. Again Haynes asked his deacons and other men to get busy. They set up pit barbecues, fueling them with downed trees, and initially cooking what was left in refrigerators cut off from power. They ended up feeding their neighbors continually for three months.[3]

So much bad news came out of the hurricane zone when it came to the work of FEMA and to the reluctance of insurers to pay for damages. (The flood insurers blamed the winds, the casualty insurers blamed the flooding, and no one answered their phones, it seemed.) As a result, loosely organized groups of churches, college students, and individuals were soon headed for the Gulf at their own expense and on their own initiative, determined to help wherever they could and to counter government ineptitude. Watching so many call-ups of these groups announced in school and churches, I noticed something that concerned me. When I was at my local Presbyterian church, they were often organizing groups to help rebuild white Presbyterian churches of pastor friends in Mississippi. In United Methodist churches I visited, they were helping rebuild United Methodist churches. At our multicultural divinity school, we were targeting New Orleans' Lower Ninth Ward. I began to wonder two things. First, were all the people who needed help getting help or just the best connected—denominationally, and otherwise? Second, I wondered were they getting the help they needed, or were they getting the help people wanted to provide? I have been around Christian mission work long enough to know that there is almost nothing that can stop twenty-five youth with thirty gallons of paint from painting your house, even if all you actually need is the storm windows cleaned. So these became two questions to ask the recipients of help and the faith-based participants in the rebuilding of their Gulf Coast communities when I hit the road nine years after Katrina struck. As for the first question, recovery efforts are ongoing, and some people were helped less—the poorest neighborhoods in New Orleans have suffered the most despite religious leaders' efforts to step up to the challenges of past neglect. The short answer to my second question was surprising. Helpers helped and even restored sagging spirits again and again for residents who felt abandoned by the powers that be. The Reverend Rod Dickson-Rishel of Long Beach United Methodist Church said it most colorfully: what the property insurance did and did not do "depending on your point of view, can make a preacher cuss," yet he hastened to add he had nothing but good to say about the church volunteers from outside his church who came to help, and kept coming.

YOU SHALL REBUILD THE CITY

New Orleans is unusual insofar as the usual southern arrangement of white evangelicals being religiously dominant does not pertain. Instead, from earliest European settlement, much of the political and economic powers have been held first and foremost in the hands of Catholics, while blacks and Creoles, and other old-line groups like Jews, Episcopalians, and Presbyterians, got an early start and have the kind of influence relative to white Methodists and Baptists one might find in New York or Chicago, rather than Baton Rouge, which is only eighty miles away. As such, Catholic presence in New Orleans meant that cleaning up after Katrina was not mere physical restoration of Catholic churches and other diocesan properties but an opportunity to tend to the broken soul of the Crescent City. In New Orleans, the money was overwhelmingly white, but the citizens themselves before the flood were overwhelmingly African American. The strategy of withdrawal into alternately respectful and tense territories—African Americans with the

Religion Is Only as Good as What It Does

mayor's office, whites with the Garden District, sharing the NFL Saints and the French Quarter—needed a reboot. Enter Michael Cowan.

After fifteen years at St. John's University in Collegeville, Minnesota, as a psychologist and counselor with strong interdisciplinary interests in theology, Cowan moved to New Orleans in January 1990 to serve on the Loyola University faculty in the Institute for Ministry. Within the first year that he was in New Orleans, he was robbed outside his home coming back from teaching a night class, and Cowan remembers, "It really frightened me." He had brought his family from a midwestern town so placid that people did not lock their doors to one where crime was endemic. But instead of leaving, he reports, he got drawn into an IAF (Industrial Areas Foundation) community organizing effort that was getting under way. Cowan put his energies from 1992 until the hurricane in 2005 and a little bit afterward into the effort to build the Jeremiah IAF organization in New Orleans. Jeremiah failed as an organization, but as a set of networked relationships that could be reenergized after Katrina, Jeremiah set up the religious community for a new set of associations to emerge in a faith-based group called Common Good. Cowan explains his pivotal role in starting the group:

> Mayor [Ray] Nagin established in October of 2005 what he called the Bring New Orleans Back Commission. One of the committees [of the commission] was government efficiency and effectiveness. These were all chaired by businesspeople, and the chair of that committee was an ally and friend of mine. He asked me (this was all volunteer work) to serve as the chief of staff of that committee and organize it. So I did that. That brought me into all of these meetings where the different committees were reporting, and our committee was working, and as we looked around, what I saw was that the business community was making its presence felt to protect its interests, as you would expect, and the government leaders were there, as they had to be there legally, but the civil society presence was just about nonexistent.[4]

All of this made Cowan think about organizing civil society participation in the planning and execution of rebuilding the city. He explored his ideas with the head of the local community foundation with whom he had worked and who had supported Jeremiah. Then he went to his boss, the president of Loyola University, and pitched the proposal of taking time away from the classroom in service to the rebuilding effort: "I said I'd like to try to organize this and what I'd really need to do it is just three years of support so that I could be free to do this work." Both Loyola's president and the community foundation president said yes. That was the genesis of Common Good.

From this timely initiative from one Catholic psychology professor with a theology degree and an expansive sense of ministry came other groups, with other such origins of their own, most notably a group of civic-minded women called Citizens for One Greater New Orleans and a faith-based community organization that is part of PICO (People Improving Communities through Organizing) called the Micah Project (Moving In Courage And Hope), which is especially strong on addressing black incarceration and poverty in New Orleans. All of this was made possible, sadly, by a hurricane.

New Orleans is different in many ways from other places in the South, and one of the chief ways is in the strength of its Catholic institutions. Cowan, a Catholic from the Midwest, tells me, "The Catholic Church is a much bigger presence both in numbers and culturally speaking here. It was certainly present in Minnesota, but it wasn't dominant in its presence as it is here in New Orleans. That's a big difference. But the Catholic Church is so big here that it thinks it can, and very often it can, function with its own resources because it has so many of them and so many concerns." That size and power, he notes, can also make it hard for the church to make common cause with other people of faith and to attend to the needs of the city. However, that line got crossed for good because of Katrina. The other big difference Cowan saw immediately, coming from white, small-town Minnesota, was "how race structured everything, including religion, in the sense that congregational life in the city was almost completely and still is completely segregated."

To Cowan and my African American interviewees, New Orleans remains a very racialized place—indeed, quintessentially so, since the landmark case *Plessy v. Ferguson* (1896) was a test (among other things) of whether there were shades of color or a strict racial binary. People have a tendency to recall that the teacher John Scopes, of the Scopes Monkey Trial (1925), was actually recruited, as was Rosa Parks later, to test a law thought to be unjust. John Scopes lost his court case but won in the popular imagination (though the struggle over evolution and creationism continues). Rosa Parks won, first in her community of Montgomery, Alabama, with the successful conclusion of the bus boycott in 1956, then in the nation. In contrast, the nearly white-skinned Homer Plessy lost in his own community of New Orleans first in 1896 and then for another half-century as racial segregation was secured in law. In that half-century and since, New Orleans has played with the race line in creative ways, but the law of the land—Washington's federal law and (more important) Baton Rouge's southern law—has been observed. All of this is to argue that a large Catholic population and Creole culture, combined with the absence of readily available sweet tea, does not make New Orleans not part of the South, except to some people who are more in touch with those markers of southern culture than with the continuing white-over-black oppression in this city, just like any population center in the Southeast.

The racial disconnect between part of New Orleans society and other segments was not the only one that Michael Cowan found as he began his part in reknitting the fabric of civil society in post-Katrina New Orleans. The very term "Common Good," the name for the organization Cowan helped found, is itself a Catholic term deriving from Thomas Aquinas's teaching that there is a natural law that applies to every human being of whatever faith and a common good that is to be pursued among all people because they are all creatures of the same Creator, no matter what church, synagogue, or mosque they may or may not attend or nation from which they may come. It is a powerful concept that allows Catholics, Protestants, Jews, Muslims, and others to work together without having to have a common confession. As religious leaders and people began to collaborate with business and civic leaders, Cowan noticed something. These leaders began to confess that after decades in New Orleans they were becoming part of conversations that they had never had before. So Cowan, the professor, began to map out the before-and-after relationships using social network analysis to get a handle on what was going on. He had asked about seventy business, civic, religious, philanthropic, and higher education leaders who they had worked with in civic betterment projects before the hurricane. His next question was, "Who have you worked with since the hurricane and flood?" The results speak for themselves, insofar as the network lines are about three times as dense after Katrina than they were before the disaster. But the real kicker is that when Cowan breaks the leaders down into sectors—business, civic, government, religious—the religious leaders looked to be the most peripheral, the least connected before the storm. And, as Cowan points out, their new degree of connection does not reflect that they are suddenly having dinner with more people; rather, "it's that they started to be engaged in the work of rebuilding the city together."

As Michael Cowan talks to me about disconnected and connected religious leaders, I flash back to the late 1990s when, as dean of a theological school, I was part of a regular lunch group in Atlanta with some older lions of the city who were hoping that younger ministers could catch the spirit of connectedness that they had in the 1960s, when Atlanta had the reputation of being "the city too busy to hate." One of those lions was the Reverend Andrew Young, a former Atlanta mayor and civil rights leader. Another was James Laney, the former president of Emory University. Both were former ambassadors, but the thing that they wanted to impress on us came from their prior commitment as ordained ministers: "Good change happened and bad things were averted because we religious leaders knew each other," said Young. "And through one another, we knew all the business and civic leaders in the community." When something came up in the community, the religious and civic leaders worked on it together. The thing that I will never forget about those lunches that sealed their testimony about the power of (southern) community when used to ethical ends came once after our meal was over and we were downstairs waiting for our cars to be brought up. An elderly guest came into the foyer, and Young went into pastor mode, expressing solicitude for him and making certain that he got into his car safely. Jim Laney explained after the guest had driven off that the elderly man was Ivan Allen, the last white mayor of Atlanta, the business leader who had reached out to black religious leaders to make way for peaceful transition when other southern cities were experiencing boycotts and reacting violently. Andrew Young had just preached his lunchtime sermon again, this time without words.

THERE WAS SOMETHING MISSING IN THE CITY

Eugenia is one of those persons who found their way into a lay ministry of leadership later in life and doubled down when Katrina flooded the neighborhood around her church. Eugenia is not her real name but a pseudonym meant to protect her identity while preserving her testimony about her experience. Like many southern Christians, she volunteered in her church to assist "the least of these" (Matt. 25) but held a day job in the private sector. And like many, the rewards of the vocation that came from volunteering through church exceeded those from paid work. Eugenia pursued opportunities for leadership training in serving the community from a Christian framework because, she says, "There was something missing in the city. The economy was great for tourists, but in the inner city and in the communities there was a missing link. In my studies and in my spiritual growth I saw that restorative justice was not happening here."[5]

Religion Is Only as Good as What It Does

Eugenia became more and more involved in a particular ministry located in one of New Orleans's perennially poorest neighborhoods. Then, in 2005, Katrina happened. While still a volunteer, she was relocating people from the community to another state and setting up schooling for their children. Because of the damage to low-lying neighborhoods in the below-sea-level bowl that is most of New Orleans, this went on for a couple of years, not just weeks or months.

When the residents Eugenia had helped finally moved back, Eugenia was looking to be a force for restorative justice, which she understands as making things right as they should be in God's justice. Yet even when we spoke eight and a half years after the storm, there still was not a new school in the neighborhood and city leaders were neglecting these residents, all the while telling them it would be better for them to get out of their neighborhood for schooling, playgrounds, and services. A public housing complex had been rebuilt, but the rest of the public services amounted to a list of unfulfilled promises to the people who had the least means to rebuild for themselves. "If the people will travel two miles outside the neighborhood to a grocery store," Eugenia explains, "then there is not going to be a grocery store built."

Scripture of course says that "one does not live be bread alone" (Luke 4:4, NRSV). What the poor neighborhoods of New Orleans lack in other services, they often have in an abundance of churches. The question becomes how to connect the richness of faith with a drive for a better future. Eugenia explains how her ministry fills in that gap. "What we do," she says, "is to build leaders, restore families, bring justice to those people. We work to be the voice for those people who do not have a voice for themselves through education, housing, and health care." As I toured Eugenia's neighborhood and several others, however, I learned that many of the churches still had not reopened in New Orleans' poor and black neighborhoods, just as many of the poorest residents left the Crescent City in 2005 never to return.[6]

In the face of the kind of continued disparities documented in the Urban League's *State of Black New Orleans: Ten Years Post-Katrina* that have white New Orleans residents reporting that their quality of life is better and black New Orleans residents saying that it is worse than pre-Katrina, how do veteran urban ministry workers keep their spirits intact?[7] "I have a good prayer life," Eugenia replies with a smile, "and I have a lot of people in New Orleans and other places who constantly support and pray for me." What gives her hope, I ask? Working with young children, she says, "Looking in their eyes and seeing hope and trying to give it back, telling them that God loves them and there is a better future waiting for them, a better future possible, sharing the Bible." She draws her strength from her understanding that it seems that "God wants me to hang on to the young generation and help them develop to be what God wants them to be as leaders in their own communities. Some days that is all that keeps me going, because everybody else has given up on them, and I can't." Everyone else sees life through the lens of Katrina, dislocation, and dispossession, but that is not good enough for the children. "You have to see it through the eyes of God," Eugenia says. "These kids are innocent of it—the disaster." More than ten years after the flood, with the Orleans Parish School Board and Recovery School District continuing to struggle over how to provide education that works for children coming from disadvantaged homes, it is a testament to Eugenia's patient, loving kindness that she continues to hold out for a higher standard—trying to look at children "through the eyes of God."

ON HIGHER GROUND

Serving in a neighborhood at the other end of the New Orleans socioeconomic scale is the Reverend Don Frampton, pastor of St. Charles Avenue Presbyterian Church (USA), whose parish overlaps the affluent Garden District as well as the Uptown and University areas. Frampton previously served a church in eastern North Carolina for eight years and before that was in Charleston. That turned out to be of benefit where Katrina was concerned, he says, because at least "Charleston and New Orleans are pretty similar. It was not a situation where I felt as if I were lost in the cosmos as pastor of a church in a city that had been decimated by a hurricane. I felt like I knew pretty much what to do, and in fact I did know what to do, and we did it and we're still doing it. We needed to reach out to the community in helping recover from this devastating calamity, and we were in a unique position to do it because we didn't get flooded."[8] That, as Frampton is quick to acknowledge, made all the difference in the world between churches that were able to come back and resume quickly and those that were not. "If you were flooded, it was months before you could return to any kind of normal operation," he notes. "If you weren't, then you could get back as soon as the city reopened and start back again, and we were able to do that. So we weren't flooded and we had plenty of resources, both financial and human resources, and if you will, we had really, really good leadership here, both lay and professional leadership, so we were positioned to take a lead role in recovery work and we

Religion Is Only as Good as What It Does

did that." What they did was to start, in late October 2005, a recovery organization named RHINO (Rebuilding Hope In New Orleans), an organization that is still making a difference. RHINO continues almost every week to host groups of volunteers from around the country who come to New Orleans to do service work. Most of the work during the school year is building with Habitat for Humanity. Sometimes the church connects volunteers with social service agencies in the city. None of the work has to do with specific Katrina cleanup anymore, but it is related to the continuing issue of people who "need to be in decent housing in relation to Habitat's mission."

As Don Frampton says, this kind of volunteering fits right into Habitat's mission in New Orleans, and Habitat is the quintessential southern domestic mission activity. Former president Jimmy Carter builds Habitat houses; so do I, with an interfaith build project each year. There is something spiritual (and oh, so concrete) about building homes for people that transcends all ideologies. Habitat identifies and vets future residents, secures the property, prepares for the build, and coordinates the volunteers. Visiting volunteers can join those builds through RHINO. As Frampton tells us, "People still like coming on down here. So we supervise them, we organize the week for them, we look after them during the week. We have a staff person who only does that and is the RHINO ministry director. We have the volunteers come here at night for supper, particularly on Wednesday night, when the church comes together for a church night supper. They eat in various members' homes one night a week as well. That's something we started back in '05 that's still going. And then they go out on their own a couple nights and have fun in a really fun city." These volunteers, housed for the first three years in a church-owned house retrofitted with dorm rooms and showers, are now housed at a guest wing of a nearby hospital. No wonder it has become a popular mission trip destination. As Frampton allows, "You can have both business and pleasure in New Orleans, which is kind of hard to offer" in other places. Not only is it still going strong, there is also Camp RHINO in the summer, which Frampton started about three years ago for junior and senior high students and is the real growth story of RHINO. "There are five weeks of Camp RHINO where youth from around the country come for a week in an urban ministry camp working with homeless shelters, soup kitchens, food banks, agencies for developmentally disabled adults, doing prayer tours at night."

I ask Frampton what difference nine years of constant mission activity has made for the host church. "It's redefined us," he replies. I ask him to go back to the August to October post-Katrina period in 2005 and try to recall what the conversations were like in his head, among his staff, and with the church's ruling elders. I ask him, somewhat bluntly, "Did Jesus speak to you to do RHINO specifically, or in the general way where Jesus always speaks to you to do good?" Frampton takes my question in stride:

> We plan our work and then we get planned. Every year, up until
> [Katrina] we, like a lot of big churches, had all kinds of plans for
> the sort of perennial events on the church calendar—among them
> stewardship—which we do in the fall. We're on a calendar year
> budget, so for '05 we'd been working on stewardship since January
> of '05 and we were going to roll that out. Actually, August 28th the
> day before the storm hit, I probably had a "minute-for-mission" on
> stewardship in that service. So when it became apparent that the city
> was uninhabitable, that people were forbidden from entering New
> Orleans, and it was going to be some time before the city reopened, I
> called my stewardship chair and I told him, "Tom, I don't think we're
> going to be doing this program this year. We're going to be directing
> all of our efforts to outreach." He said, "I know we are. That's clear."

Another initial call that Frampton made was to his finance committee chair to begin talking about ways to fund the operations of the church absent Sunday collections and people paying on pledges. Fortunately, they had (and have) an endowment that they used to bridge them over until the time when everybody was back.

Don and his family evacuated to Houston. He set up temporary shop in Houston at Memorial Drive Presbyterian with his temporary church in exile in the basement of that church, and Memorial's pastor Dave Peterson helped set the congregation up and his congregation provided for everything. Frampton says, "They were fabulous to us. I managed to get a couple of my associates to join me there along with my business manager and one or two other folks." Despite losses within the church family, the church building was relatively spared, and that made coming back sooner a possibility. The church got hit by the storm, but it didn't get flooded, Frampton says,

> Remember the floodwaters are the difference. New Orleans was
> like a bowl and there are a lot of people who live in the bottom
> of the bowl, and they had lots of feet of water in their houses and
> some churches were there, too. We're kind of on a rim, close to the
> Mississippi River levee, so we just didn't have to deal with that. We

Religion Is Only as Good as What It Does

were able to carry on as soon as we could get back to the city. That was priority number one: to track down our members and just reach out to them and let them know how they could reach us through the Internet. So for about three or four Sundays in September and then into early October we worshiped as a refugee congregation.

While they were in Houston, St. Charles Avenue Church put together the program Rebuilding Hope In New Orleans, which became their response to Hurricane Katrina. Frampton explains how it came about: "So we had it organized and I was getting tons of calls from friends in ministry from around the country saying we want to send money, we want to send people, we want to send both—what do we need to do? We knew we needed to be ready for them." Fortunately, there was an associate on the staff of St. Charles Avenue Church named Paul Seelman who, in the words of Frampton, "just eats, sleeps, and breathes this stuff," the stuff being recovery logistics. Frampton had a vision, and then Seelman just put the thing together. He gave it a name and organized it, drawing on some experience with hurricane relief in eastern North Carolina before going to seminary. He knew how a truck needed to be equipped and about bunk beds and shower rooms for volunteers. When the ministers got back to New Orleans, they really had a plan and were ready at the end of October for their first group, from Mt. Pleasant, South Carolina (itself a former hurricane congregation). It was gutting houses for about a year, and then they started building houses. At the point I visited in 2014, RHINO had built more than thirty Habitat Houses and hosted more than six thousand volunteers. RHINO is here to stay and has been for some time. Frampton looks back now: "You asked me what it was like, and it was an awful time, it was the worst of times, but it was the best of times because we knew really this was what we're supposed to do and we knew generally how to go about doing it. And we had all these friends around the country, all these wonderful Presbyterian friends who wanted to come in and help us, and we just needed to pull it together and we were able to do that."

Earlier, we learned from Michael Cowan about religious leaders becoming more connected. In my interview with Don Frampton, he brings this up, too.

As a result of Katrina, ministers and civic leaders, along with politicians, began meeting in various small groups to talk about the future of the city. For the first time I was included in those conversations as a clergyperson, and I really wanted to be in those conversations. Because the slate was wiped clean, and we were making somewhat of a new start, I don't want to say a fresh start, but a new beginning. We were invited to be a part of these groups, and we're still a part of those groups. It resulted in a lot of reform, particularly as it regarded levy boards and tax assessors, leading to the advent of an inspector general for the city of New Orleans.

It turns out that there had been a motion enacted by the city council about ten years earlier to hire an inspector general, but it never came to fruition. One of the groups of which Frampton was a part began to say, "'Why don't we look at getting back to that?' And as a result it happened, and the IG has done wonderful things and rooted out a lot of corruption already." The inspector general's work is overseen by an ethics review board, on which Frampton has served. I kid Frampton that he's put John Calvin's first and second uses of the Law to work in the public life of New Orleans, and suddenly the people are behaving well in public because they might get caught, in addition to it being their duty. He laughs and replies, "That's right. That's exactly right. But, you know, Jim, it took a storm for that to happen."[9]

ST. ROCH COMMUNITY CHURCH—ST. ROCH COMMUNITY DEVELOPMENT CORPORATION

Across the city in the Eighth Ward is another Presbyterian leader, but of the more conservative Presbyterian Church in America. His name is Ben McLeish, and when the storm came he was working at Desire Street Ministries in the Lower Ninth Ward. Meanwhile, McLeish himself was being led to create a new Christian presence in the neighborhood where he was living not far away, called St. Roch. Though I assume that the neighborhood took its name from a church named after St. Roch, the naming story is actually much more interesting.

McLeish tells me that the Catholic Church at the center of the neighborhood is actually called Our Lady: Star of the Sea, because it originally served fishermen for the 4:00 A.M. Mass. The neighborhood's original shotgun house dwellers were fishermen and working-class families, but the neighborhood also contained the largest population concentration of free people of color in the United States. It was a mixed-race neighborhood. Before that, it was a plantation belonging to Jean-Bernard Xavier Philippe de Marigny de Mandeville. After it was subdivided into the working-class

Religion Is Only as Good as What It Does

Figure 3. Statue of St. Roch, St. Roch Cemetery Chapel,
New Orleans, Louisiana. (Author's photograph)

neighborhood, there was a flu epidemic in which many of the city's residents got sick and the church's priest prayed to St. Roch, patron saint of good health (or of healing), and his congregation was spared. So they erected a shrine and then buried the city's dead in the cemetery there all around the shrine. The shrine still functions as a New Orleans sort of Lourdes (figures 3 and 4).

Our Church Is Cleaning Up after Katrina

Figure 4. St. Roch Cemetery, with Our Lady: Star of the Sea in the distance, New Orleans, Louisiana. (Author's photograph)

"So now we have a PCA Presbyterian church named after the Catholic patron saint of good health?" I ask McLeish. He smiles and goes with the flow, "Yes, in a Catholic town with mostly Baptist churches! And we're a mixed-race, socially and economically diverse PCA church, which is another anomaly all in itself. There are only a few of those."[10] I ask him which came first, the St. Roch Community Development Corporation (CDC), which he runs, or the church. McLeish tells me the church came first:

> We wanted to lead off with a church after seeing some experiences in other ministries, and looking around the nation at best practices made us just want to lead with a church first. I think it's Augustine who's quoted as saying—and I think it's debated whether he actually said this—"The church is a whore, but she's my mother." This sense that the church is just full of really broken, unfaithful people like me, right? Still, God's special presence is there, and he doesn't promise that for a nonprofit or a para-church ministry, though certainly if we believe that Christ is in us, there is something about this wacky bride (the Church) that he decides to take a special presence in. So we just thought that was the right—theologically, situationally, philosophically—the right thing to lead with was planting a church.[11]

When McLeish and a small circle of friends began, they were not sure that churches were coming back to St. Roch after Katrina. "There really were no churches open at that time in our neighborhood," McLeish says. "So we could've been it, but there's plenty that have reopened that had been around much longer. Obviously, we planted after the storm."

I assume that they went to their presbytery and asked to plant a church. "No," McLeish tells me, "that would be the conventional way to do it. We went to Desire Street Ministries—because I was on staff there and they helped fund us. They helped make this happen. For the first year they funded everything. And in that process we went to the presbytery and said, 'Hey, we want to plant a church.' Then we called J. B. [Watkins] to be our pastor. It was sort of a backwards way. Most churches plant a para-church ministry; most para-churches don't help plant a church." But of course, this is New Orleans, one of the South's places where most things are done a little differently, including starting churches to help rebuild neighborhoods after a devastating hurricane and flooding.

Daniel Schwartz is a community organizer who came to New Orleans through the religious community organizing effort composed of Christians and Jews called the Micah Project, with its center of moral gravity located in the black churches of the Lower Ninth Ward. He describes how his group's organizing focus is racism and mass incarceration. Micah's national organization, PICO, always works at helping communities attempt to reorder their power arrangements from the grass roots up by starting with a base of the most grassroots organizations of all—churches, synagogues, and mosques. Community organizing had failed in pre-flood New Orleans, but the crying needs exposed by Katrina opened up a moral vision, the ability to see things through someone else's eyes in the religious community. PICO's Micah Project came into being, and the central issue its members took on was racial justice by tackling mass incarceration, starting in New Orleans.

Making a difference in the structures of poverty in New Orleans and coastal Mississippi turns out to be about more than rebuilding the physical structures of people's homes. Public housing, access to jobs, and even food assistance are all conditioned by not having a criminal record either oneself or in one's household. The job in front of people of faith in restoring peace to ravaged communities is made more daunting by the criminal justice policies that punish low-level drug offenders early in life and then continue to penalize them and their families long after sentences have officially been served or paroles have begun. If there is a book I heard invoked as often as the Bible in the Gulf region, it was Michelle Alexander's *New Jim Crow*. The comparison is telling, for Alexander speaks a kind of prophetic truth to power, and for my interviewees she also provides the words to encapsulate the oppression that they have seen develop around them, especially over the past quarter-century.[12] As a nation, America is proud that it eschews the concept of collective punishment. It is what makes us, we teach our high school civics classes, different than Nazi Germany, Joseph Stalin's Soviet Union, and the killing fields of Cambodia. As a society we hold people responsible only for their individual actions, we say. Hurricane Katrina became the occasion for Christian helpers with resources to find out what poor people have known for many years: government charity is parsimoniously provided in long lines. American society is good at punishing children, widows, and single mothers for being poor, for being born among the poor—and doubly so if their fathers, husbands, or sons are current or former offenders.

Hurricane Katrina drove a lot of people from New Orleans, yet as with any disaster there is a whole other class of souls who have come to the city and Gulf Coast to be part of the rebuilding. One of these is the organizer Daniel Schwartz. The road that led Schwartz to New Orleans in his forties is a long one; it is fair to say that a critical point in the journey of this Chicago-born University of Pennsylvania graduate happened after college during a Sabbath lunch in Israel. He relates that a friend who was a Bible teacher at the university said, "I have this book for you." Schwartz thought, "How great of you. Another book about Judaism. I'm reading a lot." The book turned out to be *Rules for Radicals*, by fellow Chicagoan Saul Alinsky.[13] The book is all about building power in communities and holding the powerful accountable. It is the bible of community organizing. It would take twenty more years for Schwartz formally to become a community organizer; however, his earlier work in Israel and in the United States, along with his graduate education in social work, all aimed at helping people in poverty attain better lives as citizens. New Orleans is his second assignment for PICO.

The current thrust of the Micah Project centers around racial justice. As Schwartz says, "We're really looking at all of our justice system through a racial lens because we believe that it's really an underpinning of many of the major structural challenges in our system right now. Our main issue campaign is around mass incarceration; looking at that through the lens of reentry through local and state criminal justice reform."[14] Nevertheless, Micah also focuses on the school suspension policies that are the entry point for so many youth into the system. Louisiana, it must be said, has the highest rate of incarceration in the world. The state incarcerates 1,619 of every 100,000 people in its population, more than twice the U.S. average (in the nation with the highest incarceration rate in the world).[15] Three-quarters of these prisoners are African American males. New Orleans is the epicenter of state-level incarceration, and part of town called Central City turns out to be the epicenter of the epicenter of incarceration. What this means is that one in seven African American male residents in New Orleans is incarcerated, on parole, or on probation. As Schwartz warms to his subject, he tells me, "We don't believe that that is an accident. That's driven not by de jure racism, but by de facto racism."

I mention that in my research I encountered two striking maps, the map of death penalties carried out and the crime rate map for each state. Looking at the two together is astounding: the more people are executed, the more crimes there are. There is no deterrent effect evident for the death penalty. Schwartz responds, "I just had a meeting today with six clergy and one of the clergy leaders, who is African American, said, 'If incarceration made us safe, we would be the safest city in the world. And we have a murder rate that is ten times the national average.'" I ask Schwartz about Micah's religious composition, and he tells me, "We have fifteen member congregations; three are Catholic. We have a synagogue that's involved with us. And a nonde-nominational church. The rest are Baptist churches." But as diverse as those faith traditions are, Schwartz is also aware that he is a white organizer in an organization that is 90 percent African American. He asks, "What does faith have to say about that? How can we use faith as a tool to help us walk down the path of racial honesty? Getting to racial harmony, but first getting to racial honesty." He explains what he's getting at by relating an incident from the Micah Project:

> The African American pastor I just mentioned, he's actually the pastor of one of our largest congregations, was talking with a white rabbi. The pastor shared that on one Sunday he asked that everyone who has a member of their nuclear family—not a relative but in their nuclear family—who has been arrested, raise your hand or stand up. Ninety-five percent of the people stood up. The rabbi, who the pastor is telling this to says, 'It's not just that I don't know anybody that's been in jail. I don't know anybody that knows anybody.' And there was that moment for the pastor, well actually for both of them, where they were living it—the pastor also just couldn't believe that that was the case. That was a moment where two worlds are really getting some insight. And for the rabbi, he is seeing this as a religious imperative for him and his synagogue to be involved with this if they're going to have any type of faith integrity.

Schwartz relates the story to his own faith stance in the work. This, he says, "is how I also feel as a Jew myself, that there's a reason why we look at the Bible, and it begins in the book of Genesis and not the book of Exodus. The book of Genesis is a universal message, and then Exodus is a particularistic message. A rabbi once taught me, 'We need to live within the universal and the particularistic visions.'" That, says Schwartz, is the "midrash to teach us that you and you are my brothers and sisters, as is Pastor Berriere, as is Rabbi Linden."

Working in New Orleans, a city with a great sense of place, in which people speak explicitly and easily about faith, has pushed Schwartz to be able to talk in faith terms, too. "If I'm going to be working in this environment," he says, "then I have to be able to feel comfortable talking about impressions of God, which really challenged me because that wasn't in my vocabulary." As it happens, he adds,

> I work in some very dynamic Christian communities that have really informed my own Jewish experience. I have become more connected with my Jewish roots and my Jewish practice, even though I spend most of my days in churches and Sundays I'll often visit churches. For Jews, or at least in my experience, we don't talk about God. We talk about important issues. We talk about teachings, but the personal God isn't very present. I don't know if that's just in the South, but certainly within the African American community that I'm working in, it's a very personal presence of God.

But Schwartz has encouraged his partners to expand their vocabularies, too. He says, "I've been pushing or encouraging clergy that organizing should not be seen as you do church and then you do justice." He tells them that community-organizing activity is another opportunity for them to be "preaching and teaching" even when they are having a research or policy meeting with a city councilperson. Policy work is too important to leave to professionals in far-off places. As Schwartz makes the case, he tells me, "We don't need another Brookings Institution here in New Orleans. What we need is people of faith who are speaking from their own faith and personal experiences and are sharing that in a way that the other party can hear them, but that is very authentic."

Schwartz is so eloquent at this point of our talk that I ask him about his perception of the regional differences: "Do you find that a religious argument well made or an appeal to universal religion gets you farther in the public domain here than it would say in D.C. or in New York?" He quickly jumps in, "Yes. I think that the religious motifs and orientations are more present here in the South. I don't think it's an accident that the civil rights movement came out of southern churches. There's speaking out of this prophetic vision. Here we have a language of social critique. Here we have the prophets and belief. And in the South—or at least with the clergy that I'm working with—it's just communicated in a more explicit way."

Next we shift to the post-Katrina semantics Schwartz has observed. "People don't talk about Katrina," he says. "People talk to me using the construction 'Katrina and the floods that followed Katrina that destroyed our city.' So Katrina did not destroy. It's not just semantics. It was semantics, but it was saying that because the levees broke down, we were flooded. The levees were supposed to be able to save us."

"And the levees were a people problem?" I ask.

"Exactly. Nature was fine. It caused some damage," he says. New Orleanians pride themselves on being able to deal with nature, but people are responsible for what evil they do and the good they fail to do; it is hard to forgive or forget injustice.

Schwartz then begins to make the connection between flooding and the Micah Project's priorities:

> It was human failure. When the levees failed and then also how the federal government and the state government responded. I think there was a sense that if we don't take this into our own hands, this is what's going to happen. I think that was a call to arms in some ways that we can't do business as usual. We can't go back. Also I think the fact that the short-term result caused by the floods that happened after Katrina was that everyone had to get involved. And I think that some of that spirit that even as we dealt with the immediate crisis [created] something more enduring; that spirit of "Okay, I helped move trees, but now I've got to think about moving systems."

It is no accident that this conversation on mass incarceration has come after Katrina. Schwartz makes the comparison to a great training event he went to where the trainer observed, "'Most people think the economy just sort of happens. It's like the weather. We have ups and we have downs.' Then she goes on to really teach, and she shows that it isn't the weather. There are intentional decisions being made." Then Schwartz says, "So I think again, with the flooding, there were intentional decisions that were made that led to that. Intentional decisions that we're not going to supervise the building of the dam as well as we should, we're not going to invest funding as well as we should that went into that." Once you see the results of failing to think systemically, you start thinking more systemically.

At present in Louisiana, because one in seven African American males are on probation, on parole, or incarcerated, they cannot vote. One in seven. "You're taking that right off the table," Schwartz says. "It's a huge amount of

Religion Is Only as Good as What It Does

political power that is just thrown in the garbage. Well, it's being forced to be thrown in the garbage, rather. So there are other issues, I know, but I do feel that if everyone who was in the jails was white, the issue of mass incarceration would have been dealt with thirty years ago." Poverty, racism, and incarceration are tied together in Louisiana, and neither Daniel Schwartz nor the people of faith he organizes are going to stop thinking about them systemically.

Back in the Eighth Ward, Ben McLeish is trying to tackle the poverty side of things from the economic side of the table, but he is also talking about systems. He sees his work creating starter jobs as part of the fabric of ministry. He says that St. Roch CDC is all about "wanting to create a safe place to fail, and to be coached, and to be mentored." McLeish has a theology behind his work-centered approach: "We're just really feeling that work is a pre-fall condition. In the beginning, God created. It's the first thing God does as an expression to mankind—he creates, he works. And the first thing he tells Adam to do is work. That's all before sin enters in. We feel very much that it's a very redemptive thing to help create business, help get people employed." McLeish knows his Bible and elaborates his thought about the place of work in the life of people, particularly men, in his community.

> There's a verse that haunts me about John the Baptist, about how he's called to make a way for Christ but also to turn back the hearts of the fathers to their children. If a man is not working or a single mom is not working and struggling, it's really hard to keep your head up and have pride, have dignity about yourself, and deliberately raise your children. But if we can help create livable wage employment opportunities that count in this discipleship, mentoring model, then we can really begin to turn back the hearts of fathers to their children, and that alone would revolutionize families in our neighborhoods.

We talk about the intransigent systemic issues that make poverty so hard to overcome in New Orleans and other communities. Ben McLeish says that he thinks the two biggest social justice issues for Christians to be concerned about are education and mass incarceration. In his view, the war on drugs has been targeted toward low-income black and brown communities. He argues,

> It's obvious now that just as many white affluent people use marijuana because of the legalization of it in places like Colorado

and on the West Coast, but the target was black and brown minorities in poor neighborhoods. You'd get picked up for a marijuana charge because you're desperate or because you're trying to put food on the table, not just because it's your recreation, but because you're trying to make the economy work for your family. And you go to jail. You get a record. You have court fees. You can't pay them, so you spend more time in jail. You get out. You have a record. Misdemeanor. Maybe this drives you to deeper crime. Felony. You're more likely to be picked up. People call it "DWB," Driving While Black. You get pulled over just because you're black and you get profiled and all those things that happen.

So far McLeish has just given a narrative form to the system the Micah Project wants to overturn, but then he makes it personal: "A guy at our church now is serving a ten-year term because he has a drug addiction and was in a school getting food out of the cafeteria to eat. He was a prior offender, and because of that he got ten years." We ask incredulously, was it because he was near children? No, Ben tells us, it was at night. On the weekend. The charge: on school premises without permission. The sentence: ten years. So, McLeish asks us, "When he gets out what are his options for working? Who's going to hire someone who's basically spent his entire adult life in the system? But he is a really, really good cook. He's a handyman. Let's help him start his own handyman business or his own food cart. Let's get behind him and help support him in that effort." For St. Roch Church CDC, the Christian world of redemption and grace means that there are no throwaway people. Their system does not work like the incarceration state. Ben McLeish and his family and the St. Roch community are prepared to put freed prisoners to work. "I think I'm really excited long term about what that would look like," McLeish says, "how that would change the dynamics for family and community!"

Between the injuries of the flood, racism, poverty, and a criminal justice system that made intergenerational poverty a near certainty for some New Orleans residents, the religious people who vowed to help the Crescent City recover had their work cut out for them. The work is not over—it may never be over—but the faith, courage, imagination, generosity, and determination shown in the first decade since August 2005 did not and will not return empty. In the next chapter, we turn to the people who came guided by faith to help their neighbors in Mississippi and in New Orleans and to the qualities of faith that residents and helpers credit with powering them through the Katrina experience.

Religion Is Only as Good as What It Does

6

MISSISSIPPI FLOODING

The first installment in this post-Katrina examination of southern faith in the light of hurricane recovery in the Gulf states focused on the storm and what people of faith did when confronted with the newly destroyed city of New Orleans. First they dealt with flooding and loss of housing and services, and then they began to cooperate to address the ways corruption, racism, and isolation had been destroying the city from within for decades. In this chapter the focus shifts—to the kinds of people who came to help and to storm survivors, to the faith revealed by the experiences among helpers in residence. The focus also shifts somewhat east to include hard-hit Gulf Coast Mississippi, as we hear from additional voices.

PEOPLE CAME TO HELP

Driving up into the air (it seems) on the enormous Biloxi–Ocean Springs Bridge that separates one part of the mainland coastal Mississippi from another, one is struck that the gulfward side might as well be another barrier island like those that line the Gulf of Mexico from South Padre Island off Corpus Christi, Texas, all the way around to Ten Thousand Island in south Florida. It is greenly vegetated, sandy soiled, and very flat, a nice place to be on a fair-weather day and no place to be in a hurricane. But from time immemorial, people have been drawn to the sea, and Biloxi is one such place, an important center for shipbuilding, the U.S. Navy and Air Force, and more recently for gambling casinos. It is in East Biloxi, a couple of blocks off the beach, that we meet Susan Turner and James Cox at Main Street Missionary Baptist Church, the same church where the Reverend Kenneth Haynes Sr. and his deacons saved so many lives in 2005. Haynes is now at home with Parkinson's disease, but Sister Turner, the Sunday school superintendent, and Brother Cox, the church's part-time administrator bring us up-to-date on what happened next after Katrina hit. Turner's background is in education, particularly mathematics, and over the course of our conversations it becomes clear to me that Loaves and Fishes miracles happen—in part—because people like her throw themselves into helping their communities in times of need. I discovered this in asking who came to help out after Katrina and whether they were, in the judgment of locals, genuinely helpful.

Sister Turner begins by telling me how people in nearby cities, and regionally, just began showing up. "We had people coming from different places to our location who were not just our members. We had people coming from other places, in cities, like Ocean Springs, D'Iberville and Gautier. (Keesler Air Force Base was shut down.) People came in to help." FEMA never came closer than three miles away at a working bridgehead from the mainland. That was too far for disabled and elderly people to go and get their checks, so Turner, the formidable and lovely high school mathematics teacher, helped out tremendously. She convinced the government authorities to allow her to distribute the checks. She would drive her car to the church, after completing applications and collecting signatures from the older and infirm residents stranded in East Biloxi, and then she would drive to the office to turn them in. Her citizen's initiative inspired others. Turner says that helping others through the church became infectious, noting, "You didn't have to be here all day, but there was nothing else going on and we just enjoyed the camaraderie of being with each other and sharing."[1]

People from other states were moved by what they had seen on television or heard in their churches about the destruction and began showing up with replacement goods. First it was food, water, and emergency items. Turner describes the experience: "When the trucks came in, we wanted to see what they were bringing. Later, they started bringing bedroom sets and mattresses." One donor asked Turner what would be truly helpful, and

Religion Is Only as Good as What It Does

one of the men standing nearby overheard the question and interjected, "Ms. Turner, if you all could get us some bicycles, I can get to work." As she explains, though he still had a job, he did not have a car anymore. "And lo and behold, I said that to one of the ministers down in Florida," she continued, "and he came up with a big eighteen-wheeler filled with nothing but bicycles. That was the way they got their transportation—I never would have thought about it if the young man hadn't asked, but that's how they made it to work—on a bicycle." Bicycles seem so small, but as Turner explains, "Your car was gone, and there was gas but it was rationed. Many people had to go to Mobile, Alabama, to get gas, and they would take the big containers to get it, but most of the people in this area who stayed, they lost their cars."

I ask specifically about how the flooded church got repaired while its members were busy meeting the needs of people reconstructing their lives. As it turned out, someone was looking out for the church as well. "We were blessed at this church because one of our member's daughters lived in Jackson, Mississippi, at the time." Turner tells me. "She's since passed away. The young lady had cancer. Her church asked, what can we do? She sent them down, and they furnished our entire church." Turner adds that the member's daughter's church in Jackson "was an integrated church. A predominately white congregation came down and they didn't say, 'You've got to have this.' They said, 'Pick what you want,' and they paid for it." She refers to Brother Cox, who was involved with the refurbishing. Cox tells us that it was "about the middle part of 2006 when we were back in, and [the Jackson church] started putting things back together. We didn't have to change anything. It was good-quality furniture that they donated to us."

I wanted to know more about the church in Jackson and the connection between it and Main Street Missionary Baptist Church in East Biloxi. They remember that after the member's daughter helped her old church community through her new congregation, she became more ill, and her Jackson church turned to helping her. Sister Turner asks me, "What do you call the man that comes around and builds the house? They send you to Disney World?" "Do you mean Ty Pennington and *Extreme Makeover Home Edition*?" I ask. "Yeah! They built that house for her," she continues. "That congregation saw the need for her. Her husband had left her and she had three children, but they are all now doing well—graduates of college and high school graduates." I later look up the story of this impressive woman and congregation who helped this other remarkable congregation. It turns out that Sabrena Jones had arranged for her predominantly white Crossgates

Baptist Church of Brandon, Mississippi, to help Main Street Missionary Baptist Church in East Biloxi, and then her church had arranged for her to receive an *Extreme Makeover* house in 2007 because of her life of devotion to others. Sadly, she died, just as Turner said, in 2009. One of her fellow members, Tim Johnson, said of her that "to be around Sabrena was to feel the love of God. . . . Jesus walked like ten feet in front of her." Another Crossgates member, U.S. Representative Gregg Harper, described Jones as "one of the most giving people" he'd ever known.[2] There were at least two Mississippi churches that felt that way.

Turning more broadly to the kind of people who came to Biloxi to help, I ask, "Who comes to help and where do they come from?" Cox answers that in his experience all kinds of people have come to the area and have been engaged in building their (as distinct from FEMA trailer) houses. They are "mostly different religious groups coming in." Sister Turner adds that they come "from the North. We get them all the time. We're expecting some now," she says. "It's spring break. Those children came in by the busloads. They came most of time. They came on Wednesday nights and worship with us in our prayer meeting, and those young people come down and some of the men say, 'I've been here for nine years. I've been here the last ten years.'"

I ask, "Are these students on spring break from historically black colleges and universities or are they white or mixed groups?" The answer? "Most of them are white," says Turner. "I've seen them with a few black students, and mixed sometimes, but the predominant church that comes, I believe, is a white congregation, and we get them all the time."[3] This act of helping people you do not live around is a part of an American Christian active piety that is powerful and hard to explain, but it seems to tap into a need to give to those who have a need to receive—especially to those affected by the so-called acts of God—floods, tornadoes, and hurricanes. Disaster relief is also a place where racial divisions seem most susceptible to being bridged because something is being built in this American society so divided by race and class rather than being analyzed, argued over, or torn down. Last, I cannot help but feel that ten years of Gulf Coast service is like some kind of Protestant penance for a societal and governmental failure to be there when the storm arrived. It is compensatory in the same sense that Teach for America is compensatory for the failures of normal American public education. I admire the people who volunteer in each case, but I wonder when will we all get back to governing on a just basis. A report by the Institute for Southern Studies (a progressive research and advocacy center) just three years after Katrina agreed with the

Religion Is Only as Good as What It Does

bipartisan congressional investigation in finding the government's inadequate response to be a "failure of initiative," but turned its attention to the faith-led relief efforts, which consequently assumed enormous importance: "Fortunately, there was no such failure of initiative on the part of faith-based organizations. In many communities across the Gulf, volunteers from faith groups were the first to arrive after the storm and played an important role in feeding, clothing and sheltering survivors. Following the immediate humanitarian crisis, faith volunteers stayed in the region to help survivors with the hard work of cleaning flood debris and gutting ruined homes."[4]

At the time of the Institute for Southern Studies report on *Faith in the Gulf*, three years into recovery, most of the labor expended in cleanup and rebuilding had been provided by faith-based groups. The intensity of the need and the constancy of the practice of helping was changing the people engaged in helping, particularly those from the region. Helping out after Hurricanes Katrina and Rita created lasting patterns of a kind of muscular Christianity. Mississippi Baptist men in yellow T-shirts with pickup trucks, chainsaws, and tool trailers were the first helpers that my friends in Baton Rouge saw after Rita knocked out the power, flooded the roads, and knocked down enough big trees to make streets impassible, just one month after Katrina. Ten years later this action corps of middle-aged Christian responders is still going to tornadoes and other storm sites and wherever they believe they will be needed. Baptists are very visible in the South, of course, but there is reason to believe that the scale of Katrina brought more men into relief ministry than ever before. A massive feeding unit of the Mississippi (Baptist) Men's Ministry, which previously had never been needed to produce more than one hundred thousand meals in a crisis, suddenly found itself producing eighteen thousand meals every day for weeks on end.[5] And so it went across all eighty-five miles of affected Mississippi shoreline.

Thinking about what makes someone a giving person, the kind of person who feels impelled to volunteer in a crisis, I think back to something Ben McLeish said about coming to New Orleans to help others and helping himself in the process. Part of it, I remember, was that New Orleans before Katrina and after was nothing if not without pretense. In New Orleans, McLeish said, "They say being phony is the cardinal sin. It just became a very safe place to explore and sew those childhood wounds and realize some of my own need to be rescued was being flushed out." He compared himself to "the dad you see on the football field who is making his son be this all-star at ten because he wanted be an all-star but never was, trying to make up for that shortfall. But in those ruins somehow God allows for us to be a part of what he's doing." McLeish called it following the desires of his heart and having his "heart undergo surgery in many ways."[6] Now as I think about the volunteers that are still coming to the Gulf, I see more than a few people trying to work out their own troubles and their salvation in honest work, wearing honest-to-God work clothes and helping neighbors they may never see face to face.

When I asked Loyola University professor Michael Cowan about the motivations of the helpers he saw in New Orleans, he reflected, "What I saw was people who saw very intense hurt and need and found it compelling as I thought a lot of people in the country did, what happened to New Orleans; people who wanted to engage and make some contribution, wanted to do something. That very fundamental human inclination to reach out to someone who is suffering and help them—that's what I saw."[7] He told me about the changes that happen to the helpers who in a way become students of the place. One instance of this was a group that had been down every year since the year after the storm from a Unitarian church in St. Paul, Minnesota. These volunteers' thirst to learn more about New Orleans and its culture has stimulated them to become involved in interracial relations in St. Paul during the rest of the year. Quite aside from the transformations that take place because people volunteered, Cowan wanted me to leave with one big impression. "From the point of view of a resident here before and after that time, whether a group came in one time or whether they came ten times, I think I and most other people just felt a deep sense of gratitude to them for coming and making their presence felt in whatever way they did that."

Back to the Mississippi coast, and I'm driving to see Rod Dickson-Rishel, pastor of the Long Beach United Methodist Church in Long Beach. At the time Katrina hit he was pastor of Mississippi City United Methodist Church Gulfport. He is a colorful raconteur and gives a lively sense of how it felt to be responsible for others and finding it hard to maneuver. "I was at the time the disaster response coordinator, kind of the UMCOR [United Methodist Committee on Relief] guy, for the Seashore District and had been that for the Mississippi Annual Conference. So two days after the storm I'm thinking, 'Where is the cavalry? People better start showing up here quickly.' Well, what I didn't know until two or three weeks later was the cavalry was doing the same thing I was doing. They didn't have any cell phone service. They didn't have any power. They couldn't buy gasoline. The whole state of Mississippi was messed up."[8] Fortunately, in certain communities some churches

Religion Is Only as Good as What It Does

were far enough from the water to have survived. Long Beach UMC was one such church, so that, although it was out of power, the church became the center for Long Beach for all meetings and worship services. "If anyone wanted to get married, anyone needed to have a funeral, if the city needed to have a public meeting, all of that happened on this campus for probably a year and a half because the Catholics and the Baptists and the Episcopalians were all looking at the water. They were done. So this church really stood tall in that time, and the pastor here did some great work." Helping out often took the form of extraordinary neighborliness and ecumenicity.

The church Rod Dickson-Rishel was serving when Katrina hit was not so lucky as Long Beach UMC, but he still works as a pastor in the Mississippi Annual Conference's Seashore District, which is by itself an accomplishment. Many of his fellow ministers burned out or have left. I ask him what accounts for his resilience. "One of the differences I think in my experience and others was," he tells me, "I had the resources of the hospital (where his wife was the clinical psychologist). I had a place to go where I could sleep and I knew I was safe and I knew my children were safe and they were feeding us. And I know that sounds crazy, but in about two and a half days when you don't eat, things really get screwed up." What about the other ministers?

> A lot of my colleagues had either evacuated and they couldn't come back—as the civil authorities wouldn't allow them back—and some of the others, they had greater devastation to their own homes, and they didn't have anywhere to go with their families and their children, so their immediate concern was trying to take care of their families. Some of them just sat down and cried and quit. They just went away and never came back. Some of them were literally wading in the storm waters moving from place to place because they were flooded and they were trying to get away and escape.

There were horrible stories that these clergy had lived, but a group of the ministers banded together in a "covenant group" that had been formed pre-Katrina. Even though they had met before, Dickson-Rishel says, "It got real after Katrina." They continued to meet for several years.

I ask, "When help finally arrived where did it come from?" Again, as in Biloxi, people they already were connected to showed up first. "I had a brother-in-law who lived in the Jackson area at the time who brought us a bunch of gasoline and food and things," Dickson-Rishel says, and then remembers that, a morning or two after the storm,

I was back at the church and here comes a young woman. I had been her pastor when she was a high school student at a previous appointment, and now she's on the staff of a United Methodist church up in Tupelo. She's standing in the parking lot of our church saying, 'I knew that I needed to bring you this.' And she had water and camp food. We just put it in the church so that anyone who came along could find it and use it there on the church property. So help came from everywhere. And it took a little while before the really long-range stuff came.

But long-range stuff did come, in the form of checks ranging from $125,000 from a church in Kansas City to $38 from a children's Sunday school class in New England. Help also came in the person of Mississippi bishop Hope Morgan Ward, who with her husband followed the railroad tracks in to join the Dickson-Rishels' congregation meeting in the open on the very Sunday after Katrina washed the pews, pulpit, and windows right out of their sanctuary, leaving mud behind.

Thinking back nine years later, Dickson-Rishel says, "I think Bishop Ward was really at her best at that time. And I had considerable experience, as I said, in disaster responses previously. I was also aware of what had happened in Hurricane Andrew in Miami, because there the district superintendents really required that their pastors stay on the ground and work. Three or five years after that storm 80 percent of them—or some outrageous number like that—were not in the ministry anymore, not even just not at a church." So, the first time he talked to Bishop Ward, he said, "I know I'm the disaster response coordinator for the Seashore district. I hereby resign. I'm homeless. My family's homeless. My church is homeless. I cannot coordinate what is about to happen here and expect to survive. So I'm done; y'all need to go hire somebody, a full-time professional to do this." The institutional reaction to Katrina, therefore, was different than it had been to Andrew. Every volunteer team that called Bishop Morgan right after Katrina was told, "We've got to get our pastor's lives restored." She made sure that every pastor had access to a travel trailer. As Dickson-Rishel says, "We didn't always have a place to park it or a sewer to hook it up to or water or electricity, but we had one. So every pastor had somewhere to live." Nevertheless, he is the first to admit that "we all became a little Katrina crazy" in the ministry, and he is one of the only Methodist ministers who were there when the storm hit who is still appointed in the Seashore District.

Religion Is Only as Good as What It Does

For all the good that volunteers did, Dickson-Rishel confirms that there were sometimes parties of Christian folks who wanted to do things that he did not need to have done. In the big picture it was not that bad, but "bearing in mind we were all pretty fragile—it was the stuff at the time I really found to be highly offensive, but looking back on it now it wasn't." Dickson-Rishel illustrates the point by reference to some strong-willed volunteers from New York State who came with heavy equipment months after the storm:

> We had looked for weeks for the pulpit outside of that church. We couldn't find the pulpit. Finally, one day, my wife found it several blocks away from the church where it had washed up. She and a group of kids, literally young teenagers, got it and hauled it, carried it back to the church through these trash piles because it was months and months before the debris removal made any progress at all. Carried it back and put it back in the sanctuary. The stage was all warped and whacked out, but they put it in there. The pulpit to me was one of those symbols of the office [of ministry] somehow, and I had asked myself a thousand times, "Where did the pulpit go? How can it just—?" Because we found hymnals, we found choir robes, we found pews, but we couldn't find the pulpit. Well, they found it and put it in the church, and these guys came in from New York and they decided they were going to clean out the church: the old nasty, wet carpet and the remaining furniture and that chancel area, and they picked that pulpit up with a piece of machinery. They banged it all up, tore a couple pieces off of it. Took it out and threw it in the back of the yard on the debris pile. I was so angry. I had told them my policy after the storm, "We are not doing anything to this church property until the members of this church and this community are restored." I said, "We are not going to rebuild this church while I have church members who are living like animals."

The crew from New York straight up refused to do what Dickson-Rishel asked of them. He even pleaded with them, saying, "You have machinery; you can go and you can make a real difference in somebody's life." The sanctuary got gutted, but perhaps as a lingering reminder of a wide range of wounds, even today the scratched pulpit is back in place in Mississippi City United Methodist Church.

Faith-based volunteers have helped restore the Gulf region, but it only takes a few with an exaggerated sense of "saving New Orleans" or "making Mississippi better than it was" to get under the local residents' skin. Ben McLeish's St. Roch Community Church and CDC promote some definite ideas about where you have to be theologically and in terms of ethical commitments in order to be able to come and help out. As I was researching St. Roch, I noticed two things on the church website descriptions of the internships for the coming summer. First, I noticed the requirements for explicit Christian commitment, church attendance, and agreement to the central tenets of the Lausanne Covenant, and that made my eyes pop. I also noticed that interns were required to read *When Helping Hurts*, which must not have been on the reading list for Dickson-Rishel's helpers from New York.[9] I asked McLeish how he came by these requirements. He tells me that his experiences through Desire Street Ministries and learning about the dignity development movement that is happening in Christian social services informed his choices and that it is just an efficient way to bring people up to speed, "so there's some common language we can talk about, common approaches, a philosophy of ministry." What he means by that is that he wants people to see "that ultimately it's Christ who changes things" rather than bring their own messianic project into the work. "That's what ultimately changes me," he continues.

> It's what changes our community and as we're called to join into that, I want people on our team here, whether they're an intern or on our staff, to share those approaches so those are things we don't have to argue about. They'll be plenty of other things we'll have to argue about, but those are kind of fundamentals. That they're committed to the local church, again, as broken as she is, that they're committed to the local church as a way that God's bringing about redemption. And as we approach acts of mercy and development, that there's this dignity piece and there's this commonality of understanding our own poverty.

We can read all those books, McLeish argues, and still make mistakes, but maybe not as many. The Lausanne Covenant is interesting because it is a panevangelical basis for mission cooperation, not a tight Calvinistic understanding of Christian faith. I ask McLeish, why Lausanne? He tells me because "it's broad enough that it would include other people to be a part of what we're doing here. You don't have to be a PCA, John Calvin T-shirt-wearing reformer from Scotland" to intern at St. Roch. So Wesleyans and Baptists can come on those terms? I ask. "Yep," McLeish answers. "Can you be the pastor of our church? No. But if you just want to come, you love Jesus, you want to live among the poor, work among the poor, great! The other things are really meaningless arguments. Don't get me wrong, they have meaning and I'm PCA for a reason, but I'm not going let that stop the kingdom from moving forward."

One way that dignity in development takes on flesh at St. Roch is that St. Roch charges all of its visiting mission teams. McLeish explains, "We charge them forty dollars a day per person. Twenty dollars goes toward supplies, and twenty dollars goes to an indigenous leadership fund, so that I can hire this guy for a week to be the helper, so he can put food on the table for his family and kind of 'turn back the hearts of fathers to their children' and provide work in the community." McLeish actually has in mind a specific man who has rehabilitated his work history through the CDC in the manner just described. "Now I've got him hired on with a contractor here in the neighborhood. He's working full-time for him." But it is the relationship with the visiting mission groups that enables McLeish to hire the man for a week in the first place, to give him this safe environment in which to work, and to put some food on the table. After that, as McLeish says, "it allows me this real authentic opportunity to recommend him for somebody or something else." The people who come to help at St. Roch end up helping others long after they have gone back home.

THE POWER OF FAITH

For the purposes of this book, perhaps no set of testimonies from the Katrina experience are quite as revealing as the accounts of how being a person of faith shed a new light on posthurricane life. Being a Christian, seeing an area of human need and feeling a compulsion to meet that need, can make someone do uncharacteristic things, things he or she has consciously sworn never to do. That is part of the story of Alice Graham. A tenured professor of pastoral care and counseling at Hood Theological Seminary in Salisbury, North Carolina, Graham was teaching a course on "Ministry in the Midst of a Communal Disaster" and, as part of the course, brought a bus full of seminarians to the Mississippi Gulf Coast to be to help after the initial crisis was over. As a youngster hearing about Emmett Till's murder for supposedly whistling at a white woman in 1955, Graham had sworn never to set foot in such a dangerously racist and inhospitable state. Now she was doing just that.

"It was the right thing to do, but it didn't hit me until I was on the van with the students that I was going to Mississippi, and that's when the memory of Emmett Till, all the fear about Mississippi, just overwhelmed me, and I thought, 'What am I doing? I'm taking students, black and white students, into a place that will not receive them.'"[10] The anxiety built in her as she counseled her students to stay together and never go anywhere alone. The grip of fear was finally broken in a restaurant when the group stopped for a meal near their destination. Graham remembers,

> The waitress asked one of the students, "Where are you guys from and what brings you here?" Well, one of the students said, "We've come to help. We're from North Carolina." And the hostess turned around and announced to everybody gathered that these people have come all the way from North Carolina to help us. And the restaurant broke out in applause. What was significant was that the restaurant had black and white customers in it. And at that moment it was like "Woo. I'm not back twelve years old again. I am in the present now. It's not the Mississippi of my childhood. Something is different here." So I could be present and open, but it was only at that point where [reality] broke through the veil of the past, as it were.

Not only could Graham be present with her students, but she came back for a sabbatical to learn more about how to prepare ministers to be ready for work during a massive crisis like Katrina. An ordained minister in the American Baptist Church, Graham worked with a Lutheran colleague providing counseling to seniors affected by the storm through United Methodist congregations in the coastal area setting up "caring conversations," an opportunity to address the mental health and spiritual trauma brought on by storm losses. After her sabbatical, though she had a tenured professorship in North Carolina and no job in Mississippi, she discovered that she still had a calling to be part of the recovery in the state she had once sworn she would never even visit. She told her seminary president that she was resigning. Then the enormity of what she was doing set in. She explains what happened next. "So I called a friend who I had made in Mississippi, and I said, 'I've costed out what a move is going to be. It's going to be a good piece of my savings.' And she said, 'What are you talking about? We're going to come down and move you. A bunch of us have been talking about it. We knew it would be expensive so we said we'd come down and move you. Just rent the truck.'" So seven people from Mississippi came and moved Graham. After that, as in some answer to another prayer, Graham's friend RoseMary Williams, a United Methodist pastor, told her that her daughter was renovating a house that Graham could stay in as long as she needed. "Now if that's not the hand of God," Graham remembers thinking. She was also prepared to apply for early retirement from Social Security so as to self-fund her new calling. As it turned out, two weeks later there was a need for an agency director for the agency she subsequently served until 2014 (Interfaith Partnerships, formerly Mississippi Coast Interfaith Disaster Task Force), but in another twist of fate, the agency's board was rethinking its mission and moving from an emphasis on always responding to disasters toward resourcing faith-based community groups so that mental health and spiritual needs were met alongside the needs for physical recovery.[11] Though Graham does not believe in what she later called an "airy fairy" kind of faith of finding signs and wonders at every possible juncture, what she found instead was, by her own account, deeper and more challenging:

> Coming here was a faith journey of major proportions for me.
> I totally stepped out of my comfort zone and finally felt I was following the lead of God. And as I've lived into it I've discovered new capacities in myself, new levels of perseverance. So now I have an increased ability to live with uncertainty and not what I would've called "airy fairy"—you know, using God like magic. No, I'm using God like God. I am not God. God is God. And the distinction is so much clearer to me than it ever has been. God is not in my hip pocket. I can't just say some words and God appears. God is God. And God is doing God's thing and I get to show up for the party.

Graham shares what kind of party it has been in Mississippi, "When I first came I was working with a congregation's disaster coordinators, and I was trying to help them get the idea of listening to people as opposed to talking and telling them what to do. Well, these were seniors, and this one woman said, 'You mean you're asking me to go repeating what they just said, and that's going to make a difference? That's grand. I don't think you understand us.'" Graham asked her coordinator to try it and see what happened. After the coordinator promised to try, she left the meeting because, Graham thinks, "I went through a whole thing about repeating, being nonjudgmental, and all of that." To Graham's surprise, the coordinator came back to her the next meeting and said, "Dr. Graham, you planning on leaving here?" "No, no, Jean. I'm planning on staying," said Graham. To which the formerly skeptical coordinator said, "Well, you better, because I did what you said and I got information, and I need you to be here so I can answer these questions." Graham joins me in laughing, because it is so human and so funny. Yet she hastens to say that occasions like this gave her hope. "Here was this woman who just basically said this is a bunch of crap you're telling me, who then came back and said, 'I'm depending on you to be here because I told them I knew somebody who could give me some answers.'" Graham smiles, "So that gives me hope."

FINDING HOPE IN NEW ORLEANS

A couple days earlier, back in New Orleans, I had also asked Daniel Schwartz, the community organizer for the Micah Project, about the sources for his hope. He spoke of the relation between faith and the organizing work he does. Schwartz clearly holds both dearly. He tells me that lifting the powerless to the place where they have a voice is at the core of his commitments. "What keeps me in this is taking faith and community organizing both seriously," Schwartz says. "I think faith and democracy, in many ways, are not the same, but there are elements in common. Genesis gives me the idea that we're all in this together. And democracy at its best means we're all in this together."[12] He asks me if that makes sense, and I nod that I am with him. He tells me, "That's what I'm trying to live more fully into. I've been really challenged in a good way to think about faith and to [explore] how does that play out? I take clergy aside and say, 'You know, one of the problems when people talk about Dr. King is they say Dr. King. You know what he was? He was *Rev.* Dr. King." We pause for a second reflecting on the gravity of Schwartz's point—King's secularization, even his use to sell mattresses in January, comes quickly to mind. But Schwartz has more to add. "People," he says, "want to make him into a secular figure, but the 'I Have a Dream' speech was not a speech. It was a sermon."

While sermons are spoken to move hearts toward the good and toward God, the "I Have a Dream" speech depicted a future day of actual equality, not merely enlightened minds. When Schwartz and I talk about the end that he is seeking—the common good—he tells me he does not know how to answer the question of the common good theoretically. Instead, he says, "I believe we'll begin to see the common good when we begin to see the common humanity, but I only believe that we'll get there when folks who are disenfranchised have the power to drive that conversation. And that's why

Religion Is Only as Good as What It Does

I'm in organizing. It's not going to come through some type of epiphany. It's going to come when the communities that I'm working with develop the power to drive the conversation; then we're going to see movement toward the common good."

I questioned New Orleans urban ministry worker Eugenia about faith in a different frame. I asked her what was the chief spiritual issue faced by her faith-based constituency. She replied, "It's probably the connection between their faith and their quality of life. You know that a lot of our people have been conditioned that if you live too comfortably, then that's not spiritual. Or, if you're [thinking too much] about the need to have an education, or to have economic equality, then that's not spiritual. They don't understand that when Jesus speaks of having life and having it abundantly, it is not just about money, it's about all things—your health, your education, your opportunities, your access."[13] Some of what Eugenia's ministry does to promote an abundant life is so basic and yet so clever that I am reminded of Jesus' admonition to be as "wise as serpents and innocent as doves" (Matt. 10:16, ESV). Parents and grandparents will sometimes complain that they do not feel equipped to act as advocates for their children and families in school because they themselves do not know how to read. So Eugenia gets out the large-print, easy-to-read Bibles and asks, "Wouldn't you like to read the Bible?" Pretty soon she can go on to point out, "Do you know these are the same words as are in your children's books?" Here people had gone to church for thirty years and hid, even from their pastors, the fact that they could not read, but a summer program and some culturally competent literature shared between the generations makes a way out of no way and joyful readers out of everyone. For Eugenia there is a connection between her Christian faith and a better life in the here and now, and she means to share that faith every day.

When Ben McLeish and I are talking about his faith journey from being a religiously charismatic Methodist college student to a person who believes the Calvinist idea of total human depravity, I ask him about the dark side of New Orleans from a faith perspective. "What have you learned," I inquire, "about what Paul called the 'powers and principalities' which hold the greatest sway here in the St. Roch neighborhood and beyond in New Orleans?" He responds, balancing the evil and suffering he sees with the grace he has experienced. "I learned that God's stronger than them [the powers], but that they exist, that they're there." He goes on to talk about his fit with his context: "I grew up in a relatively dysfunctional family and I think, psychoanalyzing my situation, this felt comfortable being in a dysfunctional neighborhood.

It felt comfortable and familiar, and my own needs to be rescued were being worked out as I was trying to be the rescuer of other people." He hastens to add that it is "not that God didn't call. God has always called people who were broken and had bruises and weren't qualified, aren't slick and put together. But I think I've learned that more and more. New Orleans is a really safe place to let that happen because in our neighborhood there's such transparency and authenticity." McLeish illustrated the honesty of brokenness with a story: "I was renovating a house down the street one time and a guy yells to me, 'Hey! You still in that house? They foreclosed on me.' In the town I came from, Atlanta, no one would ever yell across the street about how they had been foreclosed on."

I asked the Reverend Don Frampton about the ways the Katrina experience tested and strengthened the faith of the people he ministered to at St. Charles Avenue Presbyterian Church. He replied, "It was a personal test for people in my church who had lost, who had experienced losses as a result of Katrina. Physical losses, financial losses, emotional losses, that was a hard time for them. It was hard for all of us, I guess. We all had damage. And we were living apart, away from families and things like that, but some were suffering more than others."[14] Still, the exciting part of the Katrina event, Frampton noted, "was we had this work and we knew exactly what to do. We were so focused as a church. We knew why we existed. This is why we're here. To do this for such a time as this." Frampton reports that the church has actually grown by three hundred members since Katrina, with new members joining nearly every week. Part of the attraction is the vital connection between the worshiping community and the community mission. In Frampton's words, "We're back to the full parish church, yet mission is the first thing we think about, local mission in particular. So it's changed us."

HURRICANE FATALISM AND END-TIMES HOPE

You cannot spend very long in the Gulf region without hearing about life measured in terms of natural disasters. They have people's names, but the similarity to anyone named Camille, Wilma, George, Katrina, or Rita ends with the name. These are powerfully destructive natural forces that do not care about people and their hopes and dreams. So I have to wonder, as a scholar of religion, is there fatalism at work alongside people's other ascriptive faith stances? What I mean by fatalism is an attitude of resignation in the face of past and future storms, which are thought to be inevitable and

Religion Is Only as Good as What It Does

where, if one is killed or injured, it was fated to happen. Soldiers develop this viewpoint in response to war in part to stay sane while they undertake the daily personal risks of combat. The first person I explore this with is my fellow midwesterner Michael Cowan. "Michael," I ask, "is there a natural religion aspect to being here and living close to the possibility of hurricanes in a way that a Detroiter or a Chicagoan wouldn't?" "It's a great question," he tells me, "I was forty [before I came here] and all my forty years had been spent in Illinois, Ohio, and Minnesota. And so I knew experientially what tornadoes were. They could wreak terrible havoc on lives and property. I don't know how most midwesterners feel about tornadoes, but I'm pretty sure it's not the way how people who live here feel about hurricanes." He goes on to point out that "it's a rare year when something doesn't come into the Gulf of Mexico that couldn't threaten the future of your whole city, your livelihood, the people you love, your life. And so one or more times a year you go through the anticipatory anxiety and preparation and so forth of that, and having lived through a hit by a hurricane, people who have done that I think feel it more viscerally than those who have arrived since then." Now that Cowan has had more than a few seasons in the tropical storm belt, he has thought more about hurricanes and about the moral consequences to his city. "The real difference between a hurricane and a tornado is not that they're destructive or not," Cowan says, "it's that in the one case if you're in the way of a hurricane, it's your fault unless you just flat can't get out. One of the really good things that's happened since [Katrina] is that the next time we have to evacuate the city, we're much better prepared to do it so that even if people are unable to choose, even if it isn't about choice and it's about means, there'll be a way out for everybody. There will be."

Unlike Cowan, Rod Dickson-Rishel has lived all his life in hurricane country and all his life except for higher-education years along the Mississippi coast. He even had an earlier home destroyed by a hurricane. But Katrina was different. "We talk about the storm around here like it was last week," he says. "We don't have to say Hurricane Katrina. That was before the storm. That was after the storm. It's absolutely an historical marker. In fact, when I came here and met with the Staff-Parish Relations Committee the first time, one of the things I'll never forget somebody said to me was, 'We prefer that you not use the K-word at all.'" I mention that it is hard to avoid such salient sermon material as a preacher, and Dickson-Rishel knowingly nods. But, he says, you do not need to say much: "When you stand up there and you're preaching and you say something like 'We understand about loss' and you're looking at someone who is seventy-five years old and they and their home went back to a slab—nothing. Then they rebuilt and they still live, the community still lives in the same place. They know something about loss."

Alice Graham did not herself experience the storm firsthand, but I learned as she did that how you think about surviving a hurricane has a lot to do with how you think about survival, period. She says of her first experience of working with older adult hurricane survivors in the black church during her first stint of service, "They taught me so much about the history of Mississippi in African American Caring Conversation groups where they said things to me like, 'Oh, we'll survive Katrina; we survived Jim Crow. We can survive anything.'" She experienced a surprising richness in the groups in the midst of community devastation and deprivation. Graham expresses admiration for "the way that these seniors helped each other. Many of them opening their homes to families and the residents, even in our groups, resourcing one another." Some of them she experienced living in toxic RVs, in tents, and tripled up in family homes. Some had lost their "family home that they had not had to pay a mortgage or anything on." Graham found herself committed to listening to these people who had lost so much but were working toward a fresh start against long odds. She also found herself, not surprisingly for a theological educator, listening to the clergy who were "trying to figure out what is God saying, what is God meaning in the midst of all of this?" Some, she reported, "feel guilty because their home wasn't damaged and so many people in their congregation lost homes and are so overextended. One clergywoman has since died, and I really think died because she wore herself out in the recovery traveling around the country raising money for a home for everybody who needed a home in Pass Christian." That clergywoman was the same Methodist minister who first offered Alice Graham a place to live rent-free in her daughter's renovated home. Zeal for the Lord's work and the people of her flock consumed the Reverend RoseMary Williams and perhaps led to her early death. Her self-sacrifice surely counts as one of the hidden and delayed fatalities of Katrina.

In among all the Katrina losses, some people are able to claim the kind of hope Christians associate with the sharing that is to happen at an eschatological heavenly banquet. I asked James Cox and Susan Turner of Main Street Baptist Church how people of faith were challenged in the experience. Cox told me, "I didn't find mine challenged. I knew it was a disaster," but he also allows that his boss had to point out that he was not feeling the loss so much as something else. His boss called and asked, "'James, so how are you doing?' And I said, 'I'm out here.' I was up on Cedar Lake distributing water and stuff. And

Religion Is Only as Good as What It Does

he said, 'You didn't say anything about what you lost or nothing.'" Then Cox smiles as he remembers what it felt like. "It didn't cross my mind what I lost, it was just you lost it and you put it back together and you keep going. You don't think about how much I lost or whatever. You feel like you are blessed when you see other people and what they've lost, but I was blessed." Susan Turner says that James Cox was not alone in his experience. "I think church members as a whole became stronger," she says. "They were grateful and they knew they had lost a lot, but they were grateful to God because all that material stuff was being replaced and they had their lives. They were still here. They started off really strong. They were not missing church. People who had not been coming, they were coming. And although we lost a few members, we gained."

Turner also remembers that in her neighborhood some gains in community came with the storm. "Where I live everybody had a fence, a privacy fence, and the storm just knocked them down and we all became more connected than ever before," she says. Before Katrina there were people of different denominations living in her community, Catholic, Baptist, Methodist, and so on, and neighbors would wave, but from afar, Turner says. "When those fences were pulled down we could actually touch, and they were coming over seeing if they could help and what could they do. We were blessed in that manner." Cox adds, "And amazing enough, I don't think they even got short of food [during the feeding marathon at the church]. They had freezers out in the parking lot that were full of food." Turner frames the travails with faith. "It was an experience. It was one that I will never forget, and it lets me know how grateful we are," she says. "I can't imagine how I would have taken it had I not been a Christian. I don't know, how I would have felt. There may have been some people who felt like God had let them down, but I saw renewed faith in most people."

Main Street Baptist in East Biloxi did feed people in a never-ending feast of biblical proportions after Katrina while people worked to get cleaned up and back on their feet. Interestingly, when I ask Ben McLeish how in theological terms he wants to see the city he has dedicated his adult life to, he also goes for the banquet image. "There are lots of theological angles to the city," he maintains. "For one, there's a city that resembles the coming kingdom unlike any other city in our country. One day we'll be at our banqueting table feasting before the Lord, and hopefully they'll be catering out of New Orleans because we've got some good fun, some good banquet here. We have an incredible sense of generosity. A lot of it is in the day-to-day culture, but also in the Mardi Gras season there are just parades and perfect strangers throwing out enormous gobs of stuff to you for free. It's this expression, a physical expression, of grace—just being poured out. You don't deserve it; there's nothing you did to earn the beads or the throws or the whatever." So that is like the gospel, which balances the other reality: "There's definitely a side of this city that feels cursed in many ways. Ministry here is just hard; it's just tough." Still, McLeish ends on a note of big hope. "Colossians 1:20 says God is at work redeeming all things," he says. New Orleans "is a really beautiful place to work that out, to work for God's kingdom come on earth, as it is in heaven."

I drove away from the Gulf Coast interviews with the hope that comes from humble people who believe that they are called to change the world and leave it better than they found it. No one sugarcoated problems, and from all, we heard social analysis that was cogent and compelling about the racism, poverty, and lack of government dedication to solving enduring problems. Even more compelling was the way these Christian and Jewish community leaders were living their faith in the post-Katrina context determined to light a candle while others were content to cynically curse the darkness.

Southern Louisiana and coastal Mississippi have, as we have said before, very different religious makeups. The first is much more Catholic and the second much more Baptist, but large African American populations in both regions unite them, as do the legacies of racism seen now, especially in mass incarceration and high unemployment among black males. The work that religious people have done to clean up physically from flooding and storm damage is impressive. The work that remains to heal generations of racism, poverty, and neglect is even greater, yet here, too, the religious institutions and volunteers have been largely on the side of the angels, if still unequally distributed.

As different as southern Louisiana and Mississippi can sometimes claim to be, with respect to the experience of Katrina and the aftermath, they proved resolutely both part of the South. In terms of religiosity, one other aspect sticks out for me. Daniel Schwartz said that religious speech and religious arguments get a special hearing in the South—and he had in mind, of course, New Orleans. Each of our interviewees demonstrates some of the ways that religious speech is made effective in southern community life in the context of a major natural disaster. When it came to explaining the storm, healing from the storm, choosing to help others clean up from the disaster, judging those who behave badly, and so much more, religious categories and particularly Christian beliefs and practices framed the event. If you want merely to understand cyclonic activity in the Gulf, get a weatherman. To understand the aftermath of Hurricane Katrina, a Bible is indispensable.

Religion Is Only as Good as What It Does

PART
THREE

BRAND NEW START

Southern Religious Innovations

MEGACHURCHES AND
THE REINVENTION OF
SOUTHERN CHURCH LIFE

Megachurches are big in the South. That is, the phenomenon of mega-churches—churches with approximately two thousand people in weekly worship attendance—is especially prevalent in the South. The Hartford Institute for Religion Research, which tracks all things megachurch, estimates that the southern states (including Maryland and the District of Columbia) account for 32 percent of all the nation's megachurches.[1] The significance of this figure becomes clearer when we notice that the same states account for only 25 percent of the country's population.[2] Compare that to the Northeast, with 18 percent of the population but only 5 percent of the megachurches, and the newcomer's sense that the South is a land of huge churches is no mere first impression but rather a grounded reality. Journalist Tracy Thompson calls the South "Jesusland" for a reason, and it is not just the prevalence of the bumper stickers and T-shirts she notices that say "American by birth, Southern by the grace of God." This form of exaggerated American exceptionalism, however, is part of the picture. If God sheds just a little more grace on southerners, by their reckoning, it is reciprocated in their religiosity. "The proof," says Thompson, "is in the reams of polling data that clearly show that southerners go to church more than other Americans, that more of us consider religion to be a 'very important' part of our daily lives, that we pray

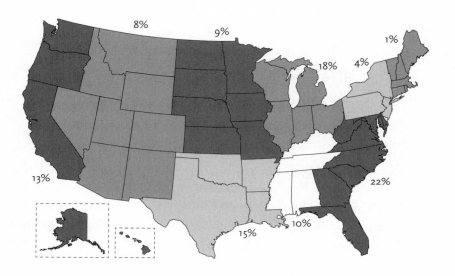

Megachurch Location by Region
Source: Warren Bird and Scott Thumma, "A New Decade of Megachurches—
2011 Profile of Large Attendance Churches in the United States,"
http://hirr.hartsem.edu/megachurch/megachurch-2011-summary-report.htm.

more often than other Americans, and that we see evidence of divine inter-cession in our daily affairs more frequently than people elsewhere."[3]

Not everyone in the South attends a megachurch, of course, but be-cause so many people do, the strong megachurch model affects the general experience of church attendance and belonging, even in small churches. To get a feel for southern megachurches in their variety, we next visit four such churches that introduce the important aspects of this innovative form of church life in the contemporary era. The first is a Southern Baptist church just outside Memphis, Tennessee, that plays an outsized role in its com-munity and in the Southern Baptist Convention. Next is the Thomas Road Baptist Church (TRBC) in Lynchburg, Virginia, a church that grew the na-tion's largest Christian college, Liberty University. After that we stop in at New Birth Missionary Baptist Church in Lithonia, Georgia, for a taste of prosperity gospel preaching. Finally, we return to Memphis and St. Andrew AME, a neighborhood church that has grown into a multifaceted resource for its largely impoverished neighborhood.

MEMPHIS: BELLEVUE BAPTIST CHURCH—
A BIG CHURCH GROWS GIANT

Driving into Memphis from the east on Interstate 40 one might be forgiven for thinking that this city is like so many other large and thriving cities of the early twenty-first century. On each side of the highway are the signs that sub-urbanites have dollars to spend; Costco, Barnes and Noble, Joseph A. Bank, Forever 21, Panera Bread, and Starbucks all beckon customers from the road. You could in fact be almost anywhere in suburban America until you see the three white steel crosses abutting the road to mark the location of Bellevue Baptist Church. With Baptist crosses of Super Bowl magnitude, you can only be in the South. The central cross, representing Christ, stands 150 feet high, with the thieves' crosses each measuring 120 feet in height. Half as tall as the Statue of Liberty, the crosses make a statement, and the church has been making a larger-than-life witness to belief in Jesus Christ for decades. In many ways the history of twentieth-century Southern Baptist success can be read in the life of this one congregation and in its changing roles and fortunes under the just four senior pastors in nearly ninety years who took Bellevue from a large but unremarkable midtown Memphis congregation of 1,430 members to the 30,000-member megachurch it is today.

The first of those four remarkable pastors was Robert Greene Lee, who always went by the euphonious name Robert G. Lee (say it out loud and you can imagine how it served as a social asset for a white southern pastor in the years 1927 to 1960). Born the son of a South Carolina sharecropper, Lee went to law school in Chicago and graduated with a degree in international law before turning his rhetorical gifts to the service of the gospel ministry. During his pastorate the church membership grew to more than nine thousand, and he was elected three times to serve as Southern Baptist Convention president. Bellevue Baptist was chosen in 1950 as one of twelve churches in *Christian Century* magazine's series on "Great Churches of America."[4] Lee himself was a major part of the attraction, and he was known far and wide for a particular sermon, "Payday Someday," which he preached the first Sunday of May every year at the municipal auditorium because the crowds were so huge. He also took this sermon on the road, and it is estimated that during his lifetime more than three million people heard him preach "Payday Someday." Every May (and whenever he was asked), Robert G. Lee retold the story of King Ahab and Queen Jezebel, who took the vineyard of poor, righteous Naboth by murderous deceit, and Elijah, who prophesied that both would die in the same dirt as their victim, trampled by horses and eaten by dogs. He took fifty-five minutes to retell the story in the most dramatic terms imaginable (think old-time radio mysteries), in Jezebel's case sparing no comparisons—to Lady Macbeth, Lucretia Borgia, and Cleopatra, among others:

> And it came to pass, when Ahab heard that Naboth was dead, that Ahab rose up to go down to the vineyard of Naboth the Jezreelite, to take possession of it (I Kings 21:16). Ahab rose up to go down—from Samaria to Jezreel. He gave orders to his royal wardrobe keeper to get out his king's clothes, because he had a little "business" trip to make to look over some property that had come to him by the shrewdness of his wife in the real estate market!

All of this was leading up to the conclusion that the judgment ways of God "often have leaden heels and travel slowly. But they always have iron hands and crush completely." The moral point about Ahab and Jezebel applied equally to Lee's modern listeners—it could easily happen to you: "'Payday Someday!' God said it—and it was done! Yes, and from this we learn the power and certainty of God in carrying out His own retributive providence, that men might know that His justice slumbereth not. Even though the mill of God grinds slowly, it grinds to powder." Then, in the last two minutes of the sermon, came the appeal to sinners to avoid Ahab and Jezebel's fate, and Lee finished with a flourish and a call to the altar of repentance and following Jesus:

> And the only way I know for any man or woman on earth to escape the sinner's payday on earth and the sinner's hell beyond—making sure of the Christian's payday on earth and the Christian's heaven beyond the Christian's payday—is through Christ Jesus, who took the sinner's place upon the Cross, becoming for all sinners all that God must judge, that sinners through faith in Christ Jesus might become all that God cannot judge. Pay Day Some Day.[5]

Robert G. Lee was not only wildly popular as a modern-day George Whitefield, a converting evangelist of the first order, he was also wholly identified with the city of Memphis and a large institutional church that dominated its space in the urban core of the city in the years before desegregation.

Bellevue's next pastor was Ramsey Pollard, who served from 1960 until 1972, establishing a suburban branch church for the congregation (satellite churches were to become a major part of the megachurch movement) and a major ministry for seniors in the church, while holding the membership steady at nine thousand and serving twice as the SBC's president. Still, when his successor, Adrian Rogers, arrived in 1972, the membership was trending older and members were moving toward the western, whiter suburbs of Memphis. In 1983, Rogers led his congregation to relocate to its present location in Cordova, Tennessee, and the building they built would be typical of Southern Baptist megachurches, a kind of faux Georgian red brick with white trim colonial that says we have been around for a while, even as the scope, storefront glass, and furnishings of the worship center call that claim into question. The original 1983 building required more than a million square feet of sheetrock to cover the walls for worship, fellowship, and classroom spaces. And speaking of classrooms, there were more than 125 Sunday school offerings.[6]

Adrian Rogers was such a lively and memorable preacher that he can still be seen and heard today on his syndicated program of preaching, *Love Worth Finding*, which is broadcast 1,852 times each week in various U.S. media markets.[7] Rogers managed to be funny and engaging, with one-liners that invariably circled back to the saving atonement of Jesus Christ alone for one's sins. He would say things like, "My wife is my number two priority, and she understands that makes me a better husband. Let me explain." He also used self-deprecation in his humor to make himself more likable, and then, with the same smile on his face, he could go on the attack against the cultural changes that represented sin to fundamentalists like himself. The problem with feminism? Just consider Genesis 3. "Eve, come here, baby," said Rogers, doing an imitation of Satan, "'I'm going to liberate you.' Adam's rib, Satan's fib, women's lib. Bang. Bang. Bang."[8] That is vintage Rogers style, and readers might wonder why we are spending so much time on a preacher, however big in his own time, who has been dead since 2005. By way of an answer, allow me to point out that Rogers rode these skills in organizing people and preaching as a culture warrior while sounding entertaining (and even more Christian than his opponents) into the SBC presidency three times, from which he helped lead the fundamentalist takeover of denominational boards and agencies. Bellevue was, and is, a conservative church, and with Rogers's leadership and the support of thirty thousand dedicated members, the SBC was made over in Bellevue's image alongside that of the equally large and influential First Baptist Church of Dallas, Texas.[9]

And what of years since then at Bellevue under the most recent pastor, Steve Gaines? Well, Gaines represents the next turn in the megachurch model, for if it still is pastor led (and the pastor needs talented preaching ability when you have thirty thousand members to try and keep interested), it is also now a house of many mansions, a church where every person has a smaller group into which to fit. Bellevue Baptist does not just have new member classes, it has a continuous cycle of classes, so that the people who have been visiting the church can jump in and attend classes at any point. Actually these classes are named "Explore 101," "Grow 201," "Discover 301," and "Serve 401," and they are presented on sequential Sundays of every month; you register for them just like they are classes in a college curriculum that advances from courses in the 100-range to the 400-range.

And why not? If you think about it, Bellevue Baptist and other megachurches of its size are larger than all but a very few American universities in the number of people they serve. The curriculum at today's Bellevue introduces a vision of where God is taking people through the church. In "Explore 101," over lunch with the pastor, staff, and members of the church family, newcomers learn about the "Vision Frame." They are taught that, like any frame, the Vision Frame has four sides, and the first side is the "Mission," which "gives us direction and points everyone in that direction," namely to "Love God, love people, share Jesus, and make disciples." The next side of the frame is called "Values," the "shared convictions that guide actions," and there are five of these: "Intimacy with Jesus, biblical truth, intentional hospitality, ministry excellence, and city renewal." The third side of the frame is for me, as a lifelong church person and theological educator, the most interesting. It is called "Our Measures," and it asks the church and individual believers "When are we successful?" and articulates measurable outcomes associated with loving God, loving people, and making disciples. Corporations and educational institutions have increasingly embraced measurable outcomes, but I have never seen a church go so far as to name the things that a Christian can do to achieve the mission Christ has set before the church.

But three sides alone do not make a square frame, and Bellevue, thinking bigger than the individual Christian, offers "Strategy" as the fourth side of its Vision Frame. Using the metaphor of a flashlight in its instructional video, Bellevue points the way so that everyone can see clearly the next steps to getting involved. The church calls this "six proven pathways to accomplishing our mission at Bellevue." Consequently, each person is guided to: (1) worship God weekly; (2) connect with others in a life group that relies on the Bible; (3) serve in the life of the congregation as a volunteer; (4) become equipped for service and knowledge through Wednesday night classes; (5) serve in Memphis and beyond; and (6) be part of spiritual awakenings through specifically evangelical activities.

Steve Gaines and Bellevue Baptist and the many other megachurches that have developed more highly articulated versions of Christian life for the twenty-first-century American have done something striking in the history of evangelicalism, particularly for the South. They have rediscovered the Christian life as a comprehensive set of God and neighbor relationships that is much more than getting saved and sinning no more. When Jerry Falwell began his ministry as a new church planter at the Thomas Road Baptist Church in 1956 in Lynchburg, southern evangelicalism had no second act beyond preaching conversion. After you realized, as Robert G. Lee preached, that it was going to be "Pay Day Some Day," either you got right with Jesus and showed up to church with a Bible in your hand and family at your side or you were doomed. The social horizon of white southern Christianity was notoriously close in those days. There was a prevailing assumption that there really was a Christian civilization that saw to it that prayer happened in the schools, the children made it home safely, the movie theaters stayed closed on Sundays, and pornography was only sold up north. If southern society policed personal sin, it also failed to see the colossal social sins of racial hatred and legal segregation of the races. Bellevue itself in those earlier days was one of the churches that turned away integrated pairs of college students presenting themselves as would-be worshippers, even as it supported missions in Africa.[10] It is in light of such history that something new can be seen to be going on even since Adrian Rogers's time at Bellevue. There is now no assumption that the society will be a moral foundation for Christians; the Constantinian age reached its last stop—the American South—and no longer serves up Christendom as a social support for the Christian church. Even that old race history is being carefully unbuilt under Steve Gaines's leadership. Even though Bellevue left downtown and left Memphis in 1983 for an address in Cordova, in 2007, under their new pastor and his philosophy of embracing the whole metropolis, a sign at the church appeared to grasp everyone's attention, saying, "Bellevue Loves Memphis." The sign represented not mere boosterism, as in "Memphis Loves the Grizzlies," but as Gaines taught, showing "Jesus' love to our city by meeting the practical needs of residents."[11]

Nearly ten years later, when one asks where religious power lies in Memphis as I did among interviewees in the evangelical, mainline, and black church communities, Steve Gaines's name came up. That is the social power of megachurch pastors in their communities, if they exercise it for their communities. Gaines and the pastor of St. Andrew African Methodist Episcopal Church, the Reverend Dr. Kenneth Robinson, have in Memphis not only name recognition but the power to form hearts and minds that popular university presidents and certain media personalities have. We will return to Memphis to spend some time in Robinson's church, but first we experience Wednesday night services at another legendary Baptist megachurch, the Thomas Road Baptist Church in Lynchburg.

LYNCHBURG, VIRGINIA—ANGRY BUMPER STICKERS AND WARM FELLOWSHIP AT TRBC

When candidate Barack Obama got himself in trouble for talking about people who cling to their guns or religion or antipathy to people who aren't like them, he might well have been talking about Lynchburg, Virginia.[12] As we arrive for Wednesday night services at the Thomas Road Baptist Church, I notice that more than a few cars feature bumper stickers that express in-your-face contempt for would-be gun controllers and for President Obama and his policies. More positively, the bumper stickers express love for the South, a reciprocal love of Jesus, and an intent to vote

Southern Religious Innovations

for Republican gubernatorial candidate Ken Cuccinelli, who had, coincidentally, lost his election the night before. One of my colleagues now teaching at the University of Virginia reminded me the prior evening that both of our mothers objected to the very idea of wearing your politics on your car bumper back in the 1960s. So I am noticing bumper stickers more than usual and thinking about them as signifiers. I also remember that my father, still a country boy at heart, told his children that he would have no objection to a nonpolitical bumper sticker, but he did not like the mess the adhesive made on the car, thus keeping the peace with my mother. Unlike in that era, when bumper stickers said simply NIXON/AGNEW or SEE ROCK CITY, today's bumper stickers are nearly all tendentious from their inception, or made so through their continued use. They often represent fear about a changing country that some people can no longer understand or accept:

REAL MEN LOVE JESUS
"Those who hammer their guns into plows will plow for those who
    do not."—Thomas Jefferson
YES WE CAN—SECEDE
WHERE'S THE BIRTH CERTIFICATE?[13]

Other bumper stickers seem to be partisan declarations of pride in voting for George W. Bush, John Kerry, John McCain, or Barack Obama long after their elections have passed. No matter what victorious presidential candidates suggest, we no longer "come together in unity as a nation" and remove the stickers but instead leave them in place to say, "I told you so." (The early disappearance of ROMNEY/RYAN bumper stickers seems to be a striking exception that proves the rule.) A friend of ours, a woman with a cabin in the rural north Georgia mountains, recounts being stopped at a divided highway traffic light when a man in a pickup pulled up beside her in the spring of 2013. He rolled his passenger side window down to get her attention. She rolled down her front driver's side window. The man in the truck said, "I just wanted to point out you have a mess on your bumper you might want to get cleaned up." Instantly she knew what he was talking about. The only thing on her bumper was an OBAMA 2012 sticker. Sometimes the bumper stickers show fear about this world or other people in, as in "God bless our troops; especially our snipers." Or, "I'm Christian and I vote. Sorry if that offends you." This fear and anger about the secular world is extended sevenfold (or so) for any claim that "this car will be driverless in case of rapture." In any event, the sense that the South was being changed by outside forces at odds with southern Christian identity was long exploited by Thomas Road Baptist Church's founder, the Reverend Jerry Falwell, to do a new thing in the name of old-time religion. The old and new and young and old are so skillfully blended (and served separately) at TRBC that there is truly something for everyone. Perhaps nowhere I know better illustrates how contemporary evangelicalism has adapted to and been transformed in the age of the Internet and cable television. The church built by a man knocking on a hundred doors a day in the 1950s, started in an old brick warehouse in the days of the Sears catalog, network radio, and broadcast TV, has managed to become a supermall megachurch for the several generations that call TRBC home.

Coming in from the parking lot, the first thing we encounter in the grand foyer, called Main Street, which connects with everything else, is an information desk on the right and a series of older elementary school kids checking themselves in like passengers using an airline ticketing kiosk. Each swipe what look like credit cards and in return get nametag stickers that say where they should be and keep track of their attendance. (Throughout the year I see variations of this system at other megachurches. It makes me reflect on what a *Leave It to Beaver* world my brothers and I grew up in: our church and parents just trusted us to go to the right classroom, even if we sometimes skipped.) Kids at TRBC have great places with attractive features geared toward their age groups; adults have lots of choices, too, either life-stage groups to belong to or EquipU classes to guide their discipleship in areas like personal finance or parenting. (Christian finance guru Dave Ramsey's Financial Peace University is the program I have encountered at even more places than I have those check-in kiosks.) We choose what appears to be the most traditional event, the Wednesday night prayer service, held in Pate Chapel on the ground floor.

The prayer service is indeed a traditional Wednesday night evangelical program that combines an inspirational and educational talk with Scripture, hymns, and prayers for members of the community in need. In our mid-fifties, my wife and I are the youngest of nearly two hundred people in the room, but this, like so much about TRBC, demonstrates the megachurch capacity of including everyone by programming for their needs. Thomas Road Baptist Church is simply a church you cannot be too young or too old for; if you can attend church, there is a group for you. At TRBC if you are an alcoholic man in need of a residential recovery center, there is a home for you. Likewise, if you are a teenage girl with an unplanned pregnancy, there is a residential center (the Godparent Foundation) for you, too. Meanwhile, here at the prayer service we hear from Rick Rasberry, a faculty member at Liberty University, on Jesus' messianic (that is, first) coming. Even though it is November, we sing what in a more liturgical tradition would be Advent hymns and are told that the rest of the month will also feature lectures from Liberty University faculty on messianic prophecy. Rasberry's interpretive technique is ample use of lower criticism, combined with the invocation of his audience's biblical knowledge of many passages, southern preacher humor, and Baptist theology: "The God that we worship does not want to be judge, but Savior, but only becomes judge when we reject his salvation." The prophet Micah's new Davidic king, "You Bethlehem though you are small . . .," is the centerpiece of prophetic expectations for a messiah, we are told. But actually such expectations were misplaced, since the real meaning of the New Testament is that Jesus comes from eternity and not from David's line. If this sounds to readers like a throwback to some of the preaching of Robert G. Lee, it should not be surprising, for once again TRBC and Liberty University itself are preserving a link to the middle of the twentieth century and earlier. They are doing so for the churchgoers around us that Wednesday night and for generations going forward in how to think about the Bible through the work of the university. The prayers that follow the talk are also a link to the past, for although the names have been printed that morning by laser printer in categories (those Ill, Awaiting Tests, In Military, Bereaved, and so on), we pray for these friends and loved ones just as Christians have done for centuries.

The next two-hour experience at TRBC is something completely different. It is called Campus Church. Thomas Road Baptist Church founded Lynchburg Christian Academy in 1967 and Liberty University in 1971. Today Liberty is the largest university in Virginia and physically surrounds TRBC. Weekday chapel attendance at Liberty is required and takes place on campus in the gym, but the voluntary Wednesday night service in the church's sanctuary is extraordinarily well attended. The service even has its own Facebook page, whose description is aspirational and captures the flavor of our experience in 2014: "This is a church for the rest of us . . . and everyone is welcome. There's no dress code or dry sermons. Skeptics and critics are our guests of honor. Each week thousands of students from dozens of campuses gather under one roof. No facades, just honest faith . . . real people. Campus Church is turning a diverse community to the heart of God."[14] The night we went there were indeed thousands of young adults present for this event that had the darkened audience and bright stage feel of a rock concert. Justin Kintzel had at that time served as Liberty's worship pastor for several years, and he was there with his guitar, band, and singers, leading worship by introducing music and stoking up the audience. We also heard a message from Liberty University campus pastor Johnnie Moore, who was introduced as the campus church teaching pastor. His message was based on the theme that "as Christians, we are supposed to be a blessing to the world." He impressed me most by the way he tapped into the anxiety of Christian college students worried about their futures and about their friends. He asked if they had it all figured out. "Job, marriage—eventually, family. Is that the way it is?" he asked. "No? That's bad, right?"[15] Then he suggested that this version of the American dream was a setup for Christians and that loving God and loving your neighbor as yourself was even better.

Johnnie Moore gave his sermon—which did not sound like a sermon—from a Lucite lectern on center stage, with a mixture of self-deprecating humor, storytelling, and patter that was closer to a first-rate standup comic than it was to most preachers, without going for gratuitous laughs. Having the audience so clearly on his side allowed him to approach a tender topic for college students at Liberty—dating, in particular what happens when you break up. "The Bible says you have to love everybody. You in the Bible sense do not have permission not to love your ex-boyfriend or ex-girlfriend in a biblical sense." Next, he moved on to the annoyance of roommates who keep hitting the snooze button and sucked them into despising their roommates and then jerked them back into the biblical reality that "the quality of your life has everything to do with how you treat other people; especially those whom you do not like." Though the message was centered on Galatians 5, Moore's message was still typical evangelical preaching in the sense that Scripture was cited from throughout the New Testament, from Romans, James, John, Colossians, and Second Peter, all used in support of his proposition that loving as God loves was a choice that they could and should make to radically improve the quality of their lives. If Moore's talk was mostly about the redemptive power of love and mercy, however, the Christian contemporary praise music that night was largely of the "Christ you are so great and I am not worthy" nature. Justin Kintzel can really sell a song, and after his closing prayer and the benediction there were still three rocking encores that had us all on our feet. But the songs still had the same themes, the kingship of Christ and our unworthiness. I listened hard, but

Southern Religious Innovations

I listened in vain for a song that said I can love my neighbors because you loved me first, Lord. Perhaps someday Moore and Kintzel will write that song together.

LITHONIA, GEORGIA—THE PROSPERITY GOSPEL
AT NEW BIRTH MISSIONARY BAPTIST

Bishop Eddie Long, a bishop in the New Testament sense of "one who oversees ministry" and not in the sense that the church has an episcopal polity, leads New Birth Missionary Baptist Church. Long took over New Birth Missionary Baptist Church in 1987, when it was an ordinary black church of three hundred members, and built it in less than twenty years to a congregation of twenty-five thousand before a scandal involving alleged coerced sex with male youths derailed its growth and cost the church some of its membership.[16] The secret to that growth, and the reason the church has not completely collapsed, is its message, commonly called the Prosperity Gospel. Prosperity preaching goes back to the earliest Pentecostal insistence that signs and wonders were still available in the present age but came to the clearest American notice in televangelist Oral Roberts's preaching that "God is a good God" eager to "bless those who call upon him" with Christ's promise that you should have life and have it abundantly. In Long's case, he was mentored by Bishop Earl Paulk, the founder and head pastor of Chapel Hill Harvester Church in Dekalb County, Georgia, from 1960 until the late 1990s.[17] By the 1970s and 1980s, the mechanical view that right-speaking and right-thinking Christians could "name and claim" their desired health and wealth had made significant inroads into Hispanic and African American churches, so much so that churches like Long's are now popularly termed Bapticostal. With white representatives of the movement such as Joel Osteen one tends to encounter something called soft prosperity, where the promises and the music are a little softer, less explicit. But with Long and his former music leader William Murphy III, one gets hard prosperity, captured nicely in the line of one of Murphy's popular New Birth choruses, "I've got more than enough, I'm coming to get my stuff."[18]

When we pull up for a Sunday morning service in February 2014, the parking lot at New Birth is not very full compared to its vast capacity, but inside probably three thousand people are at a two-hour service featuring music from a house band, singing from an excellent visiting black college choir, announcements of ways to become more educated about God's intentions for our abundant lives, and a sermon by a visiting evangelist there for a week of what might be called a revival in another setting. At New Birth, this week of Sunday through Wednesday services is called the "Recover It All ENCOUNTER," in which we are promised the opportunity to "Take Back What's Rightfully Yours & Live in Abundance!" The visiting evangelist is Apostle Renny McLean, and the whole week is premised on 1 Samuel 30:18–20. I check my iPhone to be certain of the passage, and I get the NKJV version: "So David recovered all that the Amalekites had carried away, and David rescued his two wives. And nothing of theirs was lacking, either small or great, sons or daughters, spoil or anything which they had taken from them; David recovered all. Then David took all the flocks and herds they had driven before those other livestock, and said, 'This is David's spoil.'" I am surprised, but not surprised. On the one hand this is a historical passage about what happened to David, not a teaching about how God deals with us. On the other hand, the essence of the Prosperity Gospel is to collapse that difference: as with David, so with you; God wants you to get your stuff back. McLean's message followed the same basic technique, only using the book of Hebrews and the person of Adam "made in God's image AND likeness" to also collapse a distinction between what God the Creator could get and what we could get if we accepted our image and likeness. If this sounds different from other Christian preaching, as in familiar words used in novel patterns to make new meanings, then I am conveying the experience. Another inescapable difference in a Prosperity Gospel church is the number of offerings. First, the ushers collect your 10 percent of income tithe, a requirement to be blessed; then there is a love offering for the pastor, an offering after the sermon for the guest evangelist, and last—and this is important—your seed offering. A seed offering is where you plant a seed with God to be blessed tenfold for the things that you want: good health, a job, a car, a down payment for a house, a husband. It will not work if you hold back in your obligations to tithe and be a cheerful giver in the offerings, but if you plant a seed in faith after being faithful in your offerings, God will prosper your gift.

If the number of offerings are remarkable, so, too, is the racial diversity of the congregation. Although it is predominantly black, nearly every row has someone white, Asian, or Hispanic in it. Sometimes it is obvious that these are the loved ones and family members of African American attendees, and other times it is obvious that these individuals have come by themselves. During the altar call to present oneself if one desires to be prayed over, a racial mixture of supplicants goes forward. For me, the altar call is the most

Baptist and southern note in the whole service and in many ways the most moving; it is a reminder that fixing what is broken in people's lives drives New Birth Missionary Baptist Church as much as any other church in the region.

Bishop Eddie Long Sr. died on January 22, 2017, after what was said to be a long bout with cancer. Complicating the story, he had appeared in church in October and December 2016 speaking of a health change, claiming a vegetarian diet, and denying rumors of being in hospice care. Managing the facts was the way Long lived and, in the end, the way he went out. Conservative religious websites like the Christian Post reported the story as New Birth presented it. Commentators from the Root and Essence took Long's death as an opportunity to chastise the black church for its homophobia problem as represented by clergy leaders like Long, whom they saw as hypocrites. And for New Birth? They will reorganize. There are other preachers who have been mentored by Paulk, and by Long, to step in and bring the word of faith, say people who know the situation well.[19]

MEMPHIS: ST. ANDREW AME—URBAN OASIS

In the African Methodist Episcopal Church, congregations do not call pastors and preachers do not set up their own shops. Instead, their bishops send them. This system rarely results in a megachurch. In 1991, one such bishop sent a talented physician minister away from his successful medical practice and weekend church ministry kicking and screaming to a seventy-five-member beleaguered church in southern Memphis. Over time a church of mostly elderly people who had served nobly in the civil rights era but had grown old with their church was transformed into a dynamic ministry that serves as an oasis for promotion of Christ's beloved community in a neighborhood that would otherwise be overcome with poverty, drugs, and despair. The pastor's name was Kenneth Robinson, and I first got to know him when he was appointed health commissioner for the state of Tennessee and our university hosted a luncheon in his honor because he was a much-respected former faculty member of the medical school and a graduate of Vanderbilt's Divinity School. More than most clergy, Robinson and his wife, Marilynn (who is a Yale School of Public Health graduate and an AME minister), think in terms of systems. The Reverend Kenneth Robinson has administered more than ten million dollars in external resources through the mission of his congregations from national and local foundations and local, state, and federal agencies. For that work he has received numerous national honors, including a one-hundred-thousand-dollar award for St. Andrew, granted when the Robert Wood Johnson Foundation named him one of the country's top ten community health leaders of the year. But the first days for the Robinsons at the Saint, as it is known in the community, were less than auspicious. There were about seventy people actually worshiping and involved with the work of the church in 1991. Robinson says, "They were very proud, and I was very grateful for that, but the fact was that the third floor of the now west wing had been shuttered for fifteen years because nothing was happening there and that most of the rooms on the main floor were lounges."[20] He reports that his steward said, "This is the women's lounge and the men's lounge and the young people's lounge," as he was taking him through the church the first night Robinson was on site. The steward heard himself saying that, and he said, "I guess you can see what we've been doing." So the seventy grew to understand that they had to open the church, and with Robinson's leadership they started an initial program working with what were then called at-risk youth and providing after school programs.

The repeated conceptual theme one encounters at St. Andrew today is "Ministering to Memphis—Spirit, Soul, and Body!" It is what the pastors say they are doing, and it is unapologetically actualized in the church's works. There are major programs in family life enrichment, childcare services, academic skills enhancement, economic development, and supplemental food and clothing provision. The church has an associated community housing development organization that has created thirty-three affordable single-family homes and an eighty-unit apartment community. It also sponsors the Circles of Success Learning Academy, St. Andrew's associated K–5 public charter elementary school. Altogether the church has a workforce that exceeds its 1991 membership.

When it comes to worship, Sunday mornings feature Afrocentric Christian worship that speaks to the spirit of people of south Memphis and the people who care about them. Both Reverend Robinsons will be up front in the chancel on Sunday, irrespective of who is preaching. Marilynn Robinson was called to ministry only after the couple had moved to Memphis, and she continues to hold down full-time work in public health and as a senior hospital administrator. Members therefore know that they have a power couple leading them in ministry, but the nature of that ministry is geared foremost at reaching the people in the neighborhood. Consequently, the

Harvard-educated pastors make it a point in their preaching to mix the common language of the neighborhood with occasional high-value concepts from their work and educational backgrounds. Far from seeking a lowest common denominator of speech, their preaching is an existential grappling with the meaning of the Good News for people too often at the edge of life. Two sermons I have heard Kenneth Robinson preach—one about the attractions of substance abuse and another about the tragic murder of two children by their mother—stick with me months later because of the way he refracts experience through the light of the gospel. He claims that no one would come for his preaching (next to his admitted organizational genius), but people do come—from suburban east Memphis, west Memphis, Arkansas, and northern Mississippi, as well as from revitalized downtown communities and the urban south Memphis neighborhoods surrounding the church. The church has some white members who are either married to other members or have intentionally chosen a young African American community or are students. Robinson, reflecting on the overwhelming self-segregation of the black church, says that it "really doesn't bother me. It's not high on my agenda. I think black church is as much a culture as it is a gospel and what occurs in black church tradition is cultural, and for many of our members, who live much of the rest of their lives embedded and immersed in white culture in corporate America, church for them and their children, it is an opportunity to link back to the community and to culture, and I'm okay with that." In this sense St. Andrew's is more than an oasis for the neighborhood; it also functions that way for some of its suburban neighbors who live and work in more integrated settings. Altogether, the way the Robinsons and the St. Andrew AME congregation care for their neighbors and their south Memphis neighborhood in word and deed has transformed a declining neighborhood church into a megachurch.[21]

The Robinsons retired just before Christmas 2015. By January 10, 2016, their replacement, the Reverend Dr. Byron C. Moore, was appointed by the presiding bishop and in place. He was soon to be followed by his wife, the Reverend Sharon D. Moore, as executive pastor, and the Saint was up to its full complement of power-couple pastors to continue to lead them forward.

THE MEGACHURCH IMPACT ON OTHER CONGREGATIONS

From encounters with just these four churches it should be clear that not all megachurches are alike. The scope of their ministries, the content of their preaching, and the relations to their communities and religious traditions can be strikingly different from one another. Yet they also share common elements. They feature a charismatic figure with a characteristic message that helps sustain their core identity. Their worship is ecstatic, not tepid, even though ecstatic worship is culturally variable. Their programming, including small groups, requires commitment from their members. Their place in their ecology is outsized: Bellevue loves Memphis; TRBC is the home church to America's largest Christian college or university; and St. Andrew is the largest church in its AME Episcopal conference as well as a model for how to do faith-based community development corporations right. Finally, although New Birth may have lost some of the symbolic capital that saw it gathering four former U.S. presidents in its sanctuary for the televised funeral of Coretta Scott King in 2006, before his death, Bishop Eddie Long still had more than sixty clergy who pledged themselves to his headship as they led their own Prosperity Gospel ministries. In sum, each of these churches plays a role not unlike a medieval cathedral, but this in the modern South, a region unusually devoid of Catholic cathedrals of significance. These giant churches of Protestant lineage have innovated their way into being a substitute for cathedrals, that is, churches that are more important than other congregations both as models and as actual players on the religious landscape.

How representative are these four megachurches of their type, and what is their broader significance for the experience of church in the American South? To answer the first part of that question we turn to Hartford Seminary's megachurch expert Scott Thumma and his colleague Warren Bird of the Leadership Network, who have identified the leading features of megachurches in successive sociological surveys. In their 2011 survey report they summarize their findings this way:

- **These churches are wired.** Eighty-eight percent say that their church or pastoral leadership regularly uses Facebook or other social media; nearly 75 percent do podcasts; and 56 percent blog.
- **Multisite interest has grown dramatically.** Half are multisite, and another 20 percent are thinking about it.
- **Growth is steady.** Despite occasional news reports that large churches are a baby boomer phenomenon or are in decline, a steady growth pattern remains evident, with these churches averaging 8

percent annual growth in the last five years; thus, the stated average attendance for these churches grew from 2,604 in 2005 to 3,597 in 2010.

• **The leader at the helm makes all the difference.** Seventy-nine percent say that their church's most dramatic growth occurred during the tenure of the current senior pastor.

• **Worship options extend beyond Sunday morning.** Although virtually all have multiple Sunday morning services, 48 percent have one or more Saturday evening services, and 41 percent have one or more Sunday evening services.

• **They are both big and small.** Eighty-two percent say that small groups are "central to our strategy of Christian nurture and spiritual formation," and 72 percent put a "lot of emphasis" on "Scripture studies other than Sunday school." They report that 46 percent of their attendees are involved in small groups.

• **They have a high view of their own spiritual vitality.** An overwhelming 98 percent agree that their congregations are "spiritually alive and vital." In addition, 98 percent say that they have strong beliefs and values, 95 percent report that they have a clear mission, and 93 percent say that they are willing to change to meet new challenges.

• **Newcomer orientation is constant.** Forty percent of regular participants age eighteen and older are new to the congregation in the last five years. And 70 percent of participants are under the age of fifty.

• **The dominant identity is "evangelical."** Of eight options offered, the majority chose the word "evangelical" to identify their theological outlook. Interestingly, barely 1 percent chose labels at the two theological extremes—either "fundamentalist" or "liberal."

• **The vast majority do not have serious financial struggles.** Only 6 percent say that their church's financial health is in some or serious difficulty (and only 7 percent said that for five years previously). However, 50 percent adversely felt the effects of the economic crisis, and 5 percent fewer report their financial health as "excellent" compared to five years ago.

• **Staffing costs are comparable to those of other churches.** Forty-eight percent of the average large church's total expenditures go to salary and benefits.

- **They are not independent.** Seventy percent report that their church is part of a denomination, network, fellowship, or association of churches. For those who are currently nondenominational, 33 percent say that they were once part of a denomination.[22]

Examining these findings about American megachurches from the standpoint of small and medium-size southern Christian churches of today, it is striking how many of the same features are true of smaller congregations as well. Indeed, not a small part of the genius of the modern megachurch is the marriage of the soul of a small church to the production values of a Hollywood television variety show. First among the elements that all southern congregations share is a gift for familiarity. Wednesday night suppers, small groups, and child and adult Sunday schools make Protestant Christianity in the South an experience of fellowship, a time when you will be in church so you might as well have fun, eat good food, sing, pray, and learn something. So many country and R&B singers credit singing in the church as youths to their talent and love for music, but I suppose that nearly every one of them had a mother, father, or grandparent who insisted that they go to the church where the choir was practicing. Small groups and multiple forms of involvement are a national feature of megachurches, but for southerners it is just what they know as church.

Still, preachers matter. Even in a smaller church the charismatic role may be a different one and be cast for a smaller voice or an older, sage man or (in a mainline denomination) even a bright, dynamic woman, but again the leader "makes all the difference." Increasingly even in small churches, pastors are wired. As a theological school dean of three thousand ministerial graduates over twenty years, I have been sent countless blogs, and LinkedIn, Facebook, MySpace, and Twitter invitations, and of the more than thirty-five religious traditions whose students I have worked with, everyone is represented in this new electronic church. The historian Brooks Holifield memorably writes that the early nineteenth century was a time of enormous theological literacy and that when "Robert Baird interpreted American religion for European readers in 1843, he could boast of a 'vast number of publications in every department of Christian theology,' and he might have added that American theological journals were the most scholarly publications in the culture." Holifield goes on to explain that it was the theologians who were "keepers of a language that flowed over into other fields of discourse," whether moral, philosophical, or scientific.[23] Moreover, the theologians were writing not just for each other. Holifield's basis for that assessment was the sheer amount of religious interest evidenced in published journals, letters to the editors of national periodicals for laypeople about theological issues, and specialized ecclesiastical literature received in the homes of ordinary folk. Curiously, I think, we may be living through another such time, to judge from the output on the blogosphere, on church- and movement-sponsored websites, and on Twitter accounts. Certainly not since the theological renaissance of the post–World War II era, when pastors believed that they, like Martin Luther King Jr., Paul Tillich, and Reinhold Niebuhr, might have something intelligent to say to the public, have so many tried their hands at reaching a religious public directly in writing not intended first for the pulpit. To confine ourselves here to southern pastoral writers, we encounter voices (mostly) against, and for, the death penalty, for and against gay marriage as reconcilable with Christian life and biblical teachings, for (pretty unanimously) embracing homeless brothers and sisters as the "least of these" in Matthew 25, and for and against electronic screens in church, to cite only some of the most popular topics of the day. For any practice that has too many ardent advocates in the eyes of others (for example, the Prosperity Gospel) there are websites and blogs from religious leaders passionately decrying the practice. If churches seem polite, even tepid in person, a trip to their electronic presence on the Internet and a visit with religious leaders' online avatars may convince you otherwise. Even the people who seem to be passionate only about God's generous grace can be steamed because someone else out there in person, on television, or in the virtual world is saying that God has a heavenly closed-door policy to chasten us—and so it goes. So, where are there more active players than in the South, where religion on earth is practiced as though there is a genuine fight for the keys to the kingdom of heaven? The same South where not a few of these pastoral bloggers are sensitive men and women of the cloth, who write frankly and well about how difficult it is to speak for God when everyone around them says with their lips that they want that but say with their lives that they are content to let the preacher do the hard work. Those sensitive bloggers seem to come from the less numerically successful church traditions.

Another way that even small churches in the South are wired is with screens in the worship space. I became aware of this trend when one of my seminar students wrote a terrific paper on the history of how Southern Baptist churches were furnished from the nineteenth into the twenty-first centuries.

To state the conclusions from a well-argued and extensively documented paper, it turns out that whatever pulpit and chancel arrangements the most numerically successful churches and preachers of a particular era were using soon came to dominate even country churches that had little in common with those successful—mostly county seat and big city—congregations that had started the trend. Thus, early nineteenth-century center pulpits gave way to stages where choirs and organs could appear and preachers could walk back and forth without notes like actors or dramatic revivalists. Pulpits came back in the twentieth century, but off from the center and elevated after the fashion of elegant Episcopal churches. And then at the dawn of the twenty-first-century, minimal stands, Lucite lecterns, simple stools, and wireless, over-the-ear headsets became the norm for evangelical preachers, while bands including electric guitar, electric bass, keyboard, and drums at a minimum supplanted the church organ as the instrumentation of choice. Above it all large widescreen monitors project images of the minister, words to music, Scripture, and points to remember from the message of the day. The series of images I will always remember from Matthew McCullough's paper were the little tiny Baptist churches out in rural Tennessee that had awkwardly mounted two screens up front, left and right, in order to be just like the big Nashville, Memphis, and Jackson churches. The megachurch model is that strong for other evangelical churches, too, particularly in the South. Bands, lively worship, and projecting your minister's face on the screen (even when you can see him perfectly well with your own eyes) are all things that come with the megachurch model, and it is a powerfully attractive force now. Multisite megachurches even bring the pastor's message and prayers right to the small satellite church, as for example at Bellevue Baptist, where Steve Gaines brings the same message to the gathered congregation at Arlington High School as he does to the main Cordova location. The local Arlington congregation has its own music team, small groups, and fellowship, but it is part of something bigger, too, when it comes to preaching, mission opportunities, and more.

Still, even if the evangelical megachurch model is a defining force for southern church life in the early twenty-first century, not everything on the Hartford study's list of defining characteristics is to be found in every southern church, even the evangelical ones. Smaller churches differ in important ways from the megachurches. They are not thinking about expanding to second or third locations. Smaller churches occupy a wider ideological and theological spectrum for starters, so although evangelical is a commonly found identity, so, too, are fundamentalist, mainline moderate, family chapel, sectarian holiness, storefront entrepreneurial ministry, and a liberal fellowship of displaced Yankees and southern college professors and librarians. You might think I am kidding about that last identity category, but every college town in the South has two or three of those kinds of congregations. Church life runs the gamut from hugely vital in worship mode to something more enduringly purposeful where everyone just shows up, not because they expect a great show, or sermon, or inspiring music, but because it is church—where people meet their community and, on a good day, God.

While some people new to the South marvel at the prevalence of large churches, others wonder at all the number of tiny congregations and ask how they manage to stay alive. It turns out that it is hard to kill a congregation of people who feel invested in one another and in a particular place. This is especially so in the singular rural southern congregations of Baptists, Methodists, Church of Christ, or Presbyterians known as family chapels. I remember preaching in one such congregation in Georgia known as Kelly Chapel Presbyterian Church. As is the custom, at the end of the service I greeted worshippers at the double doors at the back of the church. People introduced themselves: "I am Raymond Kelly . . . I am Carol Kelly . . . I am Raymond Kelly Jr.," and so it went for forty or so people until at last someone introduced herself as Susan Baker, and I said, "So finally I meet someone who isn't a Kelly." Then she quietly corrected me, "No. I was born a Kelly. Baker's just my married name." That is what a family chapel is like. Many small churches that do not have such close bloodlines nevertheless have the capacity to provide the close binding ties of surrogate families. If there is a downside to all of this closeness, it is that unlike the megachurches, the small congregations do not constantly look out for, greet, and orient newcomers to make them feel welcome and invite them into becoming participating new members. As such, the smaller congregations rarely grow dramatically, but at least in the South at this time one rarely hears of small congregations with door-closing financial difficulties. This is not to say that churches are constantly growing staff and programs but instead that from small churches to large ones, most come up with the resources to continue the level of service and programming they have experienced in the recent past.

One last comparison between megachurches and the not-so-large congregations of the South is on the question of independence from denominations. Because of the preponderance of Baptists in the South, of both black Baptists and predominantly white Baptists, there has been a historical preference for identifying congregations with a denominational tradition. This has also been true for Methodists and Presbyterians, the other major evangelical traditions of the region, and of course for the parts of the Pentecostal, Restoration, and Holiness traditions where theological beliefs and church practices were so distinct inside the church that it made sense to advertise those differences on the sign outside the church. Although the overwhelming majority of southern churches still relate to a historical denomination or tradition, denominations bring with them such negligible brand loyalty, and often such political baggage, that the trend over the past twenty years has been for local denominational churches to rebrand themselves as nondenominational-sounding community churches, with names like the People's Church, the Way, Christ Church, or West End Church. The point here is that the church's leadership is making the barriers to exploration as low as possible for newcomers to the extent that members may belong to a church for years before they know that it is part of an extant denomination. Even this, however, seems to be a halfway house, as an increasing number of new church starts in growing cities in the South, including Charlotte, Nashville, Raleigh, Little Rock, Birmingham, and Louisville, are truly independent of any other church body. In this respect, the South is catching up with Colorado, southern California, and the Pacific Northwest, where the word nondenominational has been stronger in new church plants for some time.

Cultural change sneaks up on us. We accept symbols and archetypes as enduring until they shift. What was a saloon is now just a bar. So, consider this: when filmmakers wanted in the past to convey the essence of southern religiosity, they showed a funeral taking place in a wooden Primitive Baptist church or a revival taking place in a tent. Moviemakers of the future demonstrating fidelity to the southern religious life of today will doubtless have to include and re-create the look and feel of the contemporary megachurch.

Southern Religious Innovations

8

THE CHANGING FACE OF
THE CATHOLIC SOUTH

Of all European faiths transplanted to what became the U.S. southern states, Roman Catholicism came first. In St. Augustine, Florida, under the Spanish; in New Orleans, Louisiana, and Mobile, Alabama, under the French; and in the Bardstown, Kentucky, area with French immigrants and transplanted Catholics from Maryland, the Church of Rome placed an early stamp on the region. But while Catholicism thrived along the Ohio and Mississippi Rivers and the port cities of the Atlantic and Gulf Coasts of the South, the interior of the South was so devoid of Catholic presence that one Catholic leader was to memorably christen the southern interior "No Priest Land" and founded a religious order, the Glenmary Home Missioners, specifically dedicated to addressing the dearth of priestly presence for Catholics living in Appalachia and the wider South. Especially in the first half of the twentieth century, we can picture a map of Christian denominations where southern Catholicism looks something like a map of Pacific Rim countries surrounding an ocean of Baptists, Methodists, and Pentecostals. In 1900, the Baltimore, New Orleans, and Louisville sees accounted for 56 percent of all the 1,178,856 Catholics in the South, including Texas and Maryland. The interior dioceses of Nashville, Little Rock, Richmond, and the Apostolic Vicariate of North Carolina, altogether, could claim only 70,100 souls.[1] Everyone else in the Catholic South was hugging some kind of river or coast. As we shall see, being Catholic in the South (even in New Orleans or Mobile) is not like being Catholic elsewhere in America, but the rapid urbanization of the South over the past half-century, culture wars realignments on some moral issues, and immigration from the Midwest and from Latin America have changed the experience of being a southern Catholic in the contemporary era.

FOUR WAVES OF SOUTHERN CATHOLIC SETTLEMENT

To get to what is new and different about Catholic life in the Now South it is useful to see the southern interior as slowly occupied by successive waves of Catholic presence. For shorthand purposes we will term these the ethnic industrial wave, the Midwest missionary wave, the Rust Belt transplants wave, and the Hispanic immigrant wave. Some Catholics, of course, lived on the interior of the southern Catholic rim; even in the nineteenth century there were enclaves of Catholic settlement, especially in railroad cities and river towns. Like the railroads themselves it was industrialization and immigration that brought more Catholics into Cullman, Alabama, in the 1870s in a manner that exemplifies the first wave.

Colonel John Gottfried Cullman, a Bavarian arriving in 1865 (first to Cincinnati, a strong German Catholic enclave), subsequently arranged in 1873 with the Louisville and Nashville Railroad to act as its agent for a tract of some 349,000 acres in Alabama. Over the next twenty years he attracted more than a hundred thousand German-speaking immigrants to the area.[2] These immigrants reached out to the Benedictine religious order to bring a strong Catholic presence into Baptist country. Though to this day the state of Alabama is one of the least Catholic of all fifty states, with just 6 percent of the population affiliated with the church (notwithstanding the early and large head start Catholicism had on the Gulf Coast), Benedictines came from Latrobe, Pennsylvania, to minister to the German population of Cullman. The brothers and priests established parishes and in 1891 a monastery, in 1892 a school, and later a college and a seminary. Saint Bernard Abbey sits in a rural pine forest setting on top of the Brindley Mountain plateau, which in the winter at least could as easily be in parts of western Europe as in the South.

Saint Bernard Abbey is for men, and the Sacred Heart Monastery, also on the grounds, serves women religious. Together with the St. Bernard Preparatory School and the Ave Maria Grotto, they preserve a particular kind of southern Catholic presence to this day. Though there is no longer a college or major seminary on the grounds, there are still Benedictine priests serving congregations in the region and yet more who are remembered fondly. The abbey is also a site for religious retreats for Catholics and non-Catholics alike. The black-robed Benedictines welcome visitors to experience their life of simple meals, the praying of the Divine Office, and the Mass. Prayer takes many forms in the Office; it is sung, said, and ritually enacted by the human body. The daily rhythms and remembrances, praises, petitions, and thanksgivings work change into the persons praying, just as St. Bernard intended. Meanwhile, St. Bernard Abbey Church is both Gothic and new in architecture in a way that suggests that the ancient monastic life has a place in this time as well as eternity.

When I visited for a retreat I was lucky enough to be there for the premiere of a documentary about the Ave Maria Grotto and Brother Joseph Zoetle, O.S.B., who fashioned miniature replicas of famous Old Testament and Christian buildings of concrete, glass, stone, and other material as a religious devotion.[3] In 1934, a garden walk through these creations was dedicated in honor of the Blessed Virgin Mary on the abbey grounds (figure 5). It has welcomed visitors every day since, as many as a million a year when US-31, right near the abbey, was the main route between Chicago and Florida. The most famous among the miniatures are the buildings of ancient Jerusalem, thus the creation's popular name, Little Jerusalem. Brother Joseph continued making miniatures throughout his long life, including scenes of ancient and papal Rome. The miniature that affected me the most deeply, however, came from Joseph's imagination and heart. It is a memorial to the boys of St. Bernard's who died serving their country in World War II (figure 6).

After the screening of the documentary, there was a social reception. This gave me a chance to talk with Abbot Cletus Meagher, O.S.B., about the film and about what it must have been like to be sent off to Alabama from Europe as Brother Joseph was as an unwanted child in the late nineteenth century and be taken in by a self-sufficient religious community. Saint Bernard's today can still feel that way. It has its own farm, bakery, church, school, and cemetery. Every monk knows where he will one day be buried on the grounds. It seems as if time stands still. Abbot Cletus and I were then joined by a lay board member for the preparatory school who told us about his long association with St. Bernard's Preparatory School and its mission, and he emphasized how much things have changed. He started with the fact that today, with 170 prep

Figure 5. Our Lady of Fatima at Ave Maria Grotto,
Cullman, Alabama. (Author's photograph)

Figure 6. St. Bernard Boys Memorial, Ave Maria Grotto,
Cullman, Alabama. (Author's photograph)

students, boys and girls, grades eight through twelve, only half are Catholic. He said that to be Catholic in the South is different: "To make it in the South as a Catholic school today, you have to be Christian more broadly." He compared this to his experience in northern Virginia in the metropolitan Washington area, where very conservative Catholic families with as many as nine children are common and keep the parochial school system running as a Catholic-only proposition. In the South, as elsewhere in these latter days, he said, there is a kind of "common course of understanding between Christians of various sorts," where the differences between Christians are not nearly so important as they once seemed and where the differences between Christians and the secular culture are greater than ever before in American life. To prove at least part of his point, today St. Bernard's is ranked as one of the top ten private schools in Alabama, a distinction that would have been unimaginable in the 1960s, when the boundaries between Catholics and other Christians were still extreme.[4]

One clear sign of this southern de facto ecumenism came the next day when a fifteen-passenger bus from the First Baptist Church of a distant Alabama town pulled up in the parking lot of the Shrine of the Most Blessed Sacrament in Hanceville, Alabama. A group of older adults, old enough to remember when Southern Baptists did not vote for John F. Kennedy for president in 1960 because he was a Catholic were coming to experience a piece of very traditional Catholic piety.

If the Benedictines in Cullman are secure in their identity and open in post–Vatican II fashion to educating other Christian youth on a more or less equal basis, the Catholicism on display at the Shrine of the Most Blessed Sacrament in Hanceville is Tridentine and Vatican I, all the way. It is conservative and out to convert even Catholics to the correct ways to think about God, to venerate the Blessed Virgin Mary, and to adore Christ in the Most Blessed Sacrament in the Eucharist of His body, reserved in a monstrance. These two sites, just thirty minutes by car from one another, are nonetheless separated by at least half a century when it comes to piety and practice. Explaining how requires a detour to Ohio.

Born Rita Rizzo on April 20, 1923, the girl who was to become Mother Angelica had a difficult childhood. As a young adult, she pursued a religious vocation and was guided by her family priest in 1944 into the St. Paul Shrine, an order of cloistered Franciscan nuns in Cleveland, Ohio.[5] The cloistered life of a Poor Clare nun had its ups and downs, including for Sister Angelica abiding back pain, which was made unbearable when she hit a wet patch of floor while working a floor-polishing machine and found herself thrown into the wall. Her health deteriorated over the next two years and eventually required spinal surgery. Before the operation she discovered her prognosis was bleak. The doctors told her there was only a fifty-fifty chance that she would ever walk again. It was at this point that she made a solemn vow to God: "Lord, if you'll let me walk again, I will build you a monastery in the South." With the help of her fellow sisters, a leg brace, and a back brace, she did recover and learn to walk again, and as Mother Angelica would later say, "The problem of making a bargain with God is that you have to hold up your end of it."[6] She and several other entrepreneurial sisters, Mary Joseph, Mary Raphael, and Mary Michael, sold fishing lures (among other things) to finance a move to the Birmingham area after securing the permission of the local ordinary bishop to locate there. Thus began Our Lady of the Angels Monastery in Irondale in 1961. Once ensconced, though she was a still a cloistered nun, Angelica began evangelizing the Bible Belt, first with speeches and pamphlets, later with vinyl records and audio cassettes. And that was just the beginning.

Before we proceed any further we might ask, why take a solemn vow to build the Lord a monastery in the South? And why Alabama, a state in which, in 1960, only 2 percent of the population was Catholic? Sister

Angelica herself could not remember why, but I suspect it had to do with the work of the Glenmary Home Missioners, founded in Ohio in 1939 by Father William Howard Bishop. Glenmary was a missionary order dedicated to addressing the needs of Catholics without access to priests in rural areas in the South and Appalachia. Bishop also had an evangelist's zeal for the truth of the Catholic faith, as even a brief extract from a typical sermon of his shows: "Every Catholic is imbued with the idea that a convert won to the faith in this world also adds jewels to his crown in the next, and every true and fervent Catholic, every Catholic who knows and loves his religion, who realizes that the true knowledge and love of God are the dearest treasures that the heart of man can possess—every such Catholic will labor and pray for conversions."[7]

Bishop had served in town and rural parishes for more than twenty years when he proposed his own missionary plan to go after the lost sheep of the rural areas and small towns of the South and Appalachia. His newsletter repeatedly stressed the view that the 1930s and 1940s were a time when paganism had the upper hand in many places across the world. That much was widely agreed upon as citizens looked overseas to Europe and Asia, but Bishop's aim was to redirect their gaze to their own country: "Yet as a matter of cold fact these millions among whom there is so much need of missionary laborers and no priests to break the bread of truth to them are even closer to us. They are our brethren and fellow citizens, sharing our own United States with us from birth to burial. They are as much Americans as we. How is it that we have delayed so long to see their needs and organize for their relief?"[8]

This sense that the American South was the mission field was sustained not only by a formidable founder but also by an advertising campaign in Catholic periodicals throughout Sister Angelica's formative years. One particular graphic that Bishop used to show the need, a map with the informal title "No Priest Land" (figure 7), ran often in the back pages of Catholic periodicals to gain the Glenmary Home Missioners financial support and vocations. While it is impossible to prove that Father Bishop or his map planted the seed in Mother Angelica's mind to go south, it is also highly likely that she had the spiritual need of the South for Catholic witness presented to her in this way before she made her vow.

The faithful Glenmary priests working the spine of the southern Appalachians and the colorful Mother Angelica can be said to be our second wave, that of the Midwest missionaries. It was back in the Midwest that Mother Angelica found further inspiration. On a trip to Chicago in 1978 to discuss one of her "little books," Mother Angelica found herself in a Baptist

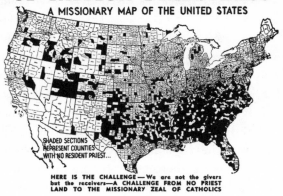

VOL. I **The Challenge** NO. I

VAST AREAS OF NATION PRIESTLESS

Almost 1,000 counties in the United States lack the advantages of resident Catholic guidance —this is the No-Priest-Land of America.

A MISSIONARY MAP OF THE UNITED STATES

AND one very striking fact: these counties include most of the areas of the United States where the birth rate is highest. Their young people settle down for life in cities, towns and open country in every section of the United States. This means that our No-Priest-Land is exercising a stronger influence upon the future destinies of America than any other sections. The populations of our cities are being kept up by the inflow from these and other rural sections in which Catholic influence is weak. They are the reservoirs of the population supply.

SHADED SECTIONS REPRESENT COUNTIES WITH NO RESIDENT PRIEST...

HERE IS THE CHALLENGE — We are not the givers but the receivers—A CHALLENGE FROM NO PRIEST LAND TO THE MISSIONARY ZEAL OF CATHOLICS

Figure 7. Father William Bishop, "Missionary Map of the United States," showing priestless counties, 1938. (Courtesy Glenmary Home Missioners)

television studio. Immediately she saw the potential of television to spread the faith, saying to herself on the way home, "Lord, I've just got to have one of those."[9] Bit by bit, that determination turned into Eternal Word Television Network (EWTN), the largest (and most conservative) Catholic television network in the world. The center of it all was Mother Angelica's teaching, which combined a slice of self-deprecating good humor with a no-nonsense return to the church's strict teachings on all matters moral and theological. There is no mollycoddling in her television programs, which are still in re-runs, or in her books. A typical bit of teaching might open with a humorous anecdote about an executive who wrote to say that he bought a satellite dish to watch pornography but ran across her on TV, and even though he had not been to Mass in twenty years, he had returned to the faith and was now feeling better about himself. Inevitably, however, Mother Angelica ends with old-fashioned church doctrine without apology:

> Adultery is a sin.
> Sexual union before marriage is a sin.
> Indulging in lust is a sin.
> Homosexual activity is a sin.
> Watching "adult" movies is a sin.

Reading sex magazines is a sin . . .
You can overcome your temptations.
God will help you.[10]

Mother Angelica's rise to stardom coincided with the beginning of the papacy of John Paul II; they shared a gift for the common touch and a love of the old piety. In the words of her biographer Raymond Arroyo, "No one in America, and perhaps in the world, did more than Mother Angelica to perpetuate and stoke interest in the rosary, Eucharistic adoration, Latin in the liturgy, the Divine Mercy Chaplet, litanies, and traditional prayers."[11] No wonder Pope John Paul II is claimed to have remarked early in the 1980s, "EWTN is the key to restoring the Roman Catholic Church in America."[12] Over time, people wanted to make pilgrimages to the studios where the programs were made in Irondale, Alabama, and this in the 1990s led Mother Angelica to be inspired to build a shrine honoring the Real Presence of Christ in the Eucharist on a four-hundred-acre former soybean farm in Hanceville. Thanks to just five donors the monastery was built and then consecrated in December 1999. Encompassing Romanesque and Gothic elements, it represents the Christendom of the High Middle Ages brought to America courtesy of rapid modern-building techniques. It is simultaneously breathtaking, a reminder that ancient European churches were not always old, and strangely out of place, a bit like a Catholic EPCOT Center.

Driving to the Shrine of the Most Blessed Sacrament, one first notes the vast number of guest houses as one goes from everyday Alabama with its Pentecostal and Baptist churches and vernacular rural housing to cute, little bed-and-breakfast guesthouses in almost suburban spacing along the road. The first clue that one is nearing sacred ground is that each B&B has a religious name—Gesu Bambino Pilgrims' House, St. Paul's Mission Hamlet, Our Lady of Lourdes, St. Clare Guest House, St. Benedict Guest House, St. Michael's Guest House, St. Mary Guest House, and so on. Still on the route but past the guesthouses runs one and a half miles of white plastic fencing that one might find around a horse farm, which leads to a rising hilltop where one can see nothing but beautiful woods all around. Then one comes out into a clearing and approaches an Italianate church and pilgrimage center surrounded by a vast parking lot. Getting out of the parking lot, visitors encounter a statue of the Blessed Virgin Mary holding a cross in her hands and flanked by God's Ten Commandments on one side and Christ's Beatitudes presented in similar tablet fashion on her right (figure 8). Moving further into the grounds visitors

Figure 8. Ten Commandments, Blessed Virgin, and Beatitudes, Shrine of the Most Blessed Sacrament, Hanceville, Alabama. (Author's photograph)

Figure 9. Entrance to the Shrine of the Most Blessed Sacrament, Hanceville, Alabama. (Author's photograph)

have the choice of going to the left to the shrine itself (figure 9) or right into Castle San Miguel, where the gift shop is located and orientations are offered.

On the day we visit the shrine we are still making up our minds where to start when we are approached by a young man, a Knight of the Holy Eucharist (a lay brother at the shrine) who asks if we "would like to hear Father's talk inside the Castle?"[13] We go inside and join a program in progress. A young Franciscan priest is giving an explanatory talk after an earlier Latin mass for a group from Langhorne, Pennsylvania, who had traveled by long-distance motor coach to tour EWTN the day before and the shrine that day in a self-identified pilgrimage. They are not unusual: the shrine is often on the top-ten list of Roman Catholic pilgrimage sites in America, attracting up to a million visitors a year. Mother Angelica's form of conservative southern Catholicism is an export from the region to the rest of the United States and, as we saw with the Alabama senior Baptists, attractive within the South as a form of conservative Christianity that is against abortion and for pious devotion to the Lord Jesus Christ. The priest, like all priests at the shrine, is of the Franciscan order (TOR) and was formed at the Franciscan University of Steubenville in Ohio, whose conservative take on Catholicism closely complements Mother Angelica's own. His talk is about mercy in the inner life of prayer, viewing prayer as relationship with God aimed at holiness. It is a good talk for most Christians of any type, whether they are too easy or hard on themselves or others. The questions that follow, however, catch me by surprise, although perhaps they should not, since this is a room full of people who chose to come to a site associated with the most conservative televised form of Catholicism. The first question is about the mechanics of indulgences: "How often can you receive one?" The next question is about the grounds of the shrine, "Where are the dead babies?" to which the priest explains that there is a memorial to a child, "Deborah," aborted at twenty weeks, but they do not have a lot of dead babies there. Then we are back to indulgences. "So even though my priest recommends confession once a month, I could be going twice a month and get a plenary indulgence for each?" Yes, the priest answers, though the object is not to rack up points but to become more merciful in one's life, more holy, as God would have us be. I sympathize with where he is going, but he is talking to a room full of people who took their first communions and were confirmed before Vatican II. At heart, they still think about the faith in the old ways and have come to the shrine to connect to a pre–Vatican II piety. The next question is in the same vein: "If you do a family rosary, do you earn a whole indulgence or just a partial one?" At this point the thirty-something priest giving the talk connected to a forty-something priest in the back row for phone-a-friend help with the answer.

Happily, after a word from the authoritative older priest, we move on to another line of questions, "How long did it take you to become a priest?" Answer: "Ten years." "Did you have to get a special dispensation to offer the Mass this morning in Latin?" There is a frisson of excitement in the room that in witnessing the rite in Latin they had experienced something either illicit or special. Answer: "No—Vatican II doesn't prohibit using Latin in its suggestion that the vernacular could be used for the Mass." This prompted a challenge from a younger person in the audience, stating that she thought that Latin needed to stay in books and that it was an abomination in the Mass. An older baby boomer priest handles this Generation X heckler fairly aggressively, saying that they were only doing as priests what they were commanded to do by the bishops and the pope. He won over most of the audience, but the happy mood of the group from Pennsylvania had dissipated somewhat. Most shuffled off to see the burial place of Baby Deborah, aborted at twenty weeks, others went to the gift shop, which was big on saints' paraphernalia, as well as items featuring Pope Benedict and Mother Teresa, and of course Mother Angelica in books, CDs, and videos.

What accounts for this Dollywood of traditional Catholicism in the middle of Alabama? Well, if Dollywood has Dolly Parton as its inspiration, the shrine has Mother Angelica as its founder. Mother Angelica envisioned the South devoid of Catholic truth, as a place that needed her, and eventually generated sufficient interest such that millions of people came to see her television studio and to see how her Poor Clares of Perpetual Adoration worshiped. Moving across the piazza to the shrine proper one enters a church of extraordinary beauty. Unlike tourist-friendly churches in Europe, this one means business—God's business. To make the point, the visitor encounters this reminder several times on the way inside:

> "MOTHER SAYS . . .": In order to show respect to our Lord Jesus
> Christ in the Most Blessed Sacrament, as well as to show a spirit
> of charity to the Nuns, the Priests and Brothers, and the other
> pilgrims who are Adoring our Lord, we request the following: 1.
> Please observe SILENCE when you enter the Shrine and the EWTN
> Chapel. 2. We encourage you to dress comfortably, but modestly.
> Please do not wear sleeveless tops, tank tops, shorts, or mini-skirts/
> skirts above the knee. Ladies may wear slacks. 3. If at all possible,
> please do not leave Mass before the Blessed Sacrament has been

exposed and the Nuns have finished singing at the Shrine. 4. Please do not take pictures inside the Shrine. There are many lovely pictures and postcards which you may purchase at the Gift Shop of El Nino in Castle San Miguel.

A pilgrimage to the Shrine of the Most Blessed Sacrament, finally, provides a place for prayer and contemplation. Pilgrims may attend Mass, silently join the nuns as they—unseen—pray the Liturgy of the Hours throughout the day, and receive the Sacrament of Confession (called Reconciliation in a more modern Catholic setting). All of it built by the faith of a tenacious nun who was not seen for the last fifteen years of her life after a series of strokes sidelined her in 2001 before she died on Easter Sunday, 2016.

RUST BELT TRANSPLANTS

Mother Angelica might just be a colorful digression in a book about the varieties of Christianity in the South were it not for two key facts about her life and faith story. First, she and her companion religious made a move to leave the Midwest, or Rust Belt, for the South, or Sun Belt, in the 1960s. They did so for reasons of opportunity, spirituality opportunity to be sure, but opportunity nonetheless. Unintentionally they prefigured massive post-1970s relocations of midwesterners, especially from Michigan, Ohio, and Illinois, to the cities and small towns of the South as the domestic auto industry relocated its plants in so-called right-to-work states mostly east of the Mississippi River, while German and Japanese companies set up business in the same region for the same reasons. The transferred management and United Auto Workers skilled-labor employees brought a great number of Catholics to the South and caused small southern dioceses suddenly to swell. At the same time, the priests they might encounter in their new parishes could be either older, more liberal priests who came of age in the aftermath of Vatican II, or younger, conservative priests ordained by bishops appointed by John Paul II. If few priests were as old-fashioned as Mother Angelica, the Catholic Church in the South was growing and beset by an unusual leadership crisis in which its youngest priests were apt to be more formal in matters liturgical and strict in matters of marriage and lay sexuality, while the experienced priests found themselves adapting to culture and their parishioners and on the outs with bishops of their own age and generation.[14] By reintroducing a strong voice for traditional Catholicism, Mother Angelica was a legitimating influence on the church and its right wing. If other women's orders adopted modernized habits or did away with them altogether after Vatican II, not so the Poor Clares or the Dominicans sisters in Nashville, who remained strict in all things and now draw as many postulates and novices as ever. So with Mother Angelica we see two important transformations in southern Catholicism: with midwestern in-migration it becomes more diverse, and with changes in the church more broadly, liberal and traditional Catholicism contend for place and leadership in the same region.

And, of course, the relocation of Rust Best Catholics is so much larger than even the Mother Angelica story. In every community where there are autoworkers who used to work up north, the Catholic Church is booming and people bring their cultural conception of Catholicism into the southern setting. Perhaps no story puts the point as forcefully as the 2010 case of St. Gerard's Catholic Church, in Buffalo, New York, a basilica-styled church that Father David Dye of Norcross, Georgia, who wanted to build a church that "didn't look like a Pizza Hut," aimed to move piece by piece to house his burgeoning parish. Some of the Norcross Catholics looked forward to worshiping in their childhood church again. Saint Gerard's was closed at the time, and although the move was blocked by sentimental Buffalo residents, it did not prevent the church from going on the block again and being sold to a group of Muslims aiming to begin a religious corporation. The Great Lakes region's loss of Catholic strength was translating into a boom in the urban South.[15] Then to all this add another wave, the coming of southern Hispanic Catholics.

THE SOUTHERN HISPANIC CATHOLICS

Though the Hispanic population is growing throughout the South, not every Roman Catholic parish offers a mass in Spanish each weekend, let alone during the week, or offers other ways to engage in the life of the parish geared toward people with origins in one of the twenty-one Latin American nations and Puerto Rico that make up the U.S. Hispanic population. This would not be necessary in every location, of course, but a national study of Catholic parishes with Hispanic ministries by Boston College professor Hosffman Ospino points to some of the reasons: lack of culturally competent priests; the low percentage of U.S.-born Hispanic pastoral leaders in parishes and dioceses; and the dependence of many Hispanic ministries on volunteers, especially from religious orders that are in increasingly short supply.[16] At the same time, the nature of the Catholic Church itself accounts for a good part of the variation.

Each Catholic bishop is pastorally responsible for the organization and activities of his diocese. Although the National Conference of Catholic Bishops works together to adopt and implement national programs, how things take shape in a given diocese heavily reflects episcopal leadership over time, together with the local assets of money and personnel available to the diocese.

The Charlotte diocese, for example, covering western North Carolina, had a long head start for its Hispanic ministry over the Raleigh diocese, even though it is the Raleigh diocese that has absorbed most of the eight hundred thousand or more Hispanics (as of 2010) in the state. The difference may be as simple as that of the charism (a church word for gift, in the sense of a gift by God for ministry) of a particular priest or nun. That was certainly the case in Charlotte, where Father Joe Waters, born in 1926, spent most of his life in the priesthood serving Spanish-speaking parishioners, including thirteen years of missionary work in Peru and Mexico. Even though he had been ordained by the bishop of Raleigh, when Waters returned from missionary service in 1974, he became a priest of the Charlotte diocese, which had been established during his absence. During his long ministry there Waters used his language and cultural skills to serve the burgeoning Latino population. When he died (appropriately enough) on Ash Wednesday, March 2015, he was remembered as a model priest by the Hispanic men who followed him into the ministry. "He had such great love and humility in the way he treated you as a human being," said Father Luis Osorio. A native of Colombia, Osorio first met Waters when Osorio visited his sister in North Carolina. "The fact that we could speak in Spanish was key. I was able to relate to him immediately. He was the first person that ever encouraged me to discover the possibility of a priestly vocation." Padre José, as he was called, displayed "such great interest in helping Hispanics. That was something that impacted me deeply when I first met him and throughout my dealings with him as priest." Charlotte's diocesan vicar for Hispanic ministry, Father Fidel Melo, called Waters "saintly" and paid him a different kind of compliment, but also for his humility: "With Padre José you never noticed if he was a moderate, conservative or liberal, as is often the case. In other words, he showed us that in order to serve God, the only thing necessary is to follow Christ as closely as we can."[17] Raleigh made up for losing Father Joe Waters to Charlotte and now employs a staff of four in the diocese to keep up with the ministries in the parishes, including offering masses in Spanish in sixty-five parishes each week.[18]

More broadly, some dioceses have geared up to embrace the challenges, and others not so much. In 2014, the Conrad N. Hilton Foundation made ten grants through Catholic Extension (a papal society that has been supporting Catholics on the margins in America since 1905) to dioceses with large populations of Hispanics and little existing capacity to serve them. Three of the ten winning dioceses (of the thirty that qualified and applied) were southern: Charleston, Richmond, and Little Rock. These dioceses will host Latin American nuns who will receive intensive pastoral leadership training to staff ministries to serve families, provide religious education, and nurture women's spirituality and youth and young adult ministry for five years. In announcing the formal launch of its U.S.–Latin American Sisters Exchange Program, Catholic Extension's president, Father Jack Wall, said, "These are women who are so motivated by a profound sense of mission and a calling to serve the Latino communities that they asked to serve on the margins where they can make a significant impact. It just so happened that these communities are here in the United States. This program will help us expand more opportunities for religious women to share their teaching and evangelizing charisms in communities with great needs."[19] So a pattern in southern Catholicism repeats itself again, with religious coming from far away to meet the spiritual needs of newly transplanted Catholics in the South.

Just as dioceses prepare in various ways to meet the needs of Hispanic Catholics, so the Benedictines and Poor Clares we met in northern Alabama, each in their own way in their own ministries, have worked to adapt to meet the needs of their Spanish-speaking sisters and brothers. The Cullman Sacred Heart Church that the Benedictines established in the nineteenth century to supply the spiritual needs of German-speaking immigrants now offers three Spanish-language masses a week, and all at prime times. The same Leaven of the Immaculate Heart of Mary nuns teach catechetics to members of the Hispanic, homeschooled, and Anglo populations, whether they go to Sacred Heart School or not. The Reverend Patrick Egan, O.S.B., is pastor to the whole congregation, and he is assisted by another Benedictine, the Reverend John O'Donnell, O.S.B., and by the Reverend Raul Ramirez V. as associate pastors. The Hispanic ministries website materials are bilingual, and the school clearly blends the congregation's cultures, but you can also see from the social activities that some things happen together, some apart, and some activities are cleverly pitched to get Anglos to affirm and participate in Hispanic fiestas. Meanwhile, over in Hanceville, Mother Angelica's Poor Clares make it a point to roll out the red carpet when feast days important to Hispanic Catholics are coming up. A typical invitation reads:

Southern Religious Innovations

The Poor Clares of Perpetual Adoration and the Shrine of the Most Blessed Sacrament invite all in the diocese to Divino Niño Day, Sept. 5. The day will be filled with Spanish and English activities for the whole family including Mass, spiritual talks, confessions, games for the children, a Eucharistic Healing Service with a Rosary Procession, and Mariachi Band. On Sunday, the Solemnity of the Divine Child Jesus, there will be a 7 A.M. Mass and 5 P.M. Benediction Service.

For cloistered nuns, these sisters know how to throw a party. Once again, you get the picture that devotion, solemnity, joy, and even laughter are meant to be companions in Mother Angelica's piety.

Alabama Catholics may be small in number, but they are hospitable to their Hispanic brothers and sisters. As we saw in chapter 4, Alabama has the archbishop of Mobile and the bishop of Birmingham, who were in the 2011 vanguard of opposition to HB 56, which sought to criminalize assistance to undocumented immigrants. As part of the research for this book, I located and read as many southern diocesan newspapers as I could for the winter of 2016, when anti-immigration feeling was running especially high in conjunction with the Donald Trump campaign for the Republican nomination for president. Contrary to anything I can cite from the mainstream Protestant press, whether mainline or evangelical, there was a remarkable amount of coverage of three types. First, there were stories taking pride in the Hispanic churches, clergy, nuns, and youth of the dioceses. Second, there was sympathetic coverage of immigration issues—including sometimes Spanish supplements on how to maintain one's immigration status under applicable law. Third, there were articles highlighting Pope Francis's trip to Mexico, and editorial material often from the bishops ordinary calling Catholics to embrace immigrants (including Syrian refugees). For me, whether attending a Catholic church, talking to Catholic friends in the South, or reading a diocesan newspaper or website, there is a shared palpable awareness that Catholics know they are different from the Protestant religious majority in the South. When it comes to people from Latin America, Catholics simply do not panic like many other southerners. They see—as they have been taught to see—the future of their church, and they see their new sisters and brothers in the faith. Moreover, because Catholicism is a sacramental faith, their first concern is usually one of sympathy: where will they (the newcomers) go to Mass? The provision of churches therefore is not left up to the immigrant community, because the provision of the sacramental ministry is first and foremost the provision of a priest, and facilities can more easily be shared in a nesting fashion among several multilingual priests serving several populations nearly simultaneously. The ethnic groups within a parish may not mix very often but may respect the fact of a mixed ministry much more than typical American Protestants, who would want their minister to serve their community exclusively. It should be noted that Hispanics are just the largest language group ministered to in this fashion, with masses in Vietnamese and Korean also being common in the South.

Multicultural sharing is at least the theory, anyway, and ever since the early 1900s the Catholic Church hierarchy has stood firmly against the idea of "national parishes" (for example, this church for Poles, that church for Italians) while letting them develop on the ground. Sharing sometimes works well, as in Cullman, but a friend of mine at the University of Notre Dame, Professor Timothy Matovina, who studies Latino Catholicism in the United States, says, "On the ground, it's one of the greatest sources of contention in the Catholic Church."[20] Because European immigrants at the beginning of the last century often moved en masse to neighborhoods and took over or built churches, their immigration and later assimilation pattern is different than what is happening today with Hispanic Catholics.[21] Matovina notes, "It's the same in the sense of strong ethnic solidarity, but the fact that (modern Hispanics) are moving (directly) into someone else's church is different."[22] That is exactly what University of North Carolina journalism student Lindsay Ruebens found in 2011 in tiny Newton Grove, North Carolina, at the rural Our Lady of Guadalupe Catholic Church, once again in the Raleigh diocese. Given that the Hispanic population has exploded in Sampson County since 2000, the Irish Lithuanian American priest Father Patrick Keane finds himself with a split congregation of one-quarter Anglos and five hundred Hispanic families making up the other three-quarters. He speaks more Spanish than English in his work, but neither that nor numerical dominance makes for easy relations. Keane says that Latinos often do not feel welcome in the church building. "Sometimes the Hispanics feel like they're renting space," he says. "They don't feel accepted when we have activities. The food tastes are different. The culture is different." Ruebens even discovered an instance where the white parishioners banned Hispanics from using the bathrooms because of the mess they made. Hugo Figueroa, forty-seven, a Mexican-born parishioner, spoke of how it feels to be at Guadalupe and to be Latino. "They think the church is theirs because they built it, but we should help each other. We need help to convince them [the white parishioners] to accept everyone, because sometimes they think the church is theirs."[23] With sixty-five of Raleigh's roughly one hundred parishes offering masses in Spanish, sharing the church is a growing southern Catholic challenge even though Newton Grove represents a single example.

Another Our Lady of Guadalupe Church, or as the only sign in front says, "Iglesia Catolica Nuestra Señora de Guadalupe," in Nashville, represents an alternative, a church equipped for and served by a Mexican immigrant population. The story of this congregation is one I have learned as it has unfolded, and I heard it from the priest who conceived of this church and acquired the funding to make it happen for his "second" set of parishioners. Father Joseph Breen was the long time pastor of St. Edward Catholic Church and the nearest church to Nolensville Road, the portion of U.S. 41 where one of the two largest populations of Hispanics in the metropolitan Nashville area had clustered, together with commercial establishments and even Pentecostal and evangelical churches serving them.[24] Part of what you get with a church organized around the Spanish language and Latin American ethnicities (or in the case of Nuestra Señora de Guadalupe, Mexican identity) is the ability to furnish the sanctuary with familiar Catholic elements that more nearly echo those of one's country of origin. A statue of the Virgin of Guadalupe, stations of the cross, even a crucifix or risen Christ that are more Spanish in style—all these make more than an aesthetic difference. That was clearly in mind when Father Breen approached former bishop Edward Kmiec, with a proposal: if he and his parishioners at St. Edward could find property for a Hispanic church for the largely Mexican worshippers that were providing more than enough Catholics for a second church in the area, would the bishop bless it? Bishop Kmiec, busy trying to get a second diocesan high school built and paid for, was reported to have replied, "You know I do not have any money for this, don't you?" Father Breen is said to have said for his part, "I am not asking for money, but for your blessing. I will get the money." And he did, with the help of Catholics throughout the diocese.[25] Bishop Kmiec's successor, Bishop David Choby, honored the commitment and was there to bless it in 2007 as the first and only Spanish-speaking Catholic church in Tennessee. Choby was there again to dedicate it as a self-sustaining church, with its own parish council, financial board, and independence, two years later.[26] Today the Nolensville corridor is a place where the signs are as likely to be in Spanish as in English, with other languages also in strong supply.

In pride of place is a large Hispanic Catholic church where a Southern Baptist church once stood.

On Sundays, in the morning, at noon, and at six in the evening, you will find families streaming in in large numbers, right up through the opening songs of praise, led by an enthusiastic group of singers and guitarists in the balcony. Visually you cannot miss five elements arrayed before you in the chancel. On the right is a traditional print of Christ exposing the Sacred Heart with an assurance of divine mercy. In the center is the altar, behind which is the small gold box, the Tabernacle, in which the consecrated host of the Body of Christ is kept. Immediately above is a clothed, crucified, and risen Christ with arms outstretched. And on the left is the most distinctive item of all, a statue representing the Virgin (Mary) of Guadalupe, together with Juan Diego, an indigenous man to whom, according to tradition, she appeared on December 9, 1531 (figure 10). The Virgin asked that a shrine in her name be built on the spot where she appeared (now in a Mexico City suburb). Juan Diego twice told his bishop about the apparition, but the bishop did not believe him and demanded a sign before he would approve construction of the shrine. On December 12 she reappeared to Juan Diego and ordered him to collect roses in his *tilmátli*, a cloak. He returned to the bishop, and when he opened his cloak, the roses fell and left behind an imprinted image of the Virgin, which is on display to this day in the Basilica de Guadalupe.[27] The Virgin of Guadalupe, with her dark skin and miraculous appearance, to the common Juan Diego made her a favorite throughout Latin America and the special pride of Mexico. The extra trimmings in this Nashville church representing the Rosary are a sign of ethnic pride and religious devotion, a bit more than one usually sees at pan-Hispanic churches and events.

When it comes to the service, the lectors, who assist with prayers and readings of Scripture, are all dressed in matching dark clothing. They and the four altar boys perform their duties with precision and grace. Families are deployed to pick up the collection, and they bring the same joy to their role that all parishioners do to the sharing of the peace, during which I start to learn how much the congregation is bilingual. The priest offering the Mass and giving the homily is Father Fernando López, who reads the liturgy carefully, but speaks without notes with a traveling microphone when he preaches. His homily is based on Jesus' parable of the prodigal son. He links the feast that the father throws for the repentant prodigal to the sacrament we are offered at the table. His message is that God is a good father who gives feasts not just for good children but for sinners, too. That is what Christ's sacrifice of himself means. He is encouraging people to come, and beyond the perennial truth

Southern Religious Innovations

Figure 10. Virgin of Guadalupe with Juan Diego surrounded with lighted rosary, Iglesia Catolica Nuestra Señora de Guadalupe, Nashville, Tennessee. (Author's photograph)

of his message I am reminded that one thing that typifies Hispanic Catholic piety is parishioners' reluctance to commune if they have not been to confession recently or if they feel themselves to be in a state of sin. Sure enough, when it is time for the Eucharist, I estimate that roughly 15 percent of the congregation goes forward. After the benediction comes a surprise; the worshippers all pray the Hail Mary. This is a so-called Leonine prayer, a prayer said by the laity after Mass that Leo XIII began in 1884 and Vatican II suppressed in 1964, when worship was understood as speech directed toward the triune God, so intercessions with the saints, even the Virgin Mary in the Ave Maria, were thought out of place. Here Marian piety is still strong, up front in painting and sculpture and in the closing words that ring out all around me:

Santa María, Madre de Dios,
ruega por nosotros pecadores,
ahora y en la hora de nuestra muerte.
Amén.
(Holy Mary, Mother of God, pray for us sinners now
    and at the hour of our death. Amen.)

A week earlier I was at the Nashville diocese's other large Hispanic ministry site, Sagrado Corazón (Sacred Heart), which is a large worshiping community run by the Hispanic ministry for the diocese and led by its director, Father David Ramírez. The ministry had been meeting in an old store in a strip mall that could "only seat seven hundred" and had outgrown its space. Where Nuestra Señora de Guadalupe is predominantly Mexican, Sagrado Corazón draws Spanish-speaking parishioners with backgrounds from all over Central and South America and the Caribbean. A year ago, after the diocese bought a former megachurch across the highway from Opryland for twelve million dollars for all its offices and other Catholic entities, Sagrado Corazón was offered the opportunity to meet in the 3,300-seat auditorium. If you can imagine a Protestant megachurch with a spare makeover (crucifix, smaller Virgin of Guadalupe, and a big painting of Christ holding the Sacred Heart, plus altar, seasonal banners, and pulpit) you can picture their new setting. Almost a year to the day after they moved in at Easter, I joined the congregation for worship. Before I even got inside, out in the parking lot I saw a sight I had not seen since my own teenage years in the early 1970s, namely families with three, four, five, and six children pouring out of cars going to church with mother and father. During worship I experience Father Ramirez as a spellbinding preacher, given to effective repetitions to bring home Jesus' points about the time to repent taught in Luke 13. Jesus talked about the Galileans slain by Romans, whose blood Pilate had mingled with their sacrifices, and asked his hearers if they thought that those people were any worse than any others. The same with people killed in a building collapse at Siloam. Then he told them, "No, I tell you; but unless you repent, you will all perish just as they did." Ramirez used this scripture to turn his message on the urgency of repentance. People should not dwell on what happened in the past. The past was over. They should not worry about the future, either. The time to act, the time to repent, was now. "Not the Past. Not the Future. Now!" (except in Spanish).

Three more things stick out as notable from my visit to Sagrado Corazón. After the Mass I saw a couple of nuns come forward to carefully clean up the altar, which was my first introduction to the strong role the Latin American religious play in this worshiping community. Next I encountered nineteen classrooms overflowing with children for Sunday school religious instruction, with nuns strategically placed to direct the right ages into the right rooms. Finally, back in the parking lot again, I realize the scale of what I have just experienced when I am faced by the number of cars, trucks, and vans that packed the multiple lots all around the old Fellowship at Twin Rivers. There were so many that I could not locate my own car until about a thousand other cars departed. Sagrado Corazón is a Catholic ministry center now, not a full-fledged Catholic church, yet it seems to me that the future of the Catholic Church in the American South is being made in those nineteen classrooms, in catechetical lessons where the faith is passed on to a new generation, and even in the parking lot where such vast numbers of large Catholic families show up for Mass together. At special ministries for Hispanics, and at blended congregations where Spanish-speaking parishioners are truly welcomed, the Catholic Church in the South is charting a new history.

PORTENTS OF THE FUTURE

Between the last two decennial censuses, southern states accounted for most of the twelve states with the fastest-growing Hispanic populations (table 1). Florida was notably missing, but it started with a huge base and still added more than 1.5 million Hispanic residents, for a 57.4 percent decade-to-decade increase, with particularly strong gains in the north and panhandle of the state, which are historically the most culturally "southern" portions. This explains why the Regional Office for Hispanic Ministry and Pastoral Institute,

Table 1. States with Fastest-Growing Hispanic Populations, 2000–2010

State	Hispanic Population, 2000	State Population, 2000 (%)	Hispanic Population, 2010	State Population, 2010 (%)	Ten-Year Population Gain (%)
Virginia	329,540	4.7	631,825	7.9	91.7
Georgia	435,227	5.3	853,689	8.8	96.1
Delaware	37,277	4.8	73,221	8.2	96.4
South Dakota	10,903	1.4	22,119	2.7	102.9
Mississippi	39,569	1.4	81,481	2.7	105.9
Maryland	227,916	4.3	470,632	8.2	106.5
North Carolina	378,963	4.7	800,120	8.4	111.1
Arkansas	86,866	3.2	186,050	6.4	114.2
Kentucky	59,939	1.5	132,836	3.1	121.6
Tennessee	123,838	2.2	290,059	4.6	134.2
Alabama	75,830	1.7	185,602	3.9	144.8
South Carolina	95,076	2.4	235,682	5.1	147.9
U.S. Totals	35,305,818	12.5%	50,477,594	16.3%	43.0%

Source: *The Hispanic Population: 2010*, 2010 Census Briefs (Washington, D.C.: U.S. Department of Commerce and Economic Statistics Administration, 2011).

SEPI, located in Miami, has more work than it can possibly do alone. Created by Catholic Bishops of the Southeast (Alabama, North Carolina, South Carolina, Florida, Georgia, Kentucky, Louisiana, Mississippi, and Tennessee) in 1978, SEPI exists to develop and train leaders for the integration of the Hispanic community in the life of the church. This development was the result of an Encuentro, a periodic meeting of the whole American Catholic Church concerned to promote ministry to, with, and by Hispanics.[28] Four times over the past half-century the church has met in this manner, and Encuentro V has been called for in 2018 to meet in Texas. As concerned parties gather and speak their hearts (for such is the nature of an Encuentro), it remains to be seen if the Catholic Church in the South can change as fast as its potential for Hispanic (and other) membership is shifting. Texas, Florida, and California are the traditional centers for Hispanic Catholicism in America, but the South is more than demonstrating its potential. Will southern Catholicism realize its full multicultural promise? More than any other large Christian body in the South, the Catholic Church has made the greatest commitment to embrace as its own people who face daily obstacles to social acceptance.

Southern Religious Innovations

9

CHRISTIAN HOMESCHOOLERS

If you sought an intimate introduction to contemporary American evangelicalism layered with southern hospitality, it would be hard to beat the Christian homeschooling movement and a visit to one of their conventions in Nashville. Each year there are roughly forty-five homeschooling conventions in the United States—concentrated in the South, the Southwest, the Midwest, and conservative bastions of the West. For Christian homeschoolers, the biggest of these conventions recently have been the Teach Them Diligently conventions offered as a ministry since 2012 by the David and Leslie Nunnery family of Greenville, South Carolina. David is the president of Worldwide Tentmakers, a mission board in Greenville dedicated to getting people to use their business skills and professions as a platform for worldwide mission and evangelism in the same way the apostle Paul supported his gospel-spreading work by making tents, according to Acts 18. The way that David and Leslie Nunnery tell their homeschooling story shapes what they are trying to do with the conventions: "Our oldest was twelve, and though he initially attended a good Christian school, the Lord began to impress on us that we needed to start homeschooling. As we prayed about this option, it became clear that this was what the Lord wanted. But the decision to homeschool was not made because of superior education in our case but for the purpose of discipleship."[1] The name Teach Them Diligently comes directly from Deuteronomy 6:7, where Moses commands all of Israel to remember the commandments they have been taught and to pass them on to their children: "You shall teach them diligently to your children, and shall talk of them when you sit in your house, when you walk by the way, when you lie down, and when you rise up" (NKJV). Consequently, a Teach Them Diligently convention lays a heavy stress on the Christian parent's duty to lead children to discipleship of Jesus Christ and to engage in mission in his name (since in the evangelical worldview the Old Testament and New Testament covenants are linked in Christ). All of this started with a family in South Carolina who believed that this kind of mission was not an option, for it was part of the Great Commission ("Therefore go and make disciples of all nations, baptizing them in the name of the Father and of the Son and of the Holy Spirit, and teaching them to obey everything I have commanded you," Matt. 28:19–20, NIV). The Nunnerys also intend to obey Jesus' last words in Acts 1:8 and to be Christ's witnesses "from Jerusalem . . . to the ends of the earth." Therefore, they say, "Our home is our Jerusalem."[2]

From a single convention in Spartanburg, South Carolina, in 2012, Teach Them Diligently rapidly expanded and now offered four such conventions, all in or near the South, when I chose to attend the convention hosted in Nashville in March 2014. My convention was to be at the Gaylord Opryland Resort and Convention Center, where the Teach Them Diligently Convention had its biggest attendance ever in 2013 and was already planning to return in 2015.[3] For sixty-five dollars my family was entitled to three days of seminars, demonstrations, showings, inspirational speeches, and access to the exhibition hall—a cornucopia of resources for Christian homeschooling families.

I had been to conventions at this enormous venue before, but the first thing I noticed was the absence of desperate smokers outside. This was a family-friendly convention; and what families they were, bigger and younger than most American families. It was not uncommon for me to see families of father and mother and four or five children under age twelve, with another child on the way. "Be fruitful and multiply" (Gen. 1:28, KJV) is an important biblical watchword for this community, and I was to learn in the exhibition hall that a number of ministries were specially focused on encouraging Christians to uphold God's countercultural command in this regard.

Before I got to the exhibition hall, however, I sampled some of the teaching sessions. The first session I went to was in a packed room of a couple hundred people watching a heavy multimedia lecture and program given by Mike Snavely defending God's intelligent design of all creatures, over against the Darwinian and scientific worldview of secular science, which argues for evolution, natural selection, and so forth. The PowerPoint slides, butterflies, and caterpillars particularly stick in my mind. So does Snavely's point: "How does the caterpillar know to head for the trees? No one is there to teach him, to educate him, to show him how to do it. He is designed by his creator to know what he is to do." Lots of similar examples from the animal kingdom were offered, of course, but the net effect was to engender awe in the created order. That is what he meant to do. For me, however, the examples caused me to think about the biological processes within the animals that were discussed, which accounted for at least some of the unlearned behaviors. These, it seemed to me, were equally miraculous. It made me wonder, Is all of Christian homeschooling science basically shouting down and disproving Charles Darwin and his intellectual descendants? I know physicians who live and work within this biblical creation worldview, so I know that one can go far with the tools of science without accepting all of its premises. Nevertheless, the awe I experience for life's processes acquired over millions of years is different than the awe Snavely and most of the audience experience; they see the direct hand of God, the busy intelligent designer of a six-thousand-year-old earth.

One room over in the convention center I found Israel Wayne speaking on the history of the homeschooling movement. Wayne is an author and a popular speaker in evangelical and homeschooling circles, and he has made his living for the past twenty-two years on the circuit. He is entertaining and engaging, and even his frequent digressions can be as informative and slyly inspiring for the audience as his prepared presentations. The way Wayne tells the story, the Christian school movement led the way for the homeschooling movement as a whole. Where once the exception to compulsory public schooling that arose in the mid-nineteenth century was available only to Catholics, Lutherans, and Mennonites, pastors in the mid-1960s in evangelical traditions began to say, "We don't care what you say, we're going to tell our children the truth." Wayne does not offer a context to his audience for those pastors' departure from evangelical Protestants' historic commitment to public schooling, but it almost certainly is the Supreme Court's decision to ban organized school prayer and religious instruction—including Bible reading—from public schools, dating from the early 1960s in *Engel v. Vitale* and *Abington School District v. Schempp*.[4] What he does tell his audience about the pastors is this: "We stand on their shoulders." From there he delineates two tracks diverging to make up the contemporary homeschooling movement that now counts three million children being educated by their parents each year. First, there are the secular homeschools associated with John Holt, and the movement Holt called "unschooling." Insofar as unschooling emphasizes allowing children to follow their natural interests so as to educate themselves about what interests them, Wayne says, that is something "Scripture speaks against," for the Bible teaches that left to our own devices we are naturally sinful, and parents are told instead that their job is to "train up a child." By contrast, Wayne dates the Christian branch of the homeschooling movement to Raymond and Dorothy Moore's 1983 book *Better Late Than Early*, in which Raymond Moore, an educator who had explored the psychological ramifications of schooling, reported a variety of findings. Wayne simplifies these findings for his audience: "What he discovered was this—that boys and girls are different! Moore's research argued that children aren't standardized, particularly boys." As Wayne expatiates on Moore's findings, I observe that the audience consists of about 45 percent men in the room. The men are nodding their heads. They were not standardized children when they went to school, but they know what it was like to be treated as though they were not up to the standard. Wayne moves on from talking about Moore, one of James Dobson's favorite guests on the *Focus on the Family* radio program (who early and often recommended taking a good child struggling with schooling out of school and teaching him until he was ready to rejoin his peers) to discussing teaching in the here and now. "Never," he says, "confuse schooling and education. Never, never, ever." Wayne goes on, "My mother homeschooled myself and my five sisters. She was a ninth-grade high school dropout, and how did I learn calculus and chemistry? She taught me to read, and I taught myself in high school."

There is a sense of God's providence in the air. The room is full of people who are homeschooling or who think they should homeschool or would like to homeschool but do not think they can, and Israel Wayne is preaching God's "Yes!" in the midst of their fears and doubts. He is clear evidence that a determined single mother with a ninth-grade education can, with God's help, lead a child to read, to get into college, and even, in Wayne's case, to obtain advanced degrees. Wayne also speaks to another fear, that of one's children being different because they are not in the mainstream. "Government-controlled schooling," he says, "is the new kid on the block." He continues, "If you sent your kids to school at five or six because you think you can't or aren't capable of teaching them to read and do math, you have bought into the matrix." Throughout this talk and throughout the convention there is a steady drumbeat against public schooling, though it is not called public schooling but "government schools." Wayne asks, "What's the best advertising for homeschooling? Government schools! (Big laughs.) They just have to be who they are. (More laughs.)" Then Israel Wayne's face changes, and his tone sobers up: "But the real reason [to homeschool] is because the Bible says to do it; that's why we homeschool."

The negativity of Israel Wayne toward public schooling is reciprocated by his audience, particularly men. Every time the term "government schools" comes up I think I am at a revival service with all the "yeses" and "amens" being voiced around me. The same goes for reactions to accounts of the harsh effects of public school on boys. These men, I surmise, did not have a great experience with school. I have to admit that I recognize the problem, since first grade was a disaster for me. My own father took me out of school several afternoons to teach me to read in the first grade during the spring, as I needed extra help. Yet there is an additional element here, an almost religious zeal to see the public school as an affront to God, the Bible, political freedom, and Christian liberty.

As I indicated earlier, there are a number of digressions in an Israel Wayne presentation, and as we have reached the end, they become of a more promotional nature. In addition to homeschooling, Wayne promotes his family renewal ministry and his book *Questions God Asks*, whose chapters are based on the dozen or so questions God is quoted as directly voicing in the Bible. He also promotes one of his publishers, which is pushing creationism as *the* core scientific lesson to be learned in a Christian home. All of us in the audience are offered a free *Evolution versus God* DVD from Master Books as long as we will give it to a non-Christian friend. The whole convention is big on what some call people friendship evangelism; this is not the ugly Fred Phelps's Westboro Baptist confront-your-neighbors-with-their-going-to-hell-lifestyle kind of witnessing, it is the give-a-friend-something-that-just-might-save-their-life kind of evangelism. So our mission, *if we accept it*, is to spread the gospel, not to hammer it into unwilling people. Wayne sends us out on a benediction of sorts: everything we teach in homeschooling, he says, can be taught from a biblical worldview, and that is important—"Even math has a biblical worldview. Remember that."

As I leave my morning sessions and head into a crowd of people changing sessions or on their way to the exhibit hall, I am struck again by how many strollers, families, and pregnancies there are in this gathering. Stuck in the crowd, I overhear two youthful mothers who cannot yet be thirty-five discussing their large families in glowing terms. One asks, "How many do you have?" The other replies, "Seven, but we haven't decided whether we are done yet. We are waiting on a Word for that." The "Word" of which she speaks is, of course, a word from the Lord, who guides those who wait.

The exhibit hall booths of books include a disproportionate number of books about dinosaurs and fossils (seriously, what kid isn't interested in dinosaurs) that stress that paleontologists and museums take facts—dinosaurs existed—and lie about them, saying that they lived millions of years ago before human beings lived, then went extinct before we evolved from lower forms of life. The basic message of these books, which are just as pretty and enticing to the eye as anything produced by DK Books or National Geographic for the mainstream audience, is that six actual days of creation in a "young Earth" are the only true science; that makes the earth between 5,700 and 10,000 years old. One memorable spread in one of these books shows Sue, the reconstructed *Tyrannosaurus rex* at the Field Museum in Chicago, and informs readers that paleontologists and museum personnel engage in lots of guesswork about how various bones get put together, sometimes using many different animals' bones and inventing missing pieces. I got the message that the next time I am in Chicago I should appreciate the fact that God made the dinosaurs but not be led astray by the scientific claims made in signs on the walls or in front of the displays. One of the best-selling of these flashy dinosaur books is creationist author Ken Ham's *Dinosaurs for Kids*. Inside his book children learn the "7F's of Dinosaur History—formed, fallen, faded, fearless, flood, found & fiction."[5] With that outline I think most readers can picture the argument made even without Bill Looney's pictures. No one who bothered to check Teach Them Diligently's Statement of Faith on the website when they signed up for the convention should be surprised by this emphasis on young earth creationism. Five of the seven articles of faith in the Statement of Faith represent core, almost generic fundamentalist and evangelical beliefs: verbal inspiration and biblical inerrancy, virgin birth, salvation by grace through faith, the ubiquity of sin, and the individual's ability to receive Christ and true belief by calling on the Lord. But two other beliefs stand out for the weight of their emphasis in the homeschooling subculture:

The earth was created by God in six literal days (Exodus 20:8–11). Discipleship in the home is not only necessary and essential, but it is also mandated in the scriptures (Deuteronomy 6:7).[6]

Nearly every booth in the large exhibition hall can be subsumed under the categories of discipleship in the home or belief in biblical creation. As I wander the exhibits, I am reminded by something else that I saw on the website as I perused the seventy-six scheduled speakers and noticed that all were—to my eyes at least—white, and that underscores that Christian homeschooling is a decidedly white enterprise. There were very few attendees of color to be seen at the convention, with the largest representation being from religious book publishers and vendors from outside the narrower field of homeschooling curricula. Statistics gathered by the National Center for Educational Statistics, part of the U.S. Department of Education, bears this out for 2007, the last year in which a phone survey was conducted. White schoolchildren represented 76.9 percent of the homeschool population even though they were just 58.3 percent of the school-age population of the United States at that time. For 2012, when the department used a statistical technique and paper self-reports in lieu of phone surveys, white children rose to 83 percent of the homeschooled population even as they accounted for only 52.2 percent of school-age children.[7] Putting this another way, white children were 1.3 times as likely (in 2007, the year of the better survey) to be homeschooled as children of all other races, while black children were only about one quarter as likely to be homeschooled as their school-age peers, with Hispanics being half as likely, and the ambiguous category of all other races—which included Asian and Pacific Islander children—to be homeschooled at close to the mean rate (that is, slightly less than the rate of white children).[8] What does it matter that homeschooling is such a white phenomenon? At least in the South it has to be seen in the context of the decades-long, racially tinged crisis in public education. When other states to the north and west were creating "normal schools" to train teachers to teach well in amply funded public schools, the South was largely rural and recovering from a devastating Civil War and then a series of depressions. Following the Supreme Court's decision in *Brown v. Board of Education* (1954), many states and localities made their education systems worse through defunding and refusal to implement desegregation except under court order. White parents began to depopulate those same school systems one family at a time by placing their children in existing private schools (remember that public schools as a rule had never been strong in the South) or into hundreds of new so-called Christian academies that were founded in the late 1960s and early 1970s just as final desegregation orders were implemented in the respective localities. Southern Christian homeschooling families stand, therefore, in a long line of parents who claim that they are only trying to do what is best for their children by protecting them from outside influences. And for them, religiously understood, they are obeying a mandate of discipleship in the home.

Still, I cannot help but be struck by the fact that forty and fifty years ago some of these very parents' parents (maybe even grandparents) took their children out of public schools to avoid mixing with black children. I am not the first person to notice the racialized dynamic of homeschooling: there is an active online, mostly defensive literature from parents claiming that wanting their children not to be exposed to the worst cultural influences found in public schools does not make them racist. One of the most intriguing social science studies on the subject, Tal Levy's "Homeschooling and Racism," noted that the best predictors for when a state legislature would vote to allow homeschooling in their state were high amounts of Christian fundamentalism, coupled with rural populations and a recent rise in public school racial integration. Not coincidentally, therefore, homeschooling became an option for most American families only in the 1980s, the decade of peak public school racial integration.[9] While other scholarly defenders of homeschooling, notably Brian Ray, downplay the racial avoidance factor, the effect of isolating children from each other still goes on.[10] This is doubly ironic in the South, a region that prides itself on the strength of its community, and among homeschoolers, who are keen on teaching the American communitarian civics that they claim are missing in public education today. Today these Christian families would be offended to be labeled as racist; many might even point out that two generations ago their families lived in the North. In any event, few are willing to grapple with the unequal educational legacy of southern history in the here and now. More important, in their minds they do what they do for their children's sake alone. James Emery White, the founding pastor of Mecklenburg Community Church in Charlotte, is one who casts the need for homeschooling in a protective light: "Homeschooling is what lets you guard and protect your child's heart and optimally mold their character in a dark and fallen world. . . . It's what lets you insulate them from the world before their maturity is ready to engage it on their own."[11] The Reverend White, like countless other parents, casts

Christian homeschooling as parental control of one's children's broader socialization and development of character. Nevertheless, the consequence of racial separation continued with homeschooling is just as real as it was in the white flight schools of the 1960s. In twenty-first-century multicultural America it is not just eleven o'clock Sunday morning that is the most segregated hour of each week, it is any time of the week in nearly any local institution that bears the name Christian. The exceptions that prove the rule are church-affiliated hospitals and some parochial schools.

Meanwhile, back in the exhibit hall, in addition to the aforementioned creation science books there is an overwhelming array of instructional materials in every conceivable kind of packaging. There are flashcards, workbooks, CDs, DVDs, textbooks, computer programs for student-paced learning, and peer learning opportunities for homeschoolers to experience field trips with other Christians like themselves. Some are incredibly glitzy and expensive, which reminds me that several of the convention's sessions are geared toward affording the Christian homeschooling lifestyle. In the middle of the exhibit hall I come to a very busy booth that is selling mimeographed lessons printed on plain, light-colored paper (like church newsletters circa 1965). Then I notice that the people helping customers and taking money are all young Mennonite women in bonnets and traditional dress. This community has been at homeschooling for a long time. If you want a simple, low-cost approach to Christian homeschooling, it appears that the Mennonites know how to do it effectively and glitz-free.

Lesson plans, curriculum materials, and books are not the only things for sale on the exhibition floor, however. There are advocacy organizations (for example, the Family Research Council) and two legal organizations, one to defend your right to homeschool your children and another to defend you against real and nuisance suits launched by neighbors attacking you because you have children home during daylight hours. ("No, you may not take my children! . . . An anonymous tip is all that separates your family from a social services investigation over issues like parental decisions regarding corporal punishment, sanctity of life, medical choices like vaccinations and midwifery, and applications of biblical standards in church and family.") Heritage Defense provides a LegalShield sort of legal services only for Christian homeschoolers for nineteen dollars a month. Talking with these legal advocates for even a few minutes starts making me alert to all the challenges and fears that homeschooling parents face. Much more prevalent than lawyers, however, are the vendors selling soup, bread, clothing, and other items that emphasize the "home" in homeschooling. If you were to guess what one does in a homeschool from what the booths are selling, you would have to say it has something to do with food and especially baking. And maybe, I think, based on the booths, kids should learn at home about baking and canning and gardening—it is a throwback to an earlier time, when at least food did not come from a store or a factory. It is both part of a Christian lifestyle for sale at this convention and a part of what some evangelicals are calling "food sovereignty," by which they mean to respond to God's command at the beginning of Genesis to have dominion over the earth and subdue it. This homeschooling emphasis on food carries another undertone as well, a suspicion that this world on the governmental and agribusiness level is broken and that no one can be trusted to provide for our family's food security except we ourselves, using God-given rain and sun to achieve localized sovereignty over the food supply. Back when I was a kid we called it planting a garden; today it is where right- and left-wing roots Christians find themselves in agreement.

In other booths alternative Christianity as a non-mall lifestyle is also fostered. Here mothers and daughters can purchase simple, natural makeup (it is called skincare, not makeup). The clothing people wear to the convention parallels what is for sale: long skirts and pants for women. Men wear beards, or not. But whatever men wear or consume, they display their masculinity without projecting misogyny on the kinds of T-shirts they wear. As I stop and compare this Christian homeschooling convention to a Las Vegas consumer electronics show with scantily clad spokesmodels, this place is the polar opposite. Sex does not sell; wholesomeness does. Or maybe I should say that sex does sell here, too, but it is the ultimate American alternative lifestyle of sex for procreation within the blessing of a large Christian family.

One of the biggest advocates of large Christian families is the organization Above Rubies, based in Franklin, Tennessee. They have a booth at the convention and are giving away issues 87 and 88 of their *Above Rubies* magazine together with other print materials advocating reversing vasectomies for men and VBACs for women. Those initials are prominent in the booth's many signs, and I have to admit that I do not initially know what they mean, so I look more closely and discover that in this context they denote "vaginal birth after cesarean." The magazines, the Above Rubies website, and the books by the group's founder, Nancy Campbell, are full of testimonies about people who thought they could physically no longer father or bear children who, with God's help, overcame obstacles to have ever-enlarging families into their late forties and fifties. The articles that do not cover these subjects are about what one does with the blessing of a large Christian family and are in keeping with Above Rubies' mission of encouraging women in their "high calling as wives, mothers and homemakers. Its purpose is to uphold and strengthen family life and to raise the standard of God's truth in the nation."[12] The name for the group is derived from Proverbs 31:10, which reads, "Who can find a virtuous woman? for her price is far above rubies" (KJV).

A couple of aisles away, a woman and her daughter have a booth and show me how they are turning their home into a resource for homeschoolers that will offer field trips, including: face time with conservative politicians; lessons in the Christian faith of the founding fathers; lessons on how to structure the "home altar," and more. Both mother and daughter are wearing dresses right out of *Little House on the Prairie*, and their booth is decorated to match in early Christian Victorian. It fits with the name of their new enterprise: Heritage Ministry Center. The business about the home altar catches my attention because I recognize in it an older piety that was extremely popular in the South in the late nineteenth and early twentieth centuries, one of Bible reading and devotions centered around a particular prayer area in the Protestant home. I learn that this is exactly what the business owner has in mind to help families re-create. The whole effort has a conservative Christian meets alternative vibe. It occurs to me that some of my most alternative students from Elon, Furman, Rhodes, Warren Wilson, Hendrix, Berry, and Berea Colleges (all in the South) actually have a lot in common with this woman and others in the room who believe in a simpler life. They all, the retro-homeschoolers and my grow-your-own-food students, may actually have more in common with Kentucky agrarian poet and essayist Wendell Berry than anybody has ever considered. Berry was born of the land and the Great Depression. These modern-day simple-life seekers have seen the damage of the past decade's recession. Many know firsthand the debt that ordinary Americans have amassed trying to chase the good life to provide for their children. The retro-homeschoolers invariably asks the emperor-has-no-clothes question: Why don't you provide *you* to your children instead of all that stuff and daycare that all that overwork, credit, and worry has brought? Did your children ask to live in a big or bigger house? My students are not thinking about kids yet, but they know they do not want to fall into the trap they watched ensnare their parents. As such, they have begun—from the left—searching for a language like the one

Wendell Berry employs. In a 2006 interview with Holly M. Brockman in the *New Southerner*, Berry mused:

> The issue of usefulness has a kind of cleansing force. If you ask, "Is it useful?" probably you're going to have fewer things you don't need. You are useful to your family if you're bringing home the things they need. Beyond that, maybe you are useful to other people by your work. The corporate world is much inclined to obscure this usefulness by making and selling a lot of things that people don't need. For instance, a lively and important question is how much light we use at night and what we use it for and need it for. I'm old enough to remember when the whole countryside was dark at night except for the lights inside the houses, and now the countryside at night is just strewn with these so-called security lights. How much of this do we need? How much of it is useful? We have a marketplace that is full of useless or unnecessary commodities. I don't want to be too much of a crank, but there are many things that people own to no real benefit, such as computer games and sometimes even computers.[13]

The convention exhibition hall is full of southern evangelicals who are living the Christian homeschooling lifestyle and asking, what's useful? Do they need the computer? Do they need to teach their child Latin? How much of the rest of American culture can their children participate in without ruining their walk with Christ? There is another question that seems to lurk in the room: Will there be a college who will accept my children when it is time for them to go to college? The answer to that question is a clear "yes." A substantial number of booths are staffed by Christian college recruiters for Liberty University, Lipscomb University, Belmont College, Trevecca Nazarene University, Welch College, Toccoa Falls College, Bob Jones University, Freed-Hardeman University, and more. Most of these schools not only want homeschooled applicants but also have pre-enrollment programs for earning college credit during the high school years. Christian homeschooling is an alternative lifestyle, but it is not an alternative that bars access to the leading Christian colleges of the South.

My last stop before leaving the exhibition hall and the Teach Them Diligently Convention is to see what is going on with all the people who are gathered around an isolated booth with a sign above saying that the vendor sells a series of books on what is called Cat and Dog Theology. The animated man at the booth tells us that in a series of four books teenagers are led to understand the basics of Christian theology and how we are supposed to behave in relation to God. It turns out that this Mechanicsville, Virginia-based publisher has developed a four-year, thirty lessons per year, biblical theology curriculum premised first on a joke. The back of the first year's book sets it all up:

> There's a joke about cats and dogs that conveys their differences perfectly—A dog says, "You pet me, you feed me, you shelter me, you love me, you must be God." A cat says, "You pet me, you feed me, you shelter me, you love me, I must be God." These God-given traits of cats ("You exist to serve me") and dogs ("I exist to serve you") are often similar to the theological attitudes we have in our view of God and our relationship to Him. Using the differences between cats and dogs in a light-handed manner, the authors compel us to challenge our thinking in deep and profound ways. As you are drawn toward God and the desire to reflect His glory in your life, you will worship, view missions, and pray in a whole new way.[14]

Each year's curriculum features a fictional story about two teenagers growing up in America's "self-absorbed culture." The banter in and around the booth leaves no doubt that parents and the series' authors are worried that teenagers are or will become cats vis-à-vis God, ungrateful and self-centered. As I leave with my Cat and Dog Theology curriculum brochure in hand I do not know about having had my thinking challenged in deep and profound ways, but I do get the point the authors are trying to make. More than that, I cannot but come away from the convention center impressed with the sincerity of conviction that these thousands of families bring to Christian homeschooling.

On the drive back home I ponder what this rising separation in children's education means for the South, for its religious outlook, and for its culture in the years to come. One thing I know is that homeschooling is on a continuum. There are degrees of separation from the common schools of yesterday. Private schools, Christian schools, Montessori schools, charter schools; few children are getting the cohort experience that Americans once had as late as the 1960s, when all first- and second-graders read about Dick and Jane and Tom and Sally. Homeschoolers just have the most atomized version of an increasingly atomized educational delivery system.

Once upon a time, we like to tell ourselves, every child went to school together with every other child in town, learned about George Washington and the cherry tree and not telling lies, and the Golden Rule, and they shared a common culture that bound them through time. When we were called to the county courthouse to sit on a jury we really were sitting with our peers, or people who had an identical education. All the witnesses could swear on the same Bible as we would. That myth is particularly strong in the South. But of course, there were two sets of southern schools—one white, one "colored." My own children were educated in a mix of public and independent schools in the 1990s to 2010s where they learned a lot about Georgia and Tennessee but precious little of those patriotic metanarratives that schools used to use to try to form citizens.

Where is all this different schooling for different subcommunities leading? I think that we are seeing it already in our politics. I believe in climate change; you do not. And we ascribe special protection to these "beliefs." You believe in creation in six literal days, I do not, and we will fight about it at the school board meeting. We have such different histories of the founding fathers' views on church and state that we advocate radically opposed jurisprudence on church-state issues. Those protected beliefs are then supported (some might say armed) by alternate facts. One thing that may bring us together or divide us all the more is that in the South, most political opponents are Christians with different views of the good, sometimes even of how to apply Scripture. As Abraham Lincoln said in his Second Inaugural Address, "Both read the same Bible and pray to the same God, and each invokes His aid against the other." Why is that? Increasingly all I can conclude is we really must have gone to different schools. Yet there are basic truths about the world—the climate *is* or *is not* at risk, for instance—and the refusal to engage looming issues of major moment out of sacrosanct prior belief commitments strikes at the heart of an educated republic. Homeschooling parents tell themselves that they are seeking something better for their children, but what if the echo chamber does not supply them with all of knowledge, skills, and perspectives that are most needed to survive the years ahead?

Southern Religious Innovations

10

SOUTHERN, CHRISTIAN, AND GAY

In perhaps no area is contemporary southern Christianity more deeply divided than over the issue of homosexuality. For conservative Christians in the South, lesbian, gay, bisexual, and now transgender persons have "chosen a lifestyle" that amounts to rejecting God's natural order of creation. Having a sexual identity that is an alternative to the conservative's prescribed heterosexual norm has become the de facto unforgivable sin, not blasphemy, not adultery, not divorce, nor any of the other things that used to make a person unwelcome around church. The "homosexual panic" (a term that formerly described a young man who was scared on the basis of feelings or experiences of possibly being gay) now describes the state of many churches, K–12 schools, and youth sports teams; and the more tied these institutions are to conservative Christian groups in the South, the greater the panic seems to be. There is an age cohort dimension to this panic about other peoples' identities, however. Younger people (including many self-described Bible-believing Christians) do not think that being gay has anything to do with one's status before God, nor should it have before the law or in the family of faith.[1] Baby boomers may be the last generation to feel otherwise, but for now gender identity and sexuality is a battleground in the South. Time may resolve this issue, but many Christians thirty-five and up hold on to sexuality as the only way to demarcate Christians from the rest of what they see as secular, value-free culture. This chapter, however, is not about the southern Christians who exclude and decry their LGBT neighbors. It is about the several million gay southerners who bear up under that pressure while often holding on to the Christian faith that supposedly drives those who would exclude them. Finally, I will focus on the LGBT Christians in the South and their allies who in the contemporary period have decided to be quiet no longer but instead to be proudly Christian and gay, and the growing minority of congregations that have staked out a publicly affirming identity of welcome. For these LGBT people of faith and their allies, the Christian message has sometimes proved stronger and more redemptive than all the resistance they have encountered from other Christians because of their identities.

A WORD ABOUT WORDS AND ACRONYMS

Though at the time of writing this book my university campus like others is using a much longer acronym, LGBTQI, to embrace and affirm at least the possible Lesbian, Gay, Bisexual, Transgender, Queer, and Intersex identities of our members, terms denoting sexualities are particularly fluid and subject to change. I have chosen to quote the terms in direct speech that my subjects have used exactly and to otherwise use the word "gay" and the acronym "LGBT," which I have seen and heard used almost exclusively in contemporary LGBT-affirming Christian church circles. The word "gay" does a lot of positive work in theses churches right now, where it is used to denote gay men and lesbian women. By contrast, the term "queer" has very little church currency, perhaps because so many people who fought for their rights to be recognized in their full identities as Christian and lesbian, gay, bisexual, or transgender were historically called queer from outside the LGBT community in hurtful ways. In any event, the church, even the gay-LGBT church, is a traditional (as opposed to radical) social institution in the larger scheme of things, and readers are asked to be attentive to how people talk about themselves.

BEFORE THE CULTURE WARS

As with any historical account, the question of when to start the narrative is a political one. In the case of southern LGBT Christians, this is particularly true. If we begin the narrative during the culture wars era of Anita Bryant,

Adrian Rogers, and Jerry Falwell, with their frequent "Adam and Eve, not Adam and Steve" jibes, we can easily fall into a recounting of historical developments that makes southern LGBT Christians look to be newcomers to the South. Starting later would also fit in with a gay historiography that sees the three-day Stonewall riots in New York in June 1969 as the watershed moment for LGBT people in America, and New York and San Francisco as the place where all southern gay men and lesbian women had to go to live their lives without daily threat of violence. As is often the case with watershed history, the real story is more complicated, and LGBT presence in southern religious life is much more interesting in the early and mid-twentieth century than we might suppose.[2] Indeed, if we wish to understand the roots of Christian resistance to antigay religiosity in the South, we would do well to examine the witness of the pre-Stonewall southern LGBT Christians and their allies.

PIONEERS

It may come as a shock to realize that the first gay-affirming denomination in the nation was formed in the South by a native southerner and the second, the Metropolitan Community Church, was founded in 1968 in California by Troy Perry, a native son of the Florida-Georgia line. The first was the tiny autocephalous Orthodox Catholic Church in America, which began in Atlanta in 1946 under the leadership of George Hyde, a Catholic convert who had recently been kicked out of seminary for asking too many skeptical questions. After hugging a fellow seminarian good-bye—but before leaving the seminary—he was brought up on charges in the school's "Chapter of Faults." The event led to a moment of prophetic resistance that also served as a fair prediction of the shape of his future life and ministry:

> One of the boys says, "I want to charge George and Carl with
> fondling one another in an immoral manner!" The [accuser] went on
> and on. Well, I'm supposed to stand up and say, "Thank you so much
> for bringing that to my attention, I had forgotten it or did not place
> great importance on it, and I'm sorry." I didn't. I got up and I said,
> "Listen, you little snot," and I walked down and I addressed the father
> superior and all the priests and all the students. And one of them later
> called it my Martin Luther speech. And I said, "You have distorted
> Christ's message, and you have gone far outside the legislations of
> Christ, and imposed your own legislation, and you with a twisted

mind, a twisted morality . . . [you say] the simple thing of expressing your feelings or friendship for another person is sinful. There's nothing sinful about two men embracing one another, but you've made it so. And you have accused me of this and that and the other," and so I said, "but you are building in every corner of the church closets in which to shut away those who have a moral standard different from yours. And I'm not going to put up with it, and I'm going to spend *my* life tearing those closet doors off the hinges!" And with that I bowed to the father superior and turned on my heels and walked out. (smiling) And they were glad to see me go.[3]

George Hyde went back to Atlanta and to Sacred Heart parish (one of two Catholic parishes in Atlanta at the time), where he ran into a young man who, having confessed his homosexuality to a priest, refused to confess that he was an abomination before God. The man was denied communion, so Hyde joined him at the railing in solidarity. They both were then refused the sacrament. Hyde put together a bigger posse of supporters, and they were all passed over as unworthy at the altar rail, and out of this judgmentalism as Hyde saw it, a new church was born, with Hyde receiving his ordination from a Greek Orthodox bishop, John Kazantks, at the first meeting of the new congregation on July 1, 1946, in the Winecoff Hotel. The congregation's expenses were initially floated by the Cotton Blossom Room, an Atlanta gay bar. By the end of the year, word of mouth had caused the congregation's membership to grow to two hundred. This foundation story is paradigmatic insofar as refusal to accept rejection of one's sexuality as the price of continuing to be Christian is at the heart of every LGBT and gay-friendly church I found in this study. What George Hyde believed throughout his ministry, that one's sexuality changed nothing about how much God loved and accepted God's sons and daughters, drives the congregations, pastors, and people who are organized to resist the prevailing Christian homophobia of the contemporary South.

Other pro–gay inclusion milestones include Bishop Bennett Sims, Episcopal bishop of Atlanta, recanting his prior theological treatise on why sexually active, self-avowed gay Christians could not be ordained to the priestly orders. A former theological professor and one of the acknowledged intellectuals of the Episcopal Church (USA), Sims became a hero to the gay community for his new stance, but his story of slow conversion over a decade was a southern story all the way through. Out of Christian charity and southern hospitality he agreed to start meeting with gay men who had partners and who worshiped in downtown Atlanta, especially at St. Luke Episcopal. Over time the power of knowing people in their full humanity did its work of testing his principles in the face of their integrity, which not incidentally was the name of the LGBT advocacy group of the Episcopal Church, Integrity, a group formed in 1974 by an English professor, Louie Crew.[4]

What Crew asked of the Episcopal Church in 1974 was to be publicly affirmed in his relationship with his partner, Ernest Clay, by his church. He was on sabbatical from Ft. Valley State College in Georgia in the San Francisco Bay area studying at Berkeley and thinking that San Francisco's Grace Cathedral, with its legendarily progressive bishop Kilmer Myers, would provide a way forward. Instead, when he called the cathedral to ask about having a ceremony of marriage performed, he heard derisive laughter over the phone, laughter that made him angry and motivated to provide an answer from below. Integrity was that answer, founded in rural Georgia and growing in time to more than sixty U.S. chapters in the Episcopal Church (USA).

Though George Hyde, Louie Crew Clay, and Troy Perry all brought the public affirmation of gay and lesbian Christians to the fore in the years 1946–75, they were not so much informing southerners that gays and lesbians existed in the South but rather trying to change the terms of cultural engagement. In a region with a strong tradition of antisodomy laws that would not be fully overturned until 2003, the precondition of southern LGBT identity could be termed "don't ask, don't tell." Writers in LGBT southern history and letters agree that before the 1970s and 1980s (and continuing in some places into the present), the South preserved an older tradition of relating sexuality and Christianity through quiet toleration rather than open acceptance. The feminist critic Mab Segrest discusses the phenomena in her book *My Mama's Dead Squirrel: Lesbian Essays on Southern Culture*, which reflects on her own growing up as a lesbian in the South. Segrest notes how southerners think of the "*eccentric* being in one's family, the *freak* in someone else's."[5] The trick of even a limited family form of acceptance is, of course, not to push one's luck and be branded a freak by one's own people. One of the informants historian Jodie Talley interviewed in 2004 for her study of gay-affirming religion in the South, Bob Beard, saw the differences in starkly regional terms:

> In the North it is OK to dislike individuals, in the South it's OK
> to dislike *groups* of people. You can dislike all those queers, but

if it's a member of *my* family or somebody *I* grew up with, we'll overlook that, you know, because he or she is our friend or our family member. And in the South we hate the groups and love the individuals, as opposed to, you know, some other parts of the country where they may love the groups and hate the individual. So I think it is a Southern thing to overlook these quirks.[6]

Such is the southern way, as Talley herself notes, "In earlier eras it would have been common for a white Southerner, for example, to disparage the African American population as a whole even while treasuring a personal relationship with a particular individual of color who seemed like family. The same would prove true with southern gays. It would be easy to make acts of sodomy illegal or to publicly reject homosexuality, but the gay person in one's own family or community would be hard to persecute, so long as that individual did not disturb the surface civil status quo."[7]

For me, a strong memory from my time as a dean of a Presbyterian seminary in Atlanta in the 1990s stands out as confirming Segrest's and Beard's views. The son of a local church whom many faculty members had known since he was a child came before a faculty panel in the middle of his time in seminary seeking to be advanced to degree candidacy, as was our custom. In this setting of vocational discernment, he let us know among other things that he was gay, HIV positive, and suffering emotionally after the death of his partner from AIDS. The men who had known him since childhood were compassionate and voted easily for advancement for his ministerial degree, even though he could not at that time hope to be ordained as an out gay man. That was my first surprise, and it carried the lesson that the totality of who you are in community in the South often trumps your sexuality, sometimes even in church systems that are guarding the doors about such matters. Another colleague who grew up out of the region, however, wasn't in the same place that day. He was vehement about our "obligation to tell Brian [not his real name] to correct his behavior." It was the faculty colleagues who were most locally connected to church structures and the community who were the most determined to maintain Brian's privacy and dignity and let him come out on his own time. Brian did eventually die of AIDS, one of the many for whom the early antiretroviral cocktail combinations did not work. Yet he did not die before he found a very public ministry as an unordained minister to others in the HIV/AIDS community in Atlanta.

Southern Religious Innovations

The AIDS crisis of the 1980s to mid-1990s profoundly disrupted the course of quiet acceptance that many LGBT people had experienced into the 1970s. Fear often knocks the "better angels of our nature" right off people's shoulders, but in the southern religious context other sources of aversive homophobia were at work besides fear of AIDS. Indeed, most contemporary observers would be quick to point to the many ways conservative and fundamentalist forms of Christianity have become known for their aversive homophobia. We might ask, therefore, when did being antigay become such a mark of true belief? The legal scholar Didi Herman contends that homophobia served as a convenient substitute for anticommunism as the prospects of godless Soviet take over began to crumble and then evaporated in the 1980s.[8] In magazines like *Christianity Today*, the secular gay rights agenda was turned aside with an increasing number of articles claiming that, as people not made according to God's plan for humanity, gays and lesbians had no rights to claim. Meanwhile, James Dobson, Pat Robertson, and Jerry Falwell helped to make the Christian heteronormative family nearly the fourth person of the American Christian Trinity, and thereby constantly raised the danger of the abomination of homosexuality not only in their radio and television programs but in every church and ministry they influenced well into the twenty-first century. The great danger of this heterosexual family idolatry was for the people who it left out—the divorced, the single, the gay, lesbian, bisexual, and transgender, and particularly the young people of churchgoing families who heard homophobic messages on Sundays and Wednesdays and at youth camps. Some of these young people learned to love the Lord and sing hymns of praise, only to wake up to their own sexuality in horror: "Am I one of *those* people whom I have heard so much about?" Even in the South, whose institutions have done much to discourage LGBT people's flourishing, 3.2 percent of the adult population self-identifies as LGBT, and the figure is more than twice as high for those age eighteen to twenty-nine.[9] Any small church with twenty or more youth at any point in time has a high chance of having one or more teens going through a LGBT gender-identity experience. The phenomenon is not isolated.

The finest book I know about the experience of LGBT people living in the South and encountering Christian antigay messages before, during, and after coming to terms with their sexual and gender identities is Bernadette Barton's *Pray the Gay Away: The Extraordinary Lives of Bible Belt Gays*. In the book she makes the point that with nearly 60 percent of the population self-identifying as fundamentalist in Kentucky, Tennessee, Mississippi, and Alabama and just over 40 percent self-identifying as fundamentalist in West Virginia, Maryland, Delaware, North Carolina, South Carolina, Georgia, and Florida, gay southerners are constantly exposed to fundamentalist rhetoric about the un-Christian lifestyle they embody. This in turn makes affirmative self-definition difficult, due to what the early twentieth-century sociologist Charles Horton Cooley termed the "looking glass self," in which the surrounding social world mirrors back to us what it sees, thus affecting our own self-perceptions.[10] In a Christian fundamentalist milieu it is, therefore, hard if not impossible to factor in the negative gaze on one's sexuality. Given how much southern Christian LGBT individuals often yearn to hold onto and affirm all aspects of their composite identities, places of alternative faithful affirmation become much more important. Passing as straight in heteronormative church settings can be painful. One of Barton's interviewees, Misty, describes going with her family to a church where homosexuals are a despised group, singled out in preaching for disapprobation: "This, for me, is a major way religion and my family colluded to keep me or anyone in the toxic closet. You see your whole immediate family, not agreeing so much like they are sitting and nodding their heads as [the preacher] speaks, but you see them in no way disagreeing. They listen intently, shake the preacher's hand on the way out with a smile and the belief system has been reinforced."[11] Misty clearly knew at the end of the church service what the looking glass of the church thought of her, and even if her family knew about or suspected her difference in sexuality, they played along with the preacher and thereby increased her sense of alienation.

Sometimes pastors and churches go even further than just using words to reinforce their belief system as, for example, when Chattanooga area detective Kat Cooper obtained partner benefits in 2013 for her same-sex spouse. The detective's mother, Linda, held her daughter's hand throughout all of the municipal hearings leading up to the positive decision. This was too much for the pastor and lay leaders of Ridgedale Church of Christ, where Linda and other family members belonged. The congregation's leaders gave the extended family an ultimatum: "They could repent for their sins and ask forgiveness in front of the congregation. Or leave the church." What about loving and supporting family members unconditionally, asked Kat Cooper, referring to what is often invoked as Christian virtue. Not in this case, thought Pastor Ken Willis, for such support constituted a clear endorsement

Southern Religious Innovations

of homosexuality: "The sin would be endorsing that lifestyle." Willis added, "The Bible speaks very plainly about that."[12]

There is another paradigmatic story of staying at home in the South, trying to come out and remain within a Christian family and church milieu— that of rejection. Sometimes parents, teachers, youth leaders, and preachers surround you, trying to pray that your gay inclinations might be taken away like a demon or a devil. Too often, there are violent breaks initiated by family refusing having anything to do with their son or daughter, brother or sister. For more than twenty years I have taught some divinity students who have been painfully kicked out of their Christian families of origin for being gay or lesbian, bisexual, or transgender but who still embrace their religious identity to the extent of wanting to spend two, three, or more expensive years studying for a religious vocation they have less of a chance of exercising than their heterosexual counterparts. Especially in the South I admire the dedication and faith; it represents that there is more to a religion than its poisonous use by others. I have little wonder that many southern LGBT folk moved to New York, San Francisco, or even Miami or Atlanta, where it was just a little easier to escape the fundamentalist gaze and live one's own life. Yet just as elsewhere in the nation other LGBT people were experiencing love, relationships, and a sphere of personal existence within the southern milieu; to a remarkable extent that sphere of personal existence has included expressions of Christian faith.

TOXIC CLOSET, SPIRITUAL WILDERNESSES, AND WELCOMING CONGREGATIONS

So what are the options for contemporary southern LGBT Christians? First there is, as we have seen, the toxic closet. Second, there is the path of nurturing one's faith outside formal religious structures (or moving in and out of a hypocritical space—like the church—where people know but do not say anything). And third, there are increasingly visible congregations of LGBT Christians and congregations who are LGBT-affirming, even though they may not be composed of a majority of LGBT attendees.

Statistically, the toxic closet may still be the most common place for LGBT Christians to find themselves living the faith in the South because sexual identity is not like race; it is not presorted into different initial church communities. You are not a gay man just because your father was a gay man attending a Gay Baptist church. Until very recently there was no gay-identity-aligned church into which to be born, and of course, contrary to what some would have you believe, gay and lesbian parents raise straight children all the time. (In more than three decades in the ministry I know how painful experiences of coming out inside the church that loved and affirmed these children of God—until they came out—has been for generations of Christians.) Not a few have done the calculations and decided to stay in place and not pay the price of rejection by their ministers and congregations, even by their families, only to live in earshot of Christian homophobic rhetoric as the cost of closeted or semicloseted existence. Some of my own seminary classmates and later my students have lived this twilight existence for decades (in the North and the South, I would note) because they (like me) were determined to be valued for the quality and character of their ministry and not for aspects of their personal lives about which others of us were never asked. Yet not to be singled out for exclusion because of your difference is not the same thing as being embraced for all of who you are. The battle for gay ordination over the past forty-plus years in several mainline denominations is nothing less than that: a battle for recognition that good people, all kinds of good, faithful people, are called to the ministry.

The next option is to leave organized religion entirely, or to "keep Jesus in my heart." It is an option that has become increasingly viable especially in urban areas of the South and for younger individuals whose cohorts are filled with others who describe themselves as "nones" when it comes to religion. If there is a central belief that unites the theistic, agnostic, and atheistic "nones," it is a strong dislike for what is seen as organized religion's hypocrisy. LGBT "nones" have additional reasons for feeling the same way as other "nones." In E. Patrick Johnson's book *Sweet Tea: Black Gay Men of the South*, the continuing need to maintain a religious connection, not necessarily with formal church adherence, is expressed this way by Anthony "First Lady" Hardaway, a man born in 1965:

> It's still important to me to commune with the divine. And what
> do I mean by that is I do not have to go to church all the time, even
> though I prefer to do that. The calling on my life now places me
> in places where I probably can't get to the church every Sunday,
> on Wednesday nights. But I make sure that the work that is being
> done would be the same as if I was in this quote/unquote place, this
> temple, this church, which means that I can do outreach in another
> city, at someone's home, to me that's still church for me. [A]nd when

I say this word, I do not mean a denomination, I mean the people—I still have to commune with the Saints. So religion, the church, it is still very much a part of me. I think that would never go away. It is just like when James Baldwin used to say it. It is just ingrained in me. I can't dismiss it, no matter how much I want to.[13]

Johnson is fascinated with the way that identities formed in churches transcend the strictures of the black church for black gay men in the South. One of his informants, Rob, born in Eden, North Carolina, in 1965, is especially pointed on the mixed messages that a church upbringing can give a person. Asked about the impact of church or religion on his childhood, Rob soon veered to the continuing impact it had on him, saying that "even to this day as a black gay male approaching 40, I still grapple with homosexuality in the church and where I fit in to that, *how* I fit into it, or even if I *do* fit into it. And just reconciling all that's been instilled in me in terms of having sexual experience with a man and whether that's right or wrong. I've been taught it was wrong; I've also been taught not necessarily that it's wrong, but God doesn't make mistakes, so you know, you're okay whoever, however you turned out to be."[14] Johnson is also interested in the apparent anomaly of what he calls "church sissies," gay men in ostensibly homophobic black churches in music and ministry leadership who do not get called out. Later, when Rob is asked why he thinks that there are so many gay men in church, he tells Johnson that it is not talking about people's differences that keeps things moving in the South, noting, "It just wouldn't be southern to talk about, that kind of thing in church." He adds, "You might acknowledge the fact that, okay, yeah, he shakes a little too much when he's directing the choir, or I wonder, I saw Pastor So-and-So with, you know, brother whoever, but as long as you don't talk about it, and don't bring it up, it really hadn't happened, it really doesn't exist."[15] So in this middle position it is southern religious and social hypocrisy that both drives some people away from religion and has also allowed others to participate religiously in a kind of suspended state—neither fully affirmed nor exiled.

In *Sweet Tea*, Patrick Johnson asked a great number of his informants about why they thought there were so many gay men in the choirs of the black church. Most of the answers were perceptive and revolved around occupying a liminal space wherein everyone knows who you are and still accepts you in the choir; maybe that is not so bad, maybe you are accepted after all in some kind of theologically provisional way in the place where your human identity was most affirmed and your sexual identity is most routinely denigrated. Many men who played by the rules to be in that liminal space were following what Atlanta's First Congregational former pastor Davita McCallister describes as a very familiar expression in the African American community, "You can be gay, but there's never any excuse for looking gay." She elaborates that what the phrase means is, "What you do in private in your home, that's fine. But we shouldn't have to see it, [and/or] to acknowledge it."[16] McCallister was not saying what was right or good for the souls of gay black folk; she was interpreting the expectations of the community for partial inclusion.

If the southern black churches will accept their gay sons and daughters under a kind of don't ask, don't tell policy, that is not always possible in conservative white churches. I have worked with students whose parents and pastors have maintained that the LGBT students can change back to being straight. Some parents have gone to elaborate lengths to enroll their teenage or adult children in residential reparative therapy programs, which usually are centered in a so-called Christian understanding of the healthy, normal (read heterosexual) person. Tales of becoming entirely alienated from one's family of origin after coming out are still not uncommon in the South. (Though neither are stories of parental attitude change despite what ministers advise.) Some of my students have struggled with the anomie that comes from being cut off and have needed substance abuse treatment and therapy to undo the soul damage done to them by their families and churches. What does such rejection feel like from the inside? Consider the story of Luke, the son of a Pentecostal minister from Tennessee who, despite being homeschooled and largely isolated from exposure to mainstream culture, came to an awareness that the same-sex attraction that his father was regularly deriding and condemning in graphic sermons was something he felt within himself. Whenever stories involving gay rights would air on the radio, Luke's father said, "They should gather all the gay people together and just kill them." Luke finally worked up the courage to come out to his mother. Her response? "If you want to live, don't tell your dad." Like so many other rejected gay teens, Luke hit the road.[17]

NEW OPTIONS FOR GAY CHRISTIANS AND THEIR ALLIES

Other options for LGBT Christians in the South are emerging. The first of these is membership in a congregation that is affiliated with denomination

or national faith group that allows, or even encourages, an open and affirming stance toward LGBT persons. These are mostly in large cities and in college and university towns, but their number is growing, and some statistics
are in order before we examine two interesting congregations that did not
develop from national denominational sexuality debates so much as they
constitute "southern originals." We opened this chapter with two southern
Christians forming gay-welcoming congregations and denominations before
1969, the so-called Stonewall watershed of gay-rights awareness. Where does
the development of such congregations in the South stand today, forty-five
and more years later? Well, thanks to the steady work of Elaine, Eric, and
Don (they do not publicize last names) at the GALIP (God's Agape Love
put Into Practice) Foundation, who have tracked and reported each open
and affirming congregation in each of the fifty states since 2003, we know
that as of January 2016 there were 1,050 LGBT-welcoming congregations in
the southern states. That sounds like a large number, until one recognizes
that in those same states in 2010, the last time a systematic census of religious
congregations was completed, those same states had 115,296 congregations.
The number of congregations in southern states, together with the subset of
congregations that affirmatively welcome LGBT persons, is shown in table 2.
For comparison's sake, however, we offer the figures for Vermont, a rural state
with old-line Congregational and Episcopal churches and many more evangelical and fundamentalist congregations on the outskirts of every town of
any size. Whereas 7.38 percent of all Vermont congregations are, by this comparison "gay-affirming," Mississippi ranks dead last in the United States, with
only 18 congregations identifying themselves as welcoming LGBT persons
in the entire state (mostly in Jackson), or 0.27 percent of all of Mississippi's
6,765 congregations. (Proportionally, there are also more big-membership,
gay-welcoming churches in New England than in the South, where a LGBT-
friendly church tends to be small to midsize.) This means, in short, that you
are 27.7 times more likely to encounter a gay-friendly congregation in Vermont than in Mississippi. To improve these odds, you want to go to Gainesville or Jacksonville in Florida, to the Research Triangle or Charlotte in North
Carolina, to Atlanta, to a college or university town, or to a state capital, like
Nashville. You can also improve your odds by looking for a church of certain
denominations. Obviously, the 44 Metropolitan Community churches in
these states would offer the certainty of an affirming congregation. Most of
the region's 147 United Church of Christ congregations are "Open and Affirming," as are 247 Episcopal Church congregations and 99 Evangelical Lutheran

Table 2. Gay-Affirming Congregations in Southern States

State	Number of Congregations	Number of Gay-Affirming Congregations	Gay-Affirming Congregations (%)
North Carolina	15,737	185	1.18
Florida	15,611	225	1.44
Georgia	12,292	122	0.99
Tennessee	11,542	87	0.75
Alabama	10,514	48	0.46
Virginia	10,088	168	1.67
South Carolina	8,051	41	0.51
Kentucky	7,745	65	0.84
Mississippi	6,765	18	0.27
Arkansas	6,697	29	0.43
Louisiana	5,841	37	0.63
West Virginia	4,413	25	0.63
For comparison:			
Vermont	854	63	7.38%

Sources: for gay-affirming congregations, http://www.gaychurch.org/;
for totals of congregations by state, 2010 U.S. Religion Census,
http://www.rcms2010.org/compare.php.

congregations. The Presbyterian Church (USA) has 121 gay-welcoming congregations in the South, but these are numerically outnumbered regionally by PC(USA) congregations who are opposed to gay ordination and Christian marriage equality, a statement that can be said to be likewise true of the 86 welcoming southern congregations in the United Methodist Church relative to the hundreds of UMC congregations in the region. The relatively small Christian Church/Disciples of Christ fields 37 GLAD Alliance (Gay and Lesbian Alliance of Disciples) congregations in the South.

As representatives of nationally strong mainline Protestant bodies, the aforementioned congregations might be somewhat expected as liberal outposts in the conservative South. Added to that, however, are more than fifty Baptist congregations and a couple dozen Roman Catholic, Old Catholic, and Independent Catholic congregations that are also open and affirming. Altogether these account for most of the LGBT-affirming churches in the South. There are, however, some interesting outliers—Pentecostal churches, nondenominational evangelical Bapticostal churches, and black churches—where the worship is nearly identical to other conservative southern congregations, with the crucial difference that homophobia has been replaced by a very deliberate message of extravagant welcome to all. We next turn to two of these churches.

TWO CONGREGATIONS

The Reverend Edwin Sanders, the young chaplain at Fisk University in Nashville (a historically black college), had run afoul of a new president who had a different sense of the role of the chapel and its chaplain. Sanders left Fisk in 1981 without a clear plan of what to do next, though many people who appreciated his ministry at Fisk urged him to start a church. But Edwin Sanders did not study anthropology at Wesleyan University and theology at Yale Divinity School to start an ordinary church in the black church tradition, of which Nashville was replete, so he turned aside the urgings of his former university flock. Seven months later, however, with some twelve diverse friends Sanders revisited the idea, and together they decided to form a different kind of church. First of all, it would be not another black church but a church for anyone, and Sanders wanted to name it Metropolitan Interdenominational to signal its openness. "Metropolitan" because Nashville was the first city in the nation to combine its cities and county into a single government, and "Interdenominational" to signal that all expressions of faith would be welcome. This would not be a church that would major in the minor issues that divided kinds of Christians but one that would claim unity in Christ. Like Christ himself, Sanders wanted to issue an invitation to "whosoever" would come. Even before they began, one of Sanders's friends warned him about the new name: did he know that "Metropolitan" was the name used by "all the gay churches across the country"? Ed Sanders said he did not care whether gay people came—everyone was welcome. If that is what people thought, he said, "So be it." In retrospect, he says, "there was a hand bigger than mine at work."[18] Sometimes people of faith make extravagant promises that later test whether their faith is as big as they claim, and sometimes keeping those promises makes their faith even bigger.

Twenty years later, when I first was getting to know the Reverend Edwin Sanders, I wondered aloud where he got his courage and imagination. He credited his education in New England to be sure, but over lunch as we prepared for our roles on a religious leaders' panel against the high rates of incarceration for drug use (and for decriminalization and harm-reduction measures), I learned that his Christian formation in courage went all the way back to growing up in Memphis and the civil rights years. His pastor then was the legendary civil rights leader and teacher of nonviolence the Reverend James Lawson. It was Lawson who taught Freedom Riders and lunch-counter sit-in demonstrators how to resist verbal hatred and even physical violence. It was Lawson who invited Martin Luther King Jr. to Memphis to help with the sanitation workers' strike that was ongoing in the spring of 1968 when King was killed by an assassin's bullet. Ed Sanders, therefore, knew what Christian courage looked like long before he left Tennessee for higher education at Wesleyan and Yale. As a fifteen-year-old he had been employed by Lawson as a runner to do the work of the Kingdom in the city of Memphis.[19] This courage was needed in the new church he founded, because among the first twelve people who gathered to form Metropolitan Interde-nominational was a gay man who would suffer and then mysteriously die of what would later become known as AIDS. Don was the one gay, black male in the original Metropolitan. The church began in February 1981, and Don died in 1984. Sanders relates that when he died, "We didn't know what was going on, and they told us he died of 'toxicosis.' I remember saying, 'What in the world is that?' I researched it and found out it had to do with cat and bird droppings, but Don didn't have cats. It was AIDS." Because one of their own members, Don, got AIDS and died, Sanders believes, "It pushed us in ministering and responding to folks with AIDS and in dealing with the issue of homosexuality."[20]

The courage to create a "whosoever church" created in turn a need for further courage—to follow through on the promise to accompany people who came to the church through any and everything they might face. The phrase itself comes from John 3:16, "For God so loved the world, that he gave his only begotten Son, that whosoever believeth in him should not perish, but have everlasting life" (KJV). The verse is so famous as to be invoked as simply "3:16" on signs held up by fans at sports events throughout the South, where the emphasis is on the invitation to believe and be saved. What Met-ropolitan Interdenominational does with the verse is something related but different. John 3:16's promise is turned into a charter for a church: Metro-politan lives to show what God's love looks like in a community of believers where literally anyone is included. One of the complaints about Jesus during his lifetime was that he ate with sinners, prostitutes, and publicans. Sanders and his church have turned that description of the wideness of Jesus' mercy into an ecclesiastical form—a place where people do not have to change as a precondition for sharing in worship and fellowship. People in gender transition, people with AIDS, people coping with addiction, prostitutes, doctors, nurses, mothers, fathers, lawyers, the formerly incarcerated, social workers, children, and divinity students have all been attracted to this vision of the beloved community at Metropolitan that looks like what Jesus was talking about but so rarely is to be found in the world of churches. (Indeed, the only church I know that pulls this off on quite this scale is Glide Memorial in San Francisco.)

From its beginning Metropolitan Interdenominational has welcomed LGBT persons to worship and welcomed them into its ministries to others. In this multiracial but predominantly African American congregation, the willingness to be open about sexuality and HIV/AIDS has made the church a magnet for people shunned by other congregations. Sometimes those churches have even used the talents of individuals with a wink and nod but without acceptance, as Sanders puts it, "It's all right for you to be here, just don't say anything, just play your little role. You can be in the choir, you can sit on the piano bench, but don't say you're gay."[21] This now 350-member church has been in HIV/AIDS work for more than thirty years and long enough to spawn the First Response Center, a primary-care clinic that provides HIV/AIDS testing, treatment, prevention services, and education.[22] Defined from the "outside," Metropolitan Interdenominational gets called the "gay church" and the "AIDS church," though less than it once did as attitudes have softened and as the church's record of ministering in Christ's name silences all but the most obtuse. Inside, however, the church is defined, not by differences, but by what members hold in common. Black History Month is not celebrated in February, nor is Gay Pride in June; instead, every corporate activity of the church underlines inclusion. Metropolitan's Core Values (LOVING, INCLUSIVE, GIVING, FELLOWSHIP, RECONCILING, SERVING, LIBERATING—each supported by scriptural warrant) all undergird the foundational messages of the living body, one of which is "Whosoever fellowships with us receives the acceptance and love of the church family."[23] Any day someone can walk into the church with a new kind of difference and be included in the body of Christ. Every Sunday that acceptance takes on flesh at the close of a fairly traditional worship service that features a choir, printed bulletins, classic hymns, use of the liturgical year, and readings from the Old and New Testaments and participatory liturgy when a giant fellowship circle is formed and everyone joins in singing:

We've come too far to turn back now;
By the grace of God we're gonna make it somehow.
Nobody knows the trouble we've seen;
We've come too far to turn back now.

For all the things that make Ed Sanders and Metropolitan Interdenominational unusual and clearly ahead of their time, they resemble most LGBT-affirming churches in one important respect. They were moved to response by the situation of a known person in their midst suffering in part because of sexuality. This is how change happens, according to the gay rights community, where it is known as "the power of one." It is hard to hate one person, whom you know well, who tells you he is gay, or she is lesbian. In the overwhelming number of Christian congregations in the South that have taken a stance for LGBT inclusion, the origin of the decision is a person or a couple, not a syllogism in a philosophical argument or a reference to Scripture. It is individuals with names like "Don" and "John" or "Victoria" and "Peggy," whose faces are known and who are loved as brothers and sisters, who make churches ask, "What would Jesus do?" and throw their doors open against the accumulated traditions and fears of centuries. There are, however, a minority of LGBT-affirming churches that start as gay-welcoming churches and more that start self-consciously as churches for gay and lesbian Christians and their families, and it is to one of these we now turn.

Covenant of the Cross is a congregation founded by the Reverend Greg Bullard in 2002 as an independent evangelical explicitly LGBT congregation for the middle Tennessee region. It is less traditional feeling than a Metropolitan Community church (the tradition in which Bullard was ordained) insofar as casual dress, praise and worship music, and a looser order of worship are the order of the day. Indeed, to walk into the services you might think you are in any of three hundred other contemporary evangelical churches in middle Tennessee until you notice two things. The first is who is seated with whom. The second is the content of the message. But before we get to these differences, let us start outside. Covenant of the Cross is physically located in an old two- or three-screen detached 1970s movie theater behind a limping strip mall in the town of Madison, twenty minutes north of downtown Nashville. When you step inside, the atmosphere changes dramatically. The interior has been attractively renovated for the church's use and the visitor is greeted again and again—not just by assigned greeters but by people who seem to have found a special church that they want to share.

I pick up a bulletin and choose a seat dead center in the middle of the action. I estimate the congregation this Sunday morning to number ninety-five adults and forty-five children with a healthy age spectrum. Though mostly white, there are black, Hispanic, and Asian worshippers, often in mixed-ethnicity family groupings. Later I am to learn from the pastor the extraordinary distances (up to ninety miles) that this congregation drives to be part of this fellowship. I also observe that not a few of the pews are packed with families with children. The appeal of this church is more and more obvious—what would it be like to be the child of two lesbian mothers in another evangelical church? School would not be a picnic either. There are also some grandmothers, making several pews a three-generation affair. Here, as we gather, the ordinary happy-to-see-you sociability of church is on display among members. It is, as Bullard told a reporter for *Out and About* (Nashville's LGBT newspaper) in 2007, a church that is clearly composed of much more than gay men and lesbian women. Bullard calculated that only 60 percent of his congregation was gay or lesbian. "The other 40 percent are children, [and people who are] straight, bisexual, asexual and those who have no clue about their sexuality," he said. "We are an affirming congregation. But not just to the GLBT community. We are 'people affirming,'"[24]The couple dyads, where people have come as couples, mostly are same-sex, and the feel of being the church is inescapably that of a close Christian congregation. So, too, are the activities that the church members undertake during the week. There is a chili challenge and game night coming up, a children's ministry workshop, and then there is the "financial facelift program" for individuals coming during the next month to help people get that part of their lives more under control.

If there are things that are strikingly similar to other healthy evangelical churches, there are real differences in the message at Covenant of the Cross reflected in its songs, in what one sees, and what one hears preached. To sum it up in a couple of words, it is unrelentingly people affirming as it seeks to offer worshippers the salvation of the great and magnanimous God of the universe. Greg Bullard and Covenant of the Cross do not need to beat people up to offer them new life in Jesus Christ. The messaging is subtle but consistent and starts with the work of the music ministry. God is magnified and worshiped without belittling the worshippers (who one supposes have heard enough misdirected personal sin talk to last several lifetimes). The opening words of the gathering song, "Hear the Sound," from the group All Sons and Daughters, serves as an example:

God of mercy, full of grace
You are forever, always forever
Slow to anger, rich in love
You are forever, always forever
We hear Your kingdom shout
And all Your praises reign
(Chorus)

So let the heavens roar
Echo across the ground
And as Your people sing of Your majesty
Lord hear the sound
Lord hear the sound[25]

Slow to anger, rich in love is the God that Covenant of the Cross sings and glorifies. Other songs and hymns sing of bringing "all that we are before the Lord" and echo Romans 8, promising that nothing can separate us from the love of God, explicitly singing that nothing means "nothing we've done, nothing we are." The best theology of Paul is used to underline the inseparable love of God in Christ Jesus for all God's children.

The message one sings at Covenant of the Cross is matched by symbols for one's eyes to take in. While making announcements Bullard picks up his crying two-year-old daughter, who broke into tears right after her other father, Brian Copeland, departed to take her older brother to Sunday school. There are no missed beats in the announcements or in the parenting; LGBT family life is celebrated. Bullard is at home with worshippers, with himself, and with his husband and his children. From the pastor to the ushers, musicians, and church officers, the language of the bodies in space is clear—we are Christian, accepted by God, by ourselves, and by each other.

Acceptance turns out to be a large part of the sermon for the day. Like most contemporary evangelical services, the Scripture and sermon points are projected on the screen. The title of the sermon is "Captive Captions," and it is based on 2 Corinthians 10:3–5: "For though we live in the world, we do not wage war as the world does. The weapons we fight with are not the weapons of the world. On the contrary, they have divine power to demolish strongholds. We demolish arguments and every pretension that sets itself up against the knowledge of God, and we take captive every thought to make it obedient to Christ" (NIV). Bullard's message is about the "stewardship of thoughts," about how our thinking can bring us closer to Jesus, rather than to worldly things.

It is Bullard's view that we dwell in self-abnegation. Discounting real compliments and blessings, we dwell on our faults and what is wrong—not on what God has done in our lives. He tells his congregation, "If we are following Jesus there is part of us that is constantly pushing on to perfection." But this does not mean that they are not good enough. He asks them to remember that "the blood of Jesus makes you worthy!" and in one of his many humorous asides he drives the point home: "I wouldn't vote for him, but Donald Trump's a man made in God's image—my job is to pray for him."[26]

Your mouth reveals your fruit, says Bullard, referencing Luke 6:43–45, and he applies the principle to Facebook, texts sent, and verbal asides to other people. We need to be careful whom we condemn. "If you are saying that someone, Hitler, Nixon, wasn't worthy of Jesus' redemption you're saying that Jesus made a mistake," Bullard says. Then, turning to the core text in 2 Corinthians, he argues that capturing your thoughts means tossing out what does not reveal Jesus. It is like guarding the gate to your mind, as when Psalm 101:3 says, "I will not set before my eyes anything that is base" (NRSV). There follows a critique of consumer cultural captivity that ends in the claim that "being in church today is a divine appointment. You are here today for a godly reason." Bullard's preaching is filled with spiritual aphorisms counseling perseverance:

> Faith doesn't make everything okay; faith makes it possible to get through anything.
>
> You are not the sin you committed.
>
> Speaking the truth in love matters.
>
> God is about making you a better person. If it's just about getting saved, you might as well get shot so you can go to heaven— but God is about making you a better person through sanctification in this world. Be changed by the renewing of your mind.

All of the Pauline acceptance theology is accompanied by a light and self-deprecating approach by the preacher. Bullard is transparent at points about his relationship with Brian and jokes about his past attention to a more svelte body with a line about a Ricky Martin T-shirt that he was able to wear before he was a father. The point of all this is to build a bridge with the lived experience of gay and lesbian people in the congregation about things that do not matter before God (even though they may have been told otherwise) so that he can get to the business of a new relationship with God and Jesus

Christ. The sermon ends in an altar call: "Do you want to become something different from what people have said you are all your life?"

Greg Bullard estimates that his congregation is 20 percent Church of Christ, 30 percent Pentecostal, and the remainder Baptist, Methodist, and other evangelical Protestants by denominational origin. They come from as far away as Bowling Green, Kentucky, to the north, Columbia, Tennessee, to the south and from McEwan and Cookeville, Tennessee, to the west and east, respectively. All those church traditions are used to altar calls and the promise of lives made new in God through Jesus Christ. On this Sunday morning in January, three people go forward and are prayed over while we sing the only old hymn of the morning:

> When peace, like a river, attendeth my way,
> when sorrows like sea billows roll;
> whatever my lot, thou hast taught me to say,
> It is well, it is well with my soul.

As I sing along I understand deep in my soul why these southern Christians have driven from such distances for this experience of worship and fellowship. Here the old-time religion of so many of their youths is carefully, joyfully mixed with total acceptance—by God, and by one another in Christ.

A 2:00 A.M. HOUR OF RECKONING FOR SOUTHERN CHURCHES

Two days later, on January 19, 2016, the Reverend Franklin Graham appeared on James Dobson's *Family Talk* program and spoke about the dangers, in his view, LGBT children and youth posed to Christian families and churches. Graham said, "I was talking to some Christians and they were talking about how they invited these gay children to come into their home and to come into the church and that they were wanting to influence them. And I thought to myself, they're not going to influence those kids; those kids are going to influence those parents' children."[27] Graham went on to warn Christians against thinking that they could fight Satan by "smiling and being real nice and loving." Instead, they needed to understand the "Enemy" and his intentions: "He wants to devour our homes. He wants to devour this nation and we have to be so careful who we let our kids hang out with. We have to be so careful who we let into the churches. You have immoral people who get into the churches and it begins to affect the others in the church and it is dangerous."[28]

As wounding as Franklin Graham's words were for people in the LGBT community and their allies, 2:00 A.M. Sunday, June 12, 2016, brought a new set of terrors compounded by some Christians. That was the hour when twenty-nine-year-old Omar Mateen attacked the Pulse Nightclub in Orlando, Florida, and carried out the worst mass shooting in U.S. history. Forty-nine people were killed and another fifty-three were wounded, making the incident both the worst single case of LGBT-directed violence in the nation's history and the largest terrorist incident since 9/11. The shooter, a security guard and self-described radical Muslim jihadist, chose Pulse because it was a well-known gay nightclub. His attack during Latin night directly targeted an especially young group of Latino/a gays and lesbians, many of whom were not out to their families. Indeed, the attack brought forth deep reflection about the role played by gay clubs in a homophobic society. Some members of the grieving LGBT community reflected on the sanctuary that clubs represented, a safe place that had been invaded. One United Methodist pastor from Chicago, the Reverend Britt Cox, told her flock: "I know for some of you, imagining a nightclub as a holy place is hard to grasp. Yet, for those of us in the Queer community, the dance floor at a gay bar is often more holy than any church has been to us. For me, it was the first place I held my wife's hand in a public place, that we danced as a couple on the dance floor, that we felt completely safe from harm and violence."[29]

There are gay bars in cities throughout the South, but in Orlando as elsewhere in the region it is not often clear where LGBT people can be fully out. Orlando is a city perched just on the edge of this book's definition of the South—where the cultural South and South Florida meet. The religious climate of Orlando is very southern, with an extra helping of Catholicism than would be characteristic of further north. And so it was that in the religious response to the Pulse shootings, southern Christianity in its diversity and (mostly) in its discomfort with sexuality played out as it has been described in this chapter. Across the nation, ministers and priests were learning about the calamity just in time for Sunday morning religious services. In California and Colorado evangelical churches there were some particularly ignorant and cruel clergy who claimed that they were glad the "earth has 50 less pedophiles today," but in the South, I can find only Pat Robertson expressing the wish that the Muslims and gays would kill one another off as far as he was concerned.[30] This kind of ugly homophobia was—thank God—absent from the southern pulpit, at least that day in the face of forty-nine dead and fifty-three wounded human beings. But the specificity of victims' ethnicity and sexuality also left Orlando's religious leaders (with some notable exceptions) and the southern clergy as a whole missing a chance to love as broadly as they might have. Even before the church services began in most of the nation, Russell Moore, president of the Southern Baptists' Ethics and Religious Liberty Commission, Tweeted to two million followers: "Christian, your gay or lesbian neighbor is probably really scared right now. Whatever our genuine disagreements, let's love and pray."[31] Albert Mohler, president of the Southern Baptist Theological Seminary, speaking the next day on *The Briefing*, his daily radio show and podcast, said, "Our response as biblically minded Christians should be first of all to respond with the absolute unconditional affirmation that every single human being, regardless of sexual behavior or sexual identity or sexual orientation, is made in the image of God."[32]

The Billy Graham Evangelistic Association sent a squad of chaplains in on the first available plane. They comforted the overwhelmed and despairing without regard to who they might be. One of the more moving things they managed to do was to quietly assemble in plastic frames color photographs of every one of the forty-nine dead and arrange them in a kind of impromptu memorial shrine.[33] Tuesday evening following the massacre, twenty-five hundred members of the Pentecostal and evangelical megachurches (including conservative mainline congregations) of the area gathered to pray for the victims. But the most moving part of the evening turned out to be when nondenominational pastor Joel Hunter of Northland, "a Church Distributed," said that he would like to cede the microphone and his speaking slot to Victoria Kirby York, national campaigns director of the National LGBTQ Task Force. York then urged compassion for LGBTQ young people who were "kicked out of their homes and churches" for being gay, leading to scandalously high suicide rates. York pled for audience members to pray for gay worshippers without requiring them to change whom they love. "There are too many people who don't think that God's love extends to them," she said.[34] She did not have to say where they might have gotten that idea.

The two largest LGBT-affirming churches in the downtown Orlando area near Pulse, Joy Metropolitan Community Church and First United Methodist, were primarily white, as were most of the other independent Catholic, mainline, Unitarian, and nondenominational churches farther out that provided what help they could in grief counseling, free funerals, and assistance. There was one church, however, Oasis Fellowship, a Pentecostal church connected with the Fellowship, associated with Bishop Yvette Flunder, a gospel singer, preacher, and advocate for full inclusion of LGBT people in the black church. In 2004, the Oasis became associated with the

Fellowship under their minister, the Reverend Brei Taylor, and now specializes in providing a Christian Family of Choice (as opposed to family of origin) to any who might come. Because of its role as the only church of color responding in the aftermath of the crisis from a prior commitment to the gay community, Oasis played a special role in connecting Latinos and Latinas to counselors and support in the community.

Aside from the gay-affirming churches and the Christians who, like Pastor Joel Hunter, led from their hearts in the crisis, the gay Christian activist Matthew Vines still heard a lot coming out of Christian leaders' mouths to upset him. At the bottom of it all was a pervasive sense that many Christians in their statements evidenced the belief that being gay and Christian were mutually exclusive. This was an especially deep comedown for Vines, who had, he wrote in an opinion article for *Time*, "gone from the happiness of celebrating a same-sex wedding in a Bible-belt church on a Saturday night, to the crushing disappointment of the next morning's news from Orlando." This was by his reasoning a reckoning time for Christian leaders to come to terms with the 50 percent of LGBT persons who are Christian. In the wake of comments that seemed to compartmentalize the categories gay and Christian, such as those heard from Moore, Mohler, and countless others, Vines had some advice:

> Unless you've long been a vocal advocate for LGBT people, you've likely contributed to that suffering—intentionally or not.
>
> Second, please mourn with us, and please do not erase the fact that the shooter targeted people for death because they were lesbian, gay, bisexual, and transgender. Lamenting only gun violence or terrorism but not the homophobic hatred that fueled them dishonors the courage that each of the victims displayed in living their lives openly in a society where that can still be a death sentence.[35]

And, Vines added, don't qualify your lamentation by saying that you disagree with someone's lifestyle but you don't want them to die. Now was the time for the sermon and actions that affirm.

Not every church in Orlando was converted to a new way of seeing LGBT victims by the Pulse massacre. Christ Church of Orlando was just five doors down from Pulse. On Sunday morning after the shootings, the nondenominational, multicultural church canceled worship services and assisted first responders. Members of the congregation delivered food, water and snacks to agencies such as the Drug Enforcement Agency, Florida Highway Patrol, Orlando Police Department, and others working the crime scene, becoming a sanctuary for many first responders, serving as a place to rehydrate and cool off from the intense summer heat. Christ Church of Orlando was proud of what it had done for the first responders, but the specificity of the victims' identity in the club two blocks away from the church is never mentioned on the church's own website or in stories about its philanthropy toward first responders.[36] On the other hand, Orlando's Episcopal cathedral's pastoral response looked different than it might have even two years earlier. On its website and social media, a word went out: "We at the Cathedral Church of St. Luke in Orlando, Florida, abhor the hateful violence perpetrated against LGBT persons in our city this past Sunday morning. We stand with the families and friends of the victims, and with the LGBT and Latin communities, praying for them daily, and for the healing of our city."[37]

There is still some of that us-them divided rhetoric that Matthew Vines points to, but the actions that followed put the faith talk to work. The cathedral performed a funeral for one of the Pulse victims, a noted gay activist, and hosted the Sunday after vigil "Prayers for Healing and Hope," including a message from Bishop Brewer on Sunday evening a week after the shooting. Members of the Orlando Gay Chorus, the Cathedral Choir, and other local choirs sang during the service just before a gathering of fifty thousand in nearby Lake Eola Park. What was remarkable was that this same church and bishop a year earlier were involved in a national news story about having refused to baptize the son of two gay men. The conservative bishop, Greg Brewer, did finally baptize the child at a main service and now was not ducking the reason the Pulse victims were targeted. He even acknowledged to the *Orlando Sentinel* that the downtown churches, including his own, had a history of being unwelcoming to gays, something he wanted to change.[38] Being a hospitable Christian had a cost of discipleship all its own.

Southern Christianity is at a crossroads, one such as it has not faced in half a century, about what loving one's neighbors requires. For many Christians like Graham, LGBT people are people whom one has a Christian license to hate as sinful and to exclude from one's fellowship as a pernicious influence on the young. For others like Sanders and Bullard, Christ's church is open to whosoever would follow him, without preconditions of any sort. In the meantime, for a surprisingly large number of younger southerners, there is a double standard, wherein LGBT people are colleagues and often friends at work and the targets of their preachers' enmity. And in the South, being the Christ-haunted place it is, there are also millions of LGBT Christians like Matthew Vines trying to make their way by faith on their own, with allies in churches, and amid the noise and dust wrought by culture warriors who believe them to be dangerous. The specter of the Pulse massacre hangs over too much of the Christian South, its lessons still to be absorbed.

CONCLUSION

Southern Christianities in Harmony and Conflict

For many months after the August 2005 Hurricane Katrina disaster, I saw a steady armada of church buses, trailers with crosses pulled by large Dodge Ram pickups, and rigs of every description transiting their way on Interstates 65 and 40 (part of my daily commute) to get to and from the Gulf Coast. Churches on the move, unorganized it seemed except by the power of faith and the need of others. That is what Christianity can do to people. It can cause you to take up a collection, give up your vacation, make you help total strangers. The months stretching through 2005–6 could be counted as some of southern Christians' (and others) finest hours in American history. They were part of healing other people's wounds from natural disaster and human neglect. That is how most southern Christians would like to see themselves most of the time—as people responding in faith, trying to make the world better.

A couple of years before Katrina hit, I visited Riverbend Maximum Security Prison in Nashville because I had been advised that my school's innovative program of educating select prisoners and divinity students in the same Monday night class was jeopardized by the warden's new ruling on religious groups. After some preliminaries, I was pleased to learn that our program was not in trouble, nor was it a problem that our mutual students were studying theology. Warden Ricky Bell pulled out his Bible from his metal desk and told my academic dean and me about his own faith, and then turned to expressing his appreciation. "These are men," I remember him saying, "they cannot leave, but these particular men have worked hard to come to terms with their lives and to be better people right here. An educational program like this gives them some way to continue to grow." Then he told us that the review of religious groups was put in place because so many of the groups simply came in to preach conversion to the incarcerated men, telling them they needed to turn their lives around without ever stopping to ask what the men needed or to establish relationships with them as individuals; it was all about what the churches wanted to do for them, the prisoners. From this I learned the unexpected humanity of a warden as a Christian and was reminded that faiths can also entice people to do things to and for other people without any thought given to what the recipients of those actions want, or their agency. Visiting a prisoner is an authentic Christian virtue. "I was in prison and you visited me," says Jesus in picturing the Last Judgment's separation of sheep from goats (Matt. 25:36, NRSV). Nowhere in Scripture does it say, "You visited me and foisted your beliefs on me."

A decade and more after Katrina as I finished this book, southern Christians were at the center of the most divisive social and political issues of the era. Some, in their roles as county clerks, have asserted a right of religious conscience not to issue marriage licenses to anyone whose (same-sex) marriages they believe are not "natural" and thus not of God. This came in acts of "interposition" to the Supreme Court's landmark ruling in *Obergefell v. Hodges* that the fundamental right to marry is guaranteed to same-sex couples by both the due process clause and the equal protection clause of the fourteenth amendment to the Constitution. Next came a spate of southern states "protecting" the public, particularly schoolchildren, from transgender youth and adults choosing the bathroom that they personally feel comfortable using, arguing instead that transgender persons must use the bathroom according to their gender at birth. (Once again views of God's "natural law" figure strongly behind the legislation.) In between these events, most of these states rejected accepting Syrian refugees, and every southern state has laws banning Sharia law under the guise of "preserving" religious freedom. In each case, legislatures have focused their fearful attentions on infinitesimally small populations in their states. The southern states, with their estimated 51,930 Muslims out of a population of more than 78 million Americans, spend enormous amounts of time worrying about an Islamic takeover. Meanwhile, this .06 percent of the southern population is a barely visible minority but a broad target for Islamophobia from Christians who do not know people outside their own faith group.[1] The transgender population in the South is of the same order of magnitude, if early population estimates are accurate.[2] Southern Christian legislators, with the strong assistance of groups like the Family Research Council, have wrapped themselves in the American flag and used evangelical and fundamentalist supporters to create a region where southern hospitality does not extend to people of embodied ethnic, sexual, or religious difference.

So which is it? How does this study of Christianities in the Now South square these two pictures? Is the dominant religious dimension of the South basically charitable and hospitable or morally judgmental and hostile to difference? The answer, as it were, is both and more. The Christianities encountered in this book are several, plural, and manifold. As such they fund the instinct to both help strangers and anathematize them. Many of the finest moral acts of southern Christians and their communities emerge out of the fact that everyone knows in their bones the stories of the good Samaritan, the prodigal son and the loving father, and the woman who gave her last coin. Southern Christians know what virtue looks like. But the family and what is "natural" are also powerful symbols that are held dear by most Christians in the South, and these symbols are easily manipulated to mean new things in new situations. Therefore, there is no simple claim, "Jesus would have us do what is right for our families," that will get total assent in the South among all Christians of all stripes if we mean that they will agree on both the sentiment (they will) and what it means (they won't). Indeed, the phrase is an almost meaningless tautology until a dialogue begins as to the meaning of the words "our" and "families." (Do they denote all families, Catholic families, just white families, or black families, too? What about Hispanic families? Immigrant families? LGBT families?) Then a similar dialogue would have to be undertaken about what "doing what is right" means. A lot of moral freight in Christian circles, and in the southern political circles that overlap with them, gets carried by ambiguous, noble-sounding rhetoric. Even harmonious-sounding Christian talk can mask a great deal of actual dissonance. For this reason, understanding the Christianities in their particularity seems more important than ever to me if we are to understand the place of religion in contemporary southern life.

When I was presenting a part of this book at a work-in-progress seminar, a bright history graduate student posed an incisive question. She asked, "What difference does it make that all these people are Christians and talking in Christian terms if they end up on such opposite sides of political questions?" In other words, might we bracket the religious rhetoric and just watch for political terms like liberty, equality, freedom, coercion, and control? After all, patriotism and religion are often fig leaves for baser motives. In the end, however, my studies and the time spent with southern Christians across the spectrum suggests that this substitution would be a mistake, for the faith-inflected fears, hopes, memories, and visions of liberation that are recorded in these pages are the primary language used by these diverse southern Christians. The variety of southern Christianities are bound together by a common set of stories—taken from the Bible—alongside experiences found in churches and society, which fund robust, sometimes bitter argument about how those stories and their lessons are applicable to this place and time. Sometimes we hear elaborate, textured harmonies. Other times, as in this moment of deep division among southern Christians about sexuality issues and personal freedom, we hear a near cacophony. Yet the thing we miss, if we turn this into pure political analysis by discarding the religious terms that diverse southern Christians use for their lives, values, motives, and aspirations, is the way that things are shaped and change happens in the largely Christian South.

A dear colleague of mine, the late professor Charles Cousar, told seminary students in a class we were teaching of his experience growing up in a conservative Chattanooga church setting during and after World War II. He said, "A bunch of segregationist Christians taught me the Bible, and the Bible taught me that segregation was wrong." Amid a tangled racial history, hurricanes, Supreme Court rulings, and new neighbors, the Christianities of the South have been generating transformations like this in individuals and churches for decades. The resources for such transformations in the Christianities of the Now South are both greater and more divergent than ever before. The faith-engendered conflicts wrought in individuals, families, churches, and communities are many, but I suspect that southern Christians would not have it any other way.

And so, we return to the theme with which this book began, hospitality. The overwhelmingly Christian South is composed of people who are divided in prayer; that is, they earnestly pray for starkly different outcomes at times. Still, this divided land of alternative Christianities is perhaps most united in wanting to be known for its Southern hospitality—a virtue that is both religious and cultural. Many, perhaps most, southern Christians have learned the New Testament verse from the Letter to the Hebrews, "Do not neglect to show hospitality to strangers, for by doing that some have entertained angels without knowing it" (Heb. 13:2, NRSV). If there is hope that these deeply committed and divided millions can transcend their fears and hostilities based in ethnicity, race, sexuality, and religious difference itself, it is that their commitment to hospitality requires that they extend themselves to strangers. That extension beyond self and clan is not perfect, and as in the Scriptures that southern Christians hold dear, hospitality beyond one's own is honored sometimes more in the breach than in practice. The lines of division are strong and reinforced by moralism and biblicism, but the resources for change, even reconciliation, come from the same sources, which demand that no one remain a stranger for long. Like rocks in a river, the Christianities of the contemporary South are still being shaped by their environment and by one another.

ACKNOWLEDGMENTS

More than for any other book I have written, my debts to others for this volume mounted quickly. The first people I need to acknowledge are the countless individuals at historic sites, churches, Christian colleges, reenactments, and public places like restaurants in each of the southern states who offered welcome, stories, and viewpoints for not much more than a respectful listening ear in return. I learned so much.

The fellow scholars and learned practitioners of religion I consulted in my travels also shaped how I thought about the culture and division of Christianities in the South. I conducted thoroughly enjoyable interviews with Willie Jennings, Ted Smith, Kate Bowler, Grant Wacker, Brooks Holifield, Alice Graham, Don Frampton, James Cox, Susan Turner, Daniel Schwartz, Michael Cowan, Chuck Campbell, Kathleen Flake, Pete Gathje, Andrew Thompson, Anne Apple, Ben McLeish, Billy Vaughn, David Forney, David Roebuck, John Portman, Laura Sugg, Luke Powery, Paul David Jones, Kenneth Robinson, Steve Haynes, Steve Montgomery, Will Willimon, Rod Dickson-Rishel, and Lee Ramsey. The astute reader will notice that not every interviewee is directly quoted in the text, but this book would not have been written without the way these gifted and thoughtful people shared of their experience and wisdom to help me see more and different things. Other such conversation partners about the project included Charles Strobel, Becca Stevens, Ed Loring, Murphy Davis, Edwin Sanders, Joe Pat Breen, Phil Breen, Tim Matovina, Tom Laney, Joe Pennel, Juan Floyd-Thomas, Melissa Snarr, Victor Judge, Ellen Armour, Phillis Sheppard, Dan Aleshire, Steve Land, and Forrest Harris.

I want to especially thank the many churches I visited that also put their services on the Internet. It is a gift to contemporary researchers who might, like me, visit a worship service in real time once to be able later to check their notes for verification and watch other weeks to compare services from week to week and season to season. One further observation about this treasure three clicks away: the confidence of the southern pulpit in its message and witness is astonishing.

I have friends and colleagues who read parts or the entirety of the manuscript. James Byrd, Dennis Dickerson, and Alexis Wells-Oghoghomeh at Vanderbilt are close colleagues and acute readers. I am also grateful to the members of the Vanderbilt Americanist History Seminar for commenting on chapter 4 in an earlier form. My good friends Guy Hicks and Phil Gehman read and commented on several early chapters and assured me that there was an audience for the book.

Vanderbilt University's Divinity School and the College of Arts and Science's History Department were my academic homes throughout the research and writing of this book, and I am grateful to Dean Emilie Townes and History chair Joel Harrington for their professional support and friendship. This book is also the second I have undertaken with the expert guidance of UNC Press senior editor Elaine Maisner, and I cannot express how fortunate I was to have a religion editor who also was attentive to southern culture. Elaine cares deeply about getting the story right, and it was a pleasure to pursue that end with her again. The rest of the UNC Press team I worked with, Jay Mazzocchi, Laura Jones Dooley, and Susan Garrett, raised the last 10 percent that makes all the difference to a first-rate professional experience for me.

Finally, this was more of a family effort than any other book I have done since I had the good fortune to begin its research on a yearlong sabbatical with my wife, Heidi, who was able to travel with me. Later on, she read every word of the manuscript with an eagle eye and a deep appreciation for how religion on the ground works. As fortune would have it, our son, Adam, became available to transcribe all the hours of interviews. I got splendid help, and he has gone on in the study of American religion in his own right. Our daughter, Julia, joined in by encouraging the project all along the way. I love you all, and I am grateful to have the best of help in bringing to light some of the surprising variety of Christianities in the South.

NOTES

Unless otherwise indicated, all Web addresses are accurate as of August 2017.

INTRODUCTION

1. John Egerton, *The Americanization of Dixie: The Southernization of America* (New York: Harper's Magazine Press, 1974); Grant Wacker, "Uneasy in Zion: Evangelicals in Postmodern Society," in *Evangelicalism and Modern America*, ed. George M. Marsden, 17–28 (Grand Rapids, Mich.: W. B. Eerdmans, 1984).

2. Two more recent books from the Religion by Region series help secure the case for continuing regional distinctiveness: Charles Reagan Wilson and Mark Silk, eds., *Religion and Public Life in the South: In the Evangelical Mode* (Walnut Creek, Calif.: AltaMira Press, 2005); and William D. Lindsey and Mark Silk, eds., *Religion and Public Life in the Southern Crossroads: Showdown States* (Walnut Creek, Calif.: AltaMira Press, 2005).

3. Warren Bird and Scott Thumma, "A New Decade of Megachurches—2011 Profile of Large Attendance Churches in the United States," Hartford Institute for Religion Research, November 22, 2011, http://hirr.hartsem.edu/megachurch/megachurch-2011 -summary-report.htm.

4. Aleksandra Sandstrom and Becka A. Alper, "Church Involvement Varies Widely among U.S. Christians," Pew Research Center, November 16, 2015, http://www .pewresearch.org/fact-tank/2015/11/16/church-involvement-varies-widely-among-u-s -christians/.

5. Michael Lipka, "Major U.S. Metropolitan Areas Differ in Their Religious Profiles," Pew Research Center, July 29, 2015, http://www.pewresearch.org/fact-tank/2015/07/29 /major-u-s-metropolitan-areas-differ-in-their-religious-profiles/.

6. Some of my excellent literary colleagues during these years of research and writing are found in these following well-thumbed volumes that convinced me I was not alone but, thank goodness, was working at a complementary angle: Bernadette Barton, *Pray the Gay Away: The Extraordinary Lives of Bible Belt Gays* (New York: New York University Press, 2012); John M. Coski, *The Confederate Battle Flag: America's Most Embattled Emblem* (Cambridge, Mass.: Belknap Press of Harvard University Press, 2005); David Fillingim, *Redneck Liberation: Country Music as Theology* (Macon, Ga.: Mercer University Press, 2003); David R. Goldfield, *Still Fighting the Civil War: The American South and Southern History*, updated ed. (Baton Rouge: Louisiana State University Press, 2013); Paul Harvey, *Freedom's Coming: Religious Culture and the Shaping of the South from the Civil War through the Civil*

Rights Era (Chapel Hill: University of North Carolina Press, 2005); Samuel S. Hill, Charles H. Lippy, and Charles Reagan Wilson, eds., *Encyclopedia of Religion in the South*, 2nd ed. (Macon, Ga.: Mercer University Press, 2005); E. Patrick Johnson, *Sweet Tea: Black Gay Men of the South* (Chapel Hill: University of North Carolina Press, 2008); Corrie E. Norman and Donald S. Armentrout, eds., *Religion in the Contemporary South: Changes, Continuities, and Contexts* (Knoxville: University of Tennessee Press, 2005); Beth Barton Schweiger and Donald G. Mathews, eds., *Religion in the American South: Protestants and Others in History and Culture* (Chapel Hill: University of North Carolina Press, 2004); Randall J. Stephens, *The Fire Spreads: Holiness and Pentecostalism in the American South* (Cambridge, Mass.: Harvard University Press, 2008); Tracy Thompson, *The New Mind of the South* (New York: Simon and Schuster, 2013); and Charles Reagan Wilson, *Flashes of a Southern Spirit: Meanings of the Spirit in the U.S. South* (Athens: University of Georgia Press, 2011).

7. Data derived from American Religious Identification Survey (ARIS) 2008, Principal Investigators: Barry A. Kosmin and Ariela Keysar. For more, see http://commons .trincoll.edu/aris/publications/2008-2/aris-2008-summary-report/.

8. See, e.g., Thomas A. Tweed, "Our Lady of Guadalupe Visits the Confederate Memorial," *Southern Cultures* 8 (Summer 2002): 72–93; Steven W. Ramey, "Temples and Beyond: Varieties of Hindu Experiences in the South," in *Religion in the Contemporary South: Changes, Continuities, and Contexts*, ed. Corrie Norman and Don Armentrout, 207–24 (Knoxville: University of Tennessee Press, 2005); and Jeff Wilson, *Dixie Dharma: Inside a Buddhist Temple in the American South* (Chapel Hill: University of North Carolina Press, 2012). In addition, David Goldfield, in *Region, Race and Cities: Interpreting the Urban South* (Baton Rouge: Louisiana State University Press, 1997), has a terrific chapter on "Jews, Blacks, and Southern Whites" that spells out the fraught relations of being Jewish in the South in a concise and historically elegant manner.

9. Samuel S. Hill, *Southern Churches in Crisis* (New York: Holt, Rinehart and Winston, 1967).

10. Erskine Clarke, *Dwelling Place: A Plantation Epic* (New Haven, Conn.: Yale University Press, 2005).

CHAPTER 1

1. John Beck, Aaron J. Randall, and Wendy Jean Frandsen, *Southern Culture: An Introduction*, 2nd ed. (Durham, N.C.: Carolina Academic Press, 2009).

2. David Hackett Fischer, *Albion's Seed: Four British Folkways in America* (New York: Oxford University Press, 1989), 613–17, 727–31.

3. Kim Severson, "S. Truett Cathy, Chick-fil-A Founder, Dies at 93," *New York Times*, September 8, 2014.

4. Ibid.

5. John B. Boles, "The Southern Way of Religion," *Virginia Quarterly Review* 75, no. (Spring 1999): 226.

6. "Religious Landscape Study," Pew Forum on Religion and Public Life, , http://www .pewforum.org/religious-landscape-study/.

7. Kendra Bailey Morris, "Fatback and Foie Gras: An Ode to My Southern Baptist Food Roots," Fatback and Foie Gras, May 26, 2010, http://fatbackandfoiegras.blogspot .com/2010/05/ode-to-my-southern-baptist-food-roots.html.

8. Ibid.

9. Wendy Ashley, "Obesity in the Body of Christ," SBCLife, January 2007, http://www
.sbclife.net/Articles/2007/01/sla8.

10. "History & Founders," Southern Foodways Alliance, https://www.southernfoodways
.org/about-us/history-founders/.

11. "Nashville Author John Egerton Dies" *Tennessean*, November 23, 2013.

12. John Egerton, *Speak Now against the Day: The Generation before the Civil Rights
Movement in the South* (New York: Alfred A. Knopf, 1994). Earlier, Egerton had
focused on why civil rights leaders had stayed in the South given their ambivalence
about the region in *A Mind to Stay Here; Profiles from the South* (New York:
Macmillan, 1970).

13. John Egerton, Ann Bleidt Egerton, and Al Clayton, *Southern Food: At Home, on the
Road, in History* (New York: Alfred A. Knopf, 1987).

14. Pew Forum, "Religious Landscape Study."

15. "Food Insecurity in the United States," Feeding America, map.feedingamerica.org
/county/2014/overall.

16. Hemant Mehta, "Tennessee Legislator Files Bill to Put 'In God We Trust'
on All License Plates," Friendly Atheist, January 12, 2017, http://www.patheos.com
/blogs/friendlyatheist/2017/01/12/tennessee-legislator-files-bill-to-put-in-god-we
-trust-on-all-license-plates/; "'In God We Trust' Plates Proposed by Ga. Legislators,"
Americans United for Separation of Church and State, January 2012, https://www
.au.org/church-state/january-2012-church-state/au-bulletin/%E2%80%98in-god
-we-trust%E2%80%99-plates-proposed-by-ga; Christine Vestal, "On Medicaid
Expansion, a Question of Math and Politics," July 8, 2015, Pew Charitable Trusts,
http://www.pewtrusts.org/en/research-and-analysis/blogs/stateline/2015/07/08
/on-medicaid-expansion-a-question-of-math-and-politics.

17. "Deterrence: States without the Death Penalty Have Had Consistently Lower
Murder Rates," Death Penalty Information Center, http://www.deathpenaltyinfo.org
/deterrence-states-without-death-penalty-have-had-consistently-lower-murder-rates.

18. Michele Reese, "Midtown Church Cited for Helping the Homeless," WREG.com,
November 7, 2013, http://wreg.com/2013/11/07/midtown-church-cited-for-helping
-the-homeless/.

19. "State Minimum Wages: 2017 Minimum Wage by State," National Conference
of State Legislatures, January 5, 2017, http://www.ncsl.org/research/labor-and
-employment/state-minimum-wage-chart.aspx.

20. On health clinics, see Jill M. Johnson, "Health Ministries and Local Churches,"
Ministry Matters, November 25, 2013, http://www.ministrymatters.com/all/entry/4476
/health-ministries-and-local-churches; and Dave Boucher and Holly Fletcher, "Beth
Harwell Creates Health Care Task Force; Critics Call It a 'Joke,'" *Tennessean*, April 12,
2016. On food banks, see Marisol Bello, "Food Banks Run Short as Federal Government
Hands Out Less," *USA Today*, September 8, 2012.

21. "History—More Than 3 Decades of Ministry," Society of St. Andrew, http://
endhunger.org/history/.

22. "Why Feed America First?," Feed America First, http://www.feedamericafirst
.com/why.

23. "News," Feed America First, http://www.feedamericafirst.com/news.

24. Charles F. Strobel, *Room in the Inn* (Nashville, Tenn.: Abingdon Press, 1992); "Room in the Inn Annual Report, 2013–2014," Room in the Inn, http://roomintheinn .org/sites/default/files/RITI-AnnualDashboard2014-v4.pdf.

25. "Who We Serve & How You Help," Room in the Inn, http://roomintheinn.org /shine-your-light/who-we-serve-how-you-help.

26. Pete Gathje, interview by author, Memphis, Tenn., November 19, 2013. Additional quotations in this chapter are from this interview.

27. Room in the Inn—Memphis, http://www.roomintheinn-memphis.org/.

28. Pete Gathje, "Manna House Volunteer Guide," Radical Hospitality, October 16, 2012, http://radical-hospitality.blogspot.com/2012/10/manna-house-volunteer-guide .html.

29. "Central Presbyterian Church," National Park Service, Atlanta, https://www.nps .gov/nr/travel/atlanta/cen.htm.

30. Tom Wilemon, "Uninsured Still Rely on Faith-Based Clinics Even after ACA," *Tennessean*, August 4, 2014, http://www.tennessean.com/story/news/health /2014/08/04/uninsured-still-rely-faith-based-clinics-even-aca/13604537/.

31. "Our Partners," Good Samaritan Clinic, http://goodsamaritansc.org/about-us /partners/.

32. "Story," Open Table Nashville, http://opentablenashville.org/story.

33. Ibid.

34. Dry Bones Rattling, https://drybonesrattling.wordpress.com/.

35. Dry Bones Rattling, "The State of the Dream and Why I Stopped Serving the Poor," January 18, 2016, https://drybonesrattling.wordpress.com/2016/01/18/ the-state-of-the-dream-and-why-i-stopped-serving-the-poor-3/.

36. G. K. Chesterton, *What I Saw in America* (1992), in *The Collected Works of G. K. Chesterton*, vol. 21 (San Francisco: Ignatius Press, 1990), 41.

37. Sidney E. Mead, "The 'Nation with the Soul of a Church,'" *Church History* 36, no. 3 (1967): 262–83.

38. Pew Forum, "Religious Landscape Study."

39. "Proper Charity," Gateway Rescue Mission, March 4, 2016, https://gatewaymission .org/proper-charity/.

40. Willie Jennings, interview by author, Durham, N.C., March 4, 2014.

41. See Mary McClintock Fulkerson, *Places of Redemption: Theology for a Worldly Church* (Oxford: Oxford University Press, 2007), for the deep factors at play that make true inclusion so exceptional in modern congregations.

42. Luke Powery, telephone interview by author, March 25, 2014.

43. David Roebuck, interview, Church of God (Cleveland, Tennessee) Archives, July 17, 2014.

44. Kate Bowler, interview by author, Durham, N.C., March 5, 2014.

45. Powery, interview.

46. *Obergefell et al. v. Hodges, Director, Ohio Department of Health, et al.*, 576 U.S. (2015).

47. WAFF 48 Digital Staff, "More Counties Issue Marriage Licenses," WAFF.com, February 10, 2015, http://www.waff.com/story/28070797/more-counties-issue -marriage-licenses.

48. "Womick Asks County Clerks to Ignore Supreme Court Ruling on Gay Marriage," *USA Today*, https://www.usatoday.com/story/news/2015/07/28

/state-rep-asks-county-clerks-to-ignore-scotus-ruling-on-gay-marriage/30772805/; Scott Broden and Michelle Willard, "Womick Seeks Haslam Impeachment over Gay Marriage," *Daily News Journal* (Murfreesboro, Tenn.), July 14, 2015.

49. Jonathan M. Katz, "North Carolina Allows Officials to Refuse to Perform Gay Marriages," *Boston Globe*, June 12, 2015.

50. Melanie Eversley, "Kim Davis Is No Rosa Parks, Critics Say," *USA Today*, September 10, 2015.

51. Alan Rappeport, "Mike Huckabee (Not Ted Cruz) Captures Spotlight at Kim Davis Event," First Draft, New York Times, September 8, 2015, http://www.nytimes.com/politics/first-draft/2015/09/08/mike-huckabee-captures-spotlight-not-ted-cruz-at-kim-davis-event/.

CHAPTER 2

1. William Faulkner, *Requiem for a Nun* (1951; New York: Vintage Books, 2012), 73.

2. John Bell Hood, *Advance and Retreat: Personal Experiences in the United States and Confederate States Armies* (New Orleans, La.: Published for the Hood Orphan Memorial Fund [by] G. T. Beauregard, 1880), 280–93.

3. "Spring Hill Gallery," Civil War Trust, https://www.civilwar.org/learn/galleries/spring-hill.

4. "Ten Facts: The Battle of Franklin," Civil War Trust, https://www.civilwar.org/learn/articles/10-facts-battle-franklin; James M. McPherson, *Battle Cry of Freedom: The Civil War Era* (New York: Oxford University Press, 1988), 812.

5. Our guide seemed to believe that economic reparations for slavery were tried and proved wanting. The audacity of the plan and the all-too-predictable failure to implement it is quite a different story. See Henry Louis Gates Jr., "The Truth behind '40 Acres and a Mule," Root, January 7, 2013, http://www.theroot.com/the-truth-behind-40-acres-and-a-mule-1790894780.

6. "Charge to the Sons of Confederate Veterans," Sons of Confederate Veterans, http://www.scv.org/new.

7. Edward Alfred Pollard, *The Lost Cause: A New Southern History of the War of the Confederates* (New York: E. B. Treat, 1866).

8. Charles Reagan Wilson, *Baptized in Blood: The Religion of the Lost Cause, 1865–1920* (Athens: University of Georgia Press, 2009), 10.

9. Ibid., 11.

10. Indeed, after Wilson, scholars have debated whether other groups like the United Daughters of the Confederacy and ladies' memorial associations may have been more effective promoters of the Lost Cause civil religion. Arthur Remillard, *Southern Civil Religions: Imagining the Good Society in the Post-Reconstruction Era* (Athens: University of Georgia Press, 2011), has capably argued that the Lost Cause was just one civil religion competing for guarantor of social unity in the South. See also Karen L. Cox, *Dixie's Daughters: The United Daughters of the Confederacy and the Preservation of Confederate Culture* (Gainesville: University Press of Florida, 2003); and Caroline E. Janney, *Burying the Dead but Not the Past: Ladies' Memorial Associations and the Lost Cause* (Chapel Hill: University of North Carolina Press, 2008).

11. Quoted in Wilson, *Baptized in Blood*, 25.

12. For an elegant synopsis of how the casus belli were all about defending slavery to southern secessionists in their own minds, see Ta-Nehisi Coates, "What This Cruel War Was Over," Atlantic, June 22, 2015, http://www.theatlantic.com/politics /archive/2015/06/what-this-cruel-war-was-over/396482/.

13. The best guide to the vexed question of the history and meaning of black Confederates is Kevin M. Levin, "The Myth of the Black Confederate Soldier," Daily Beast, August 8, 2015, http://www.thedailybeast.com/articles/2015/08/08/the-myth -of-the-black-confederate-soldier.html; Levin is writing to respond both to historians like John Stauffer and to even more exaggerated claims of neo-Confederate authors. See Stauffer's "Yes, There Were Black Confederates. Here's Why," Root, January 20, 2015, http://www.theroot.com/yes-there-were-black-confederates-here-s-why-1790858546.

14. "'Stonewall' Jackson and His Presbyterian Journey," Presbyterian College Blue Notes," February 1, 2013, https://www.presby.edu/archives-blog/2013/02/01 /stonewall-jackson/.

15. Ben Cleary, "The Death of Jackson," Opinionator, New York Times, May 3, 2015, http://opinionator.blogs.nytimes.com/2013/05/03/the-death-of-jackson/.

16. Thomas Kidd, "'An Army of the Living God': Stonewall Jackson's Death and Southern Memory," Anxious Bench, May 7, 2013, http://www.patheos.com/blogs /anxiousbench/2013/05/an-army-of-the-living-god-stonewall-jackson-death-and -southern-memory/.

17. H. Rondel Rumburg, ed., Chaplain's Handbook: Sons of Confederate Veterans (Columbia, Tenn.: Sons of Confederate Veterans, 2005).

18. See Gardiner H. Shattuck, A Shield and Hiding Place: The Religious Life of the Civil War Armies (Macon, Ga.: Mercer University Press, 1987).

19. "Chaplains' Corps Chronicles: June 2015," SCV Chaplain-in-Chief, http:// chaplain-in-chief.com/custom3_1.html.

20. For a detailed history of this position, see Euan Hague and Edward H. Sebesta, "The U.S. Civil War as a Theological War: Neo-Confederacy, Christian Nationalism, and Theology," in Neo-Confederacy: A Critical Introduction, ed. Euan Hague, Edward H. Sebesta, and Heidi Beirich, 50–74 (Austin: University of Texas Press, 2008).

21. "Ministering since 1979," Re-Enactor's Missions for Jesus Christ, http://www.rmjc .org/33-years-of-ministry.

22. "Sam Davis," American Civil War Story, http://www.americancivilwarstory.com /sam-davis.html.

23. "Sons of Confederate Veterans in Its Own Civil War," Southern Poverty Law Center, Intelligence Report, March 5, 2002, http://www.splcenter.org/get-informed /intelligence-report/browse-all-issues/2002/spring/a-house-divided.

24. "Battleflag Resolution from Anderson Reunion," September 3, 2010, http://www .scv.org/pdf/2010BattleFlagResolution.pdf.

25. Russell Moore, "The Cross and the Confederate Flag," June 19, 2015, http://www .russellmoore.com/2015/06/19/the-cross-and-the-confederate-flag/.

26. Sari Horwitz et al., "What We Know So Far about Charleston Church Shooting Suspect Dylann Roof," Washington Post, June 20, 2015.

27. Frances Robles, "Dylann Roof Photos and a Manifesto Are Posted on Website," New York Times, June 20, 2015. "Council of Conservative Citizens," Southern Poverty

Law Center, http://www.splcenter.org/get-informed/intelligence-files/groups/council -of-conservative-citizens.

28. Peter Holley and DeNeen L. Brown, "Woman Takes Down Confederate Flag in Front of South Carolina Statehouse," *Washington Post*, June 27, 2015.

29. Brad Paisley, LL Cool J, and Lee Thomas Miller, "Accidental Racist" (song), 2013.

30. Lilly Workneh, "Starbucks Wants Employees to Start Conversations about Race with Customers," Huffington Post, March 17, 2015, http://www.huffingtonpost.com /2015/03/17/starbucks-race-together-c_n_6884100.html; Whitney Filloon, "Starbucks Nixes Its Terrible 'Race Together' Cup-Writing Campaign," Eater, May 22, 2015, http://www.eater.com/2015/3/22/8272697/starbucks-race-together-cup-writing- campaign-ended.

31. "History of Juneteenth," Juneteenth.com, http://www.juneteenth.com/history.htm.

32. Moore, "Cross and Confederate Flag."

33. "Americans Are 'Infected' with Country's 'Legacy of Racial Inequality,'" Equal Justice Initiative, https://eji.org/videos/americans-infected-by-legacy-racial-inequality.

34. Amy Steele, "#CharlestonShooting: 'Hood Blacks, Good Blacks, He Just Saw Blacks,'" Rhetoric, Race, and Religion, June 20, 2015, http://www.patheos.com/blogs /rhetoricraceandreligion/2015/06/charlestonshooting-hood-blacks-good-blacks-he-just -saw-blacks.html.

35. Khushbu Shah and Eliott C. McLaughlin, "Your Creator . . . He's Coming for You," CNN.com, January 11, 2017, http://www.cnn.com/2017/01/11/us/dylann-roof-sentencing /index.html.

36. "John Grisham, Greg Iles and Kathryn Stocket Lead Charge to Remove Confederate Flag in Mississippi," Writers Write, August 18, 2015, http://www.writerswrite.com/john -grisham-greg-iles-and-kathryn-stocket-lead-charge-81820151.

CHAPTER 3

1. Dennis Covington, *Salvation on Sand Mountain: Snake Handling and Redemption in Southern Appalachia* (Reading, Mass.: Addison-Wesley, 1995).

2. Kevin Hardy and Mary Helen Montgomery, "Charges against Serpent-Handling Tennessee Pastor Dismissed," Timesfreepress.com (Chattanooga, Tenn.), January 8, 2014, http://www.timesfreepress.com/news/2014/jan/08/charges-against-tennessee -serpent-handling-pastor-/128545/.

3. Andrew Hamblin, video interview, http://www.tennessean.com/viewart/20140112 /NEWS06/301120062/TN-snake-handling-pastor-won-t-get-53-serpents-back, accessed January 24, 2014 (discontinued).

4. The notoriously colorful A. J. Tomlinson suggested that mountain nonbelievers brought the first serpents to a Pentecostal service to try and point out the folly of the believers' faith in a literal restoration of biblical gifts. What was meant in scorn was taken according to this account as a challenge to faith and then became a cornerstone of demonstrating the depth of one's faith. Homer A. Tomlinson, *"It Came to Pass in Those Days": The Shout of a King* (Queens Village, N.Y.: Church of God, U.S.A. Headquarters, 1968), 41. See also David L. Kimbrough, *Taking Up Serpents: Snake Handlers of Eastern Kentucky* (Chapel Hill: University of North Carolina Press, 1995), 39–48; Randall J. Stephens, *The Fire Spreads: Holiness and*

Pentecostalism in the American South (Cambridge, Mass.: Harvard University Press, 2008), 251–54.

5. Hamblin, video interview.

6. Ralph W. Hood, "Serpent-Handling Sects," in *Encyclopedia of Christianity in the United States*, ed. George Thomas Kurian and Mark A. Lamport, 2081 (Lanham, Md.: Rowman and Littlefield, 2016).

7. For early history and theological disputes, see Michael J. McVicar, "Take Away the Serpents from Us: The Sign of Serpent Handling and the Development of Southern Pentecostalism," *Journal of Southern Religion* 15 (2013): http://jsr.fsu.edu/issues/vol15 /mcvicar.html. See also Kimbrough, *Taking Up Serpents*; Jimmy Morrow and Ralph W. Hood, *Handling Serpents: Pastor Jimmy Morrow's Narrative History of His Appalachian Jesus' Name Tradition* (Macon, Ga.: Mercer University Press, 2005); and Thomas G. Burton, *Serpent-Handling Believers* (Knoxville: University of Tennessee Press, 1993).

8. Charles Darwin, *The Life and Letters of Charles Darwin, Including an Autobiographical Chapter*, vol. 2 (New York: D. Appleton, 1888), 105.

9. Samuel S. Hill, *Southern Churches in Crisis* (New York: Holt, Rinehart and Winston, 1967); Samuel S. Hill, *Religion and the Solid South* (Nashville, Tenn.: Abingdon Press, 1972); Samuel S. Hill, ed., *Religion in the Southern States: A Historical Study* (Macon, Ga.: Mercer University Press, 1983); Kenneth Cauthen, *I Don't Care What the Bible Says: An Interpretation of the South* (Macon, Ga.: Mercer University Press, 2003); John Lee Eighmy, *Churches in Cultural Captivity: A History of the Social Attitudes of Southern Baptists* (Knoxville: University of Tennessee Press, 1972).

10. Donald G. Mathews, *Religion in the Old South* (Chicago: University of Chicago Press, 1977); Bertram Wyatt-Brown, *Southern Honor: Ethics and Behavior in the Old South* (New York: Oxford University Press, 1982); Bertram Wyatt-Brown, *Honor and Violence in the Old South* (New York: Oxford University Press, 1986); Christine Leigh Heyrman, *Southern Cross: The Beginnings of the Bible Belt* (Chapel Hill: University of North Carolina Press, 1997).

11. Heyrman, *Southern Cross*, 256.

12. Stephens, *Fire Spreads*, 4.

13. Paul Keith Conkin, *Cane Ridge, America's Pentecost* (Madison: University of Wisconsin Press, 1990).

14. James Leo Garrett, *Baptist Theology: A Four-Century Study* (Macon, Ga.: Mercer University Press, 2009), 213–14.

15. T. H. L. Parker, *Calvin: An Introduction to His Thought* (Louisville, Ky.: Westminster /John Knox Press, 1995), 78–86.

16. John Wesley, *A Plain Account of Christian Perfection*, 36th ed. (New York: Carlton and Lanahan, 1870).

17. Edith L. Blumhofer, "Holiness Movement," in *Encyclopedia of Religion in the South*, 2nd ed., ed. Samuel S. Hill, Charles H. Lippy, and Charles Reagan Wilson, 379–82 (Macon, Ga.: Mercer University Press, 2005).

18. For an excellent discussion of how newspapers spread the word even more effectively than preachers, see Randall J. Stephens, "'There Is Magic in Print': The Holiness-Pentecostal Press and the Origins of Southern Pentecostalism," in *Southern Crossroads: Perspectives on Religion and Culture*, ed. Walter H. Conser and Rodger M. Payne, 194–230 (Lexington: University Press of Kentucky, 2008).

19. "Weird Babel of Tongues. New Sect of Fanatics Is Breaking Loose. Wild Scene Last Night on Azusa Street. Gurgle of Wordless Talk by a Sister," *Los Angeles Times*, 18 April 1906.

20. Marne L. Campbell, "'The Newest Religious Sect Has Started in Los Angeles': Race, Class, Ethnicity, and the Origins of the Pentecostal Movement, 1906–1913," *Journal of African American History* 95, no. 1 (2010): 1–25.

21. "Women with Men Embrace: Whites and Blacks Mix in a Religious Frenzy," *Los Angeles Times*, September 3, 1906.

22. A. J. Tomlinson, as quoted in Stephens, *Fire Spreads*, 227.

23. *Bridegroom's Messenger*, October 1, 1907, 2.

24. Stephens, *Fire Spreads*, 2008, 228.

25. Grant Wacker, *Heaven Below: Early Pentecostals and American Culture* (Cambridge, Mass.: Harvard University Press, 2001), 268–69.

26. David Roebuck, interview by author, Cleveland, Tenn., July 17, 2014.

27. Chris Tomlin, Jesse Reeves, Jonas Myrin, and Matt Redman, "Our God" (song), 2010.

28. Henry Seeley, Joth Hunt, and Liz Webber, "The Anthem" (song), 2007.

29. Jason Clayborn, Gabrielle Hatcher, and Hezekiah Walker, "Better" (song), 2016.

30. "Spirit and Power—A 10-Country Survey of Pentecostals," Pew Research Center, October 5, 2006, http://www.pewforum.org/2006/10/05/spirit-and-power/.

31. See Charles Reagan Wilson and Mark Silk, eds., *Religion and Public Life in the South: In the Evangelical Mode* (Walnut Creek, Calif.: AltaMira Press, 2005), 56. See also William D. Lindsey and Mark Silk, eds., *Religion and Public Life in the Southern Crossroads: Showdown States* (Walnut Creek, Calif.: AltaMira Press, 2005), 25. The only state where Pentecostals and Holiness adherents rise above this general trend is in West Virginia, where they account for 11.5 percent of religious adherents.

CHAPTER 4

1. "Women in State Legislatures 2017," CAWP, http://www.cawp.rutgers.edu/women-state-legislature-2017; "State by State Information," CAWP, http://www.cawp.rutgers.edu/state-by-state.

2. Richard Fausset, "For Alabama Chief Justice, Soldiering in Name of God Is Nothing New," *New York Times*, February 9, 2015.

3. For instance, of the 396 members of the Mobile Bar Association surveyed before the 2012 election, only 3 deemed Moore "best qualified to serve." "Mobile Baldwin Alabama Politics," Mobile Bay Times, http://www.mobilebaytimes.com/roundup021012.html.

4. Joseph J. Ellis, *American Sphinx: The Character of Thomas Jefferson* (New York: Alfred A. Knopf, 1997).

5. Fausset, "Alabama Chief Justice."

6. Ibid.

7. Alabama Chief Justice Roy S. Moore to Governor Robert Bentley, January 27, 2015, available at media.al.com/news_impact/other/Read%20Chief%20Justice%20Moore%20letter.pdf.

8. For instance, the influential pastor Matthew Trewhella writes, "There are only three reasons for open defiance to the higher civil authority. First, they are to oppose and

resist any laws or edicts from the higher authority that contravene—violate, oppose, or contradict—the law or Word of God. Second, they are to protect the person and property of those who reside within their jurisdiction from any unjust or immoral laws or actions by the higher authority. Third, they are not to implement any laws or decrees made by the higher authority that violate the U.S. Constitution or their state constitution, and if necessary, resist them." See Trewhella, "If SCOTUS Mandates Same-Sex Marriage, Must States Follow Suit?," CNS News, June 22, 2015, http://www.cnsnews.com/commentary/matthew-trewhella/if-scotus-mandates-same-sex-marriage-must-states-follow-suit. Another advocate working along these lines is Mathew D. Staver, the founder and chairman of Liberty Counsel, the legal group that provided most of the legal support for the county clerks who refused to issue same-sex (or any) marriage licenses in the wake of the U.S. Supreme Court's June 2015 ruling.

9. "Jefferson's Gravestone," Monticello, https://www.monticello.org/site/research-and-collections/jeffersons-gravestone.

10. Jay T. Robertson, assistant professor of Christian Studies, School of Christian Studies, University of Mobile, offers a fairly typical reading of Galatians 5:1–15 in the Alabama Baptist. See more at http://www.thealabamabaptist.org/print-edition-article-detail.php?id_art=11486&pricat_art=5#sthash.E9RVehOS.dpuf "The Alabama Baptist—A Resource for Christian Living," accessed September 1, 2015, http://www.thealabamabaptist.org/print-edition-article-detail.php?id_art=11486&pricat_art=5 (discontinued).

11. Mark Berman, "Alabama Supreme Court Chief Justice Roy Moore Suspended for Defiance over Same-Sex Marriage," *Washington Post*, September 30, 2016.

12. Jay Reeves, "Churches Speak out against Alabama Immigration Law," Tuscaloosa News.com, June 18, 2011, http://www.tuscaloosanews.com/news/20110618/churches-speak-out-against-alabama-immigration-law.

13. Ibid.

14. Quoted in Edward B. Arroyo and Sue Weishar, "That 'Merciless Law': The Faith Response to Alabama's HB 56," Jesuit Social Research Institute, *Just South Quarterly*, Winter 2011, 1–3.

15. Greg Garrison, "United Methodist Bishop Will Willimon Calls Alabama Immigration Law Meanest in Nation," AL.com, June 15, 2011, http://blog.al.com/spotnews/2011/06/united_methodist_bishop_will_w.html.

16. "Forty-eight years ago, while sitting in a Birmingham jail cell, Dr. Martin Luther King Jr. wrote that, just as Christians have a moral duty to obey just laws, they also have a moral duty to disobey unjust ones. We are a group of United Methodist ministers from all across the state of Alabama who believe that HB 56 is an unjust law." William H. Willimon, "An Open Letter on Immigration," Day1.org, June 14, 2011, http://ht.ly/5hvSJ.

17. Kim Chandler, "Alabama House Passes Arizona-Style Immigration Law," *Birmingham News*, April 5, 2011.

18. *Parsley v. Bennet*, Complaint for Declaratory and Injunctive Relief, CV-ll-S-2736-NE.

19. Ibid.

20. Ibid.

21. "Alabama Citizens for Constitutional Reform Honor Bishop Parsley," *Alabama Episcopalian*, November–December 2011, 20.

22. William Willimon, interview by author, Durham, N.C., March 4, 2014.

23. William H. Willimon, *Bishop: The Art of Questioning Authority by an Authority in Question* (Nashville, Tenn.: Abingdon, 2012), 72–73.

24. Ibid., 75, quoting the Theological Declaration of Barmen, in *Book of Confessions: Study Edition* (Louisville, Ky.: Geneva Press, 1996), 311.

25. Ibid., 68.

26. Michele Reese, "Midtown Church Cited for Helping the Homeless," WREG.com, November 7, 2013, http://wreg.com/2013/11/07/midtown-church-cited-for-helping-the-homeless/.

27. National Coalition for the Homeless, *Share No More: The Criminalization of Efforts to Feed People in Need* (Washington, D.C.: National Coalition for the Homeless, October 2014).

28. Lerone Bennett, *What Manner of Man: A Biography of Martin Luther King, Jr* (Chicago: Johnson, 1964), 55–86.

29. "Why We Are Here Today," NAACP of North Carolina, April 29, 2013, http://carolinajustice.typepad.com/ncnaacp/2013/05/why-we-are-here-today.html.

30. Ibid.

31. Herman Schwartz, "One Party System: What Total Republican Control of a State Really Means," Reuters Blogs, August 19, 2015, http://blogs.reuters.com/great-debate/2015/08/19/one-party-system-what-total-republican-control-of-a-state-really-means/; Ben Jealous, "Moral Mondays: A Model Grassroots Movement," Huffington Post, June 14, 2013, http://www.huffingtonpost.com/benjamin-todd-jealous/moral-mondays-a-model-gra_b_3441695.html.

32. Courtney Ritter, as reported in Ari Berman, "North Carolina's Moral Mondays," Nation, July 17, 2013, http://www.thenation.com/article/175328/north-carolinas-moral-mondays#.

33. Willie Jennings, interview by author, Durham, N.C., March 3, 2014.

34. Georgia Parke, "Youth Takes on Moral Monday Movement," Chronicle, September 17, 2013, http://www.dukechronicle.com/article/2013/09/youth-takes-moral-monday-movement.

35. "In North Carolina, 'Moral Mondays' a Day for Protest," NPR, June 23, 2013, http://www.npr.org/templates/story/story.php?storyId=194945099.

36. Rev. Dr. William Barber II, "We Are in a Crisis—a Moral Crisis," Sojourners, May 13, 2014, https://sojo.net/articles/faith-action/we-are-crisis-moral-crisis.

37. Ibid.

38. Rev. Dr. William J. Barber II and Barbara Zelter, *Forward Together: A Moral Message for the Nation* (Saint Louis, Mo.: Chalice Press, 2014), 179.

39. The Forward Together movement's DNA is religious, but there is some evidence that not every religious leader has been prepared to defend its prophetic premises on scriptural grounds, so a lectionary with core biblical texts, along with theological reflections on those texts for use with congregations, was produced in downloadable format. In the lectionary Rodney Sadler, William Turner, and Peter Wherry provide reflections on Genesis 1:26–27 (made in image of God), 1 Samuel 8:11–17 (on the need for prophets to balance kingly or governmental power), Isaiah 1:10–17 (what God calls for from believing communities), Matthew 25:31–46 ("as you have treated the least of

these"), and Acts 2:43–47 (an example of a just and diverse community). See "'Forward Together' Lectionary: Wrestling with the Crises in our State through Scriptural and Theological Lenses," Democracy North Carolina, https://democracync.org/resources /forward-together-lectionary/.

40. Anne Blythe, "NC NAACP Leader William Barber Stepping Down to Help National Effort on Poverty," *(Raleigh) News and Observer*, May 11, 2017.

CHAPTER 5

1. Sheri Fink, "Strained by Katrina, a Hospital Faced Deadly Choices," *New York Times*, August 25, 2009.

2. "President Arrives in Alabama, Briefed on Hurricane Katrina," White House press release, September 2, 2005, available at http://georgewbush-whitehouse.archives.gov /news/releases/2005/09/20050902-2.html.

3. Chris Joyner, "Biloxi Church Fights Storm, Feeds the People after Katrina," *USA Today*, August 29, 2010.

4. Michael Cowan, interview by author, New Orleans, La., April 7, 2014. Additional quotations in this chapter are from this interview.

5. "Eugenia," interview by author, New Orleans, La., April 8, 2014. Additional details from Eugenia's story besides her name, including her neighborhood, church, and place of work, have been expurgated to preserve anonymity. Additional quotations in this chapter are from this interview.

6. Samuel G. Freedman, "Long, Slow Return for Black Churches in New Orleans," *New York Times*, August 27, 2010.

7. Urban League of Greater New Orleans, *State of Black New Orleans: Ten Years Post-Katrina* (New Orleans, La.: Urban League of Greater New Orleans, 2015), available at http://urbanleaguela.org/ul/wp-content/uploads/2015/08/StateofBlackNewOrleans_ TenYearsPostKatrina.pdf.

8. Don Frampton, interview by author, New Orleans, La., April 7, 2014. Additional quotations in this chapter are from this interview.

9. Since Calvin, Reformed thinkers posit that the Law has three uses: the elenctic or pedagogical use (driving sinners to despair of their righteousness); the civil use (curbing evil and injustice in society); and the didactic or normative use (guiding believers in a life of grateful obedience).

10. Ben McLeish, interview by author, New Orleans, La., April 7, 1014.

11. McLeish is actually quoting Tony Campolo's paraphrase of Augustine. Those who cannot find those words in the Augustinian corpus might take comfort in the quotation from a sermon upon which it seems to be based, "Let us honor her [the church], because she is the bride of so great a Lord. And what am I to say? Great and unheard of is the bridegroom's gracious generosity; he found her a whore, he made her a virgin. She mustn't deny that she was once a whore, or she may forget the kindness and mercy of her liberator." Augustine, *Sermon 213.* Augustine.

12. Michelle Alexander, *The New Jim Crow: Mass Incarceration in the Age of Colorblindness* (New York: New Press, 2010).

13. Saul David Alinsky, *Rules for Radicals: A Practical Primer for Realistic Radicals* (New York: Random House, 1971).

14. Daniel Schwartz, interview by author, New Orleans, La., April 7, 2014.

15. Cindy Chang, "Louisiana Is the World's Prison Capital," NOLA.com, May 13, 2012, http://www.nola.com/crime/index.ssf/2012/05/louisiana_is_the_worlds_prison .html. The comparison figures for incarceration per 100,000 residents are telling: Louisiana 1,619, United States 730, Russia 525, Rwanda 450, Iran 333, China 122, Afghanistan 62.

CHAPTER 6

1. Susan Turner and James Cox, interview by author, East Biloxi, Miss., April 10, 2014. Additional quotations in this chapter are from this interview.

2. "'ABC's Extreme Makeover' Winner Buried," WAPT.com, December 27, 2009, http://www.wapt.com/-ABC-s-Extreme-Makeover-Winner-Buried/5998042.

3. One reason that Susan Turner and James Cox did not know the names of the congregations that sent so many volunteers to the Biloxi area is because this work is managed by Back Bay Mission, a United Church of Christ mission founded ninety-three years ago to meet health, education, and, later, housing needs of residents. Two seminaries—Eden and Chicago Theological—have longstanding programs with the mission that have led to a continuous presence whether the cities along the coast have been booming, in a downturn, or recovering from periodic storms. See http://www .thebackbaymission.org/.

4. U.S. House of Representatives, *A Failure of Initiative: Final Report of the Select Bipartisan Committee to Investigate the Preparation for and Response to Hurricane Katrina*, H. Rept. 109-377, February 2006. Desiree Evans, Chris Kromm, and Sue Sturgis, *Faith in the Gulf: Lessons from the Religious Response to Hurricane Katrina* (Durham, N.C.: Institute for Southern Studies, 2008), 7.

5. William Perkins, "Mississippi Continues Recovery," Baptist Message, September 4, 2006, http://www.baptistmessage.com/node/2868, accessed May 31, 2015 (discontinued).

6. Ben McLeish, interview by author, New Orleans, La., April 7, 2014. Additional quotations in this chapter are from this interview.

7. Michael Cowan, interview by author, New Orleans, La., April 7, 2014. Additional quotations in this chapter are from this interview.

8. Rod Dickson-Rishel, interview by author, Long Beach, Miss., April 10, 2014.

9. Steve Corbett et al., *When Helping Hurts: How to Alleviate Poverty without Hurting the Poor . . . and Yourself,* new ed. (Chicago: Moody, 2014). Another popular guide along these lines in evangelical circles is Robert D. Lupton, *Toxic Charity: How Churches and Charities Hurt Those They Help (and How to Reverse It)* (New York: HarperOne, 2011).

10. Alice Graham, interview by author, Biloxi, Miss., April 10, 2014. Additional quotations in this chapter are from this interview.

11. After our interview, Graham was hired to become the executive director of the Back Bay Mission, in Biloxi, starting January 5, 2015. "Announcing Rev. Alice Graham, Ph.D., as Our Executive Director," Back Bay Mission, January 6, 2015, https://thebackbaymission. org/2015/01/announcing-rev-alice-graham-ph-d-as-our-executive-director/.

12. Daniel Schwartz, interview by author, New Orleans, La., April 9, 2014. Additional quotations in this chapter are from this interview.

13. "Eugenia," interview by author, New Orleans, La., April 8, 2014. Additional quotations in this chapter are from this interview.

14. Donald Frampton, interview by author, New Orleans, La., April 7, 2014. Additional quotations in this chapter are from this interview.

CHAPTER 7

1. Warren Bird and Scott Thumma, "A New Decade of Megachurches—2011 Profile of Large Attendance Churches in the United States," Hartford Institute for Religion Research, November 22, 2011, http://hirr.hartsem.edu/megachurch/megachurch-2011 -summary-report.htm.

2. U.S. Census National, State, and Puerto Rico Commonwealth Totals Datasets: Population, population change, and estimated components of population change: April 1, 2010 to July 1, 2013, http://www.census.gov/popest/data/national/totals/2013/NST -EST2013-alldata.html.

3. Tracy Thompson, *The New Mind of the South* (New York: Simon and Schuster, 2013), 106.

4. "Great Churches of America, IV: Bellevue Baptist," *Christian Century*, April 19, 1950, 490–96.

5. Robert G. Lee, "Payday Someday," News for Christians, http://www.newsfor christians.com/clser1/lee-rg001.html.

6. Randall H. Balmer, *Grant Us Courage: Travels along the Mainline of American Protestantism* (New York: Oxford University Press, 1996), 78, 82.

7. "LWF," Love Worth Finding, http://www.lwf.org/site/PageServer?pagename= all_tv#tennessee.

8. Adrian Rogers as reported by Balmer, *Grant Us Courage*, 80–81.

9. For three views of the takeover and its aftermath, see Nancy Tatom Ammerman, *Baptist Battles: Social Change and Religious Conflict in the Southern Baptist Convention* (New Brunswick, N.J.: Rutgers University Press, 1990); Barry Hankins, *Uneasy in Babylon: Southern Baptist Conservatives and American Culture* (Tuscaloosa: University of Alabama Press, 2002); David S. Dockery, ed., *Southern Baptist Identity: An Evangelical Denomination Faces the Future* (Wheaton, Ill.: Crossway Books, 2009). The last book features essays by principals holding responsibility in the remade SBC who still are finding a way forward more than two decades after coming to power.

10. Stephen R. Haynes, *The Last Segregated Hour: The Memphis Kneel-Ins and the Campaign for Southern Church Desegregation* (New York: Oxford University Press, 2013), 26–27. Two students were caught by a policeman and eventually charged with disrupting worship, a state crime. Subsequently, the church responded to such visitors by offering segregated seating. Nearly every white church in Memphis has a lot to live down and seek reconciliation for.

11. "Bellevue Loves Memphis," Bellevue Baptist Church, http://www.bellevue.org /bellevue-loves-memphis.

12. The exact quotation reads, "It's not surprising, then, they get bitter, they cling to guns or religion or antipathy to people who aren't like them or anti-immigrant sentiment or anti-trade sentiment as a way to explain their frustrations." It was offered in the context of the 2008 Democratic Pennsylvania primary and was intended as a sympathetic

explanation of voters' reluctance to trust in government after being neglected by successive administrations. The statement, often misquoted, took on a life of its own, to the point where in the 2012 Republican primary Texas governor Rick Perry said, "I happily cling to my guns and my God, even if President Obama thinks that that is a simpleminded thing in his elitist heart."

13. Though all of these bumper stickers seen in the Lynchburg vicinity caught our attention, the statement attributed to Thomas Jefferson sent us to the Internet, where we found that it was one of several spurious quotations about the second amendment from Jefferson that researchers at the Jefferson Library work hard to dispel. See http://www .monticello.org/site/jefferson/those-who-hammer-their-guns-plowsquotation.

14. "Liberty University Campus Church," Facebook, https://www.facebook.com /pages/Liberty-University-Campus-Church/129642457085676?sk=info.

15. Johnnie Moore, vice president of communications, message on Galatians 5 at Liberty University Campus Church, at Thomas Road Baptist Church, Lynchburg, Va., November 6, 2013, https://www.youtube.com/watch?v=uOPIoeioYPc.

16. The coverage of the scandal is well documented and analyzed by Anthea D. Butler, "The Fall of Eddie Long," *Religion in the News* 13, no. 2 (Spring 2011), http://www.trincoll .edu/depts/csrpl/RINVol13No2/FallofEddieLong.htm.

17. Paulk himself was accused of multiple sexual scandals, including fathering his brother's wife's child. Shirea L. Carroll, "10 Sex Scandals That Rocked the Christian Church," Essence.com, September 28, 2010, http://www.essence.com/2010/09/28 /sex-scandals-christian-church-eddie-long.

18. Kate Bowler and Wen Reagan, "Bigger, Better, Louder: The Prosperity Gospel's Impact on Contemporary Christian Worship," *Religion and American Culture: A Journal of Interpretation* 24, no. 2 (Summer 2014): 186–230.

19. Kyle Nazario, "Who Is Bishop Eddie Long?," *Atlanta Journal Constitution*, January 23, 2017; Leonardo Blair, "Eddie Long Funeral: Thousands Celebrate Life of New Birth Pastor (Video)," Christian Post, January 25, 2017, http://www .christianpost.com/news /eddie-long-funeral-thousands-celebrate-life-of-new-birth-pastor-watch-live-173453 /; Lawrence Ware, "Eddie Long's Death and Homophobic Theological Legacy," Root, January 15, 2017, http://www.theroot.com/eddie-longs-death-and-homophobic -theological-legacy-1791231305; Charreah K. Jackson, "The Death [of] Bishop Eddie Long and the Reckoning of the Black Church," Essence.com, January 17, 2017, http:// www.essence.com/news/death-bishop-eddie-long-and-reckoning-black-church.

20. Kenneth Robinson, interview by author, Memphis, Tenn., November 19, 2013.

21. As this book was being finished, the Robinsons announced their retirements from the active ministry, which was celebrated in January 2016. The Saint's new pastor is the Reverend Dr. Byron C. Moore, who is also married to an AME Intinerant Elder, the Reverend Sharon D. Moore. David Waters, "Robinsons Retiring as Co-Pastors of St. Andrew AME," Commercial Appeal, December 14, 2015, http://www.archive .commercialappeal.com/news/robinsons-retiring-as-co-pastors-of-st-andrew-ame -26e59030-8fdb-13b4-e053-0100007fc81d-362074601.html.

22. Bird and Thumma, "2011 Summary Research Report," 2–3.

23. E. Brooks Holifield, *Theology in America: Christian Thought from the Age of the Puritans to the Civil War* (New Haven, Conn.: Yale University Press, 2003), 3.

CHAPTER 8

1. James M. Woods, *A History of the Catholic Church in the American South: 1513–1900* (Gainesville: University Press of Florida, 2011), 371.

2. "Cullman's History," Cullman County, Alabama, http://co.cullman.al.us/history.html.

3. *Brother Joseph and the Grotto*, Red Clay Pictures, DVD, December 2013, 82 mins. See http://www.brotherjosephmovie.com/.

4. Leada Gore, "2016's Best Private High Schools in Alabama," AL.com, February 23, 2016, http://www.al.com/news/index.ssf/2016/02/2016s_best_private_high_school.html.

5. Raymond Arroyo, *Mother Angelica: The Remarkable Story of a Nun, Her Nerve, and a Network of Miracles* (New York: Doubleday, 2005), 38.

6. M. Angelica and Christine Allison, *Mother Angelica's Answers, Not Promises*, 2nd ed. (San Francisco: Ignatius Press, 1996), 17.

7. William Howard Bishop, Sermon, Second Sunday after Easter, April 22, 1917, Glenmary Home Missioners, http://www.glenmary.org/site/epage/106020_919.htm.

8. William Howard Bishop, *Challenge* vol. 1, no. 1 (February 1938): 1, 4.

9. M. Angelica and Allison, *Mother Angelica's Answers, Not Promises*, 19.

10. Ibid., 113–14, 132.

11. Arroyo, *Mother Angelica*, 330.

12. Ibid., 195.

13. "The Knights of the Holy Eucharist," Laybrother.com, February 23, 2012, http://laybrother.com/the-knights-of-the-holy-eucharist/.

14. See Peter Steinfels, *A People Adrift: The Crisis of the Roman Catholic Church in America* (New York: Simon and Schuster 2003); and John Portmann, *Catholic Culture in the USA: In and Out of Church* (New York: Continuum, 2010), for contemporary accounts of the generational divide in the church.

15. Jake Whitman, "N.Y. Basilica Style Church to Be Moved 900 Miles to Georgia," ABC News, November 7, 2010, http://abcnews.go.com/WN/church-move-buffalo -nybasilica-moved-900-miles-georgia/story?id=12081499; Melinda Miller, "St. Gerard Church and Rectory Heading for Sale," *Buffalo News*, January 17, 2017.

16. Hosffman Ospino, *Hispanic Ministry in Catholic Parishes: A Summary Report of Findings from the National Study of Catholic Parishes with Hispanic Ministry* (Boston: Boston College School of Theology, 2014), 42–43.

17. "Local Hispanics Recall 'Padre José' with Love" (sidebar), "Father Joe Waters, Pioneer of Hispanic Ministry in the Charlotte Diocese, Dies," *Catholic News Herald*, February 27, 2015, 5.

18. "Horario de Misas," Catholic Diocese of Raleigh," http://dioceseofraleigh.org /hispanic-ministry/community/masses-in-spanish.

19. "U.S.-Latin American Sisters Exchange Program Launched to Serve Growing Hispanic Population," Catholic Extension, October 7, 2014, https://www.catholic extension.org/news-media/media-room/in-the-news/us-latin-american-sisters -exchange-program-launched-serve-growing.

20. Lindsay Ruebens, "Catholic in a Small Southern Town: A New Kind of Segregation," Endeavors, May 31, 2011, http://endeavors.unc.edu/catholic_in_a_ small_southern_town_a_new_kind_of_segregation.

21. Timothy M. Matovina, *Latino Catholicism: Transformation in America's Largest Church* (Princeton, N.J.: Princeton University Press, 2012), 24–25.

22. Ruebens, "Catholic in a Small Southern Town."

23. Ibid.

24. James Chaney, "The Formation of a Hispanic Enclave in Nashville, Tennessee," *Southeastern Geographer* 50, no. 1 (2010): 17–38.

25. "40 Days: Save Our Lady's for Nashville Hispanics," Political Salsa, May 21, 2008, http://politicalsalsa.blogspot.com/2008/05/save-our-ladys-for-nashville-hispanics.html.

26. "An Interview with Reverend Joseph P. Breen of Saint Edward Church," http://www.espanglishmagazine.com/archive/55-breen.html (discontinued). "Nashville Diocese Establishes Tennessee's First All-Hispanic Parish," *Catholic Review*, January 19, 2012, http://catholicreview.org/article/life/style/nashville-diocese-establishes-tennessees-first-all-hispanic-parish.

27. "Our Lady of Guadalupe," Catholic Online, http://www.catholic.org/about/guadalupe.php.

28. Mario J. Paredes, *The History of the National Encuentros: Hispanic Americans in the One Catholic Church* (New York: Paulist Press, 2014).

CHAPTER 9

1. David and Leslie Nunnery, "Who We Are and What We Are Doing," Teach Them Diligently, https://teachthemdiligently.net/about/who-and-what.

2. Ibid.

3. Total paid attendance, not including exhibitors, for the 2013 conventions exceeded 25,000 persons for all venues, according to Teach Them Diligently. For 2015 and 2106, TTD moved to three big locations, Atlanta, Nashville, and the giant Cedar Point amusement park in Sandusky, Ohio.

4. *Engel v. Vitale*, 370 U.S. 421 (1962), outlawed official school prayers, including New York State's official school prayer, "Almighty God, we acknowledge our dependence upon Thee, and we beg Thy blessings upon us, our parents, our teachers and our country. Amen." *Abington School District v. Schempp*, 374 U.S. 203 (1963), invalidated a Pennsylvania law requiring that "at least ten verses from the Holy Bible [be] read, without comment, at the opening of each public school on each school day." Both sets of state practices were found to have violated the Establishment Clause of the U.S. Constitution.

5. Ken Ham and Bill Looney, *Dinosaurs for Kids* (Green Forest, Ark.: Master Books, 2009).

6. "Statement of Faith," Teach Them Diligently, https://teachthemdiligently.net/about/statement-of-faith.

7. "Number and Percentage of Homeschooled Students Ages 5 through 17 with a Grade Equivalent of Kindergarten through 12th Grade, by Selected Child, Parent, and Household Characteristics: 2003, 2007, and 2012," National Center for Education Statistics, http://nces.ed.gov/programs/digest/d13/tables/dt13_206.10.asp. The National Center for Education Statistics estimates that "approximately 3 percent of the school-age population was homeschooled in the 2011–12 school year. Among children who were homeschooled, a higher percentage were White (83 percent) than Black (5 percent),

Hispanic (7 percent), or Asian or Pacific Islander (2 percent)." https://nces.ed.gov /fastfacts/display.asp?id=91.

8. U.S. Department of Education, National Center for Education Statistics, Homeschooling in the United States: 2003; and Parent Survey (Parent:1999) and Parent and Family Involvement in Education Survey (PFI:2003 and PFI:2007) of the National Household Education Surveys Program.

9. Tal Levy, "Homeschooling and Racism," *Journal of Black Studies* 39, no. 6 (July 2009): 905–23.

10. Brian D. Ray, *Strengths of Their Own—Home Schoolers across America: Academic Achievement, Family Characteristics, and Longitudinal Traits* (Salem, Oreg.: National Home Education Research Institute, 1999).

11. James Emery White, "Why Homeschool?," *Crosswalk*, May 30, 2013, http://www .crosswalk.com/blogs/dr-james-emery-white/why-homeschool.html.

12. *Above Rubies*, no. 88, 3.

13. Holly M. Brockman, interview with Wendell Berry, New Southerner, January– February 2006, http://www.newsoutherner.com/Wendell_Berry_interview.htm.

14. Bob Sjogren and Gerald Robison, *Cat and Dog Theology: Rethinking Our Relationship with Our Master*, rev. ed. (Downers Grove, Ill.: IVP Books, 2003).

CHAPTER 10

1. Caryle Murphy, "Most U.S. Christian Groups Grow More Accepting of Homosexuality," Pew Research Center, December 18, 2015, http://www.pewresearc h.org/fact-tank/2015/12/18/most-u-s-christian-groups-grow-more-accepting -of-homosexuality/.

2. For a more complex twentieth-century history of LGBT life in the South, see John Howard, *Men Like That: A Southern Queer History* (Chicago: University of Chicago Press, 1999); John Howard, ed., *Carryin' On in the Lesbian and Gay South* (New York: New York University Press, 1997); Suzanne Pharr, *Homophobia: A Weapon of Sexism* (Inverness, Calif.: Chardon Press, 1988); and John Howard, "Gays," in *The New Encyclopedia of Southern Culture*, ed. Charles Reagan Wilson et al., 4:79–83 (Chapel Hill: University of North Carolina Press, 2006).

3. Archbishop George Hyde, interview by Jodie Talley, Belleair, Fla., December 10, 2005, in Talley, "A Queer Miracle in Georgia: The Origins of Gay-Affirming Religion in the South," (M.A. thesis, Georgia State University, 2006), 40.

4. Louie Crew, "Founding," Integrity USA, http://www.integrityusa.org/archive /History/founding.htm.

5. Mab Segrest, *My Mama's Dead Squirrel: Lesbian Essays on Southern Culture* (Ithaca, N.Y.: Firebrand Books, 1985), 25.

6. Robert Beard, interview by Jodie Talley, Atlanta, Ga., November 1, 2004, in Talley, "Queer Miracle in Georgia," 30.

7. Talley, "Queer Miracle in Georgia," 34.

8. Didi Herman, *The Antigay Agenda: Orthodox Vision and the Christian Right* (Chicago: University of Chicago Press, 1997).

9. The 3.2 percent figure comes from Gary J. Gates and Frank Newport, "Special Report: 3.4% of U.S. Adults Identify as LGBT," Gallup.com, October 19, 2012, http://www.gallup

.com/poll/158066/special-report-adults-identify-lgbt.aspx, and compares to a national average of 3.4 percent for all adults, with 6.2 percent of adults ages eighteen to twenty-nine nationally self-identifying as LGBT. These figures are corroborated by Gary J. Gates, of the Williams Institute, who carefully documents LGBT demographics in, e.g., "How Many People Are Lesbian, Gay, Bisexual and Transgender?," Williams Institute, April 2011, http://williamsinstitute.law.ucla.edu/research/census-lgbt-demographics-studies /how-many-people-are-lesbian-gay-bisexual-and-transgender/.

10. Bernadette Barton, *Pray the Gay Away: The Extraordinary Lives of Bible Belt Gays* (New York: New York University, 2012), 19–20.

11. Ibid., 32.

12. Kevin Hardy, "After Same-Sex Couple Victory in Collegedale, Church Ousts Gay Detective's Family," Timesfreepress.com (Chattanooga, Tenn.), August 21, 2013, http:// www.timesfreepress.com/news/local/story/2013/aug/21/repent-or-leave/116579/.

13. E. Patrick Johnson, *Sweet Tea: Black Gay Men of the South* (Chapel Hill: University of North Carolina Press, 2008), 215.

14. Ibid., 245–46.

15. Ibid., 249.

16. The Rev. Davita McCallister, interview by Jodie Talley (First Congregational Church), September 7, 2004, in Talley, "Queer Miracle," PAGE.

17. Alex Morris, "The Forsaken: A Rising Number of Homeless Gay Teens Are Being Cast Out by Religious Families," Rolling Stone.com, September 3, 2014, http://www .rollingstone.com/culture/features/the-forsaken-a-rising-number-of-homeless-gay -teens-are-being-cast-out-by-religious-families-20140903.

18. Gary David Comstock, *A Whosoever Church: Welcoming Lesbians and Gay Men into African American Congregations* (Louisville, Ky.: Westminster John Knox Press, 2001), 141.

19. Ibid., 148.

20. Ibid., 140.

21. Ibid., 150.

22. "HIV/AIDS at 30: Edwin Sanders Ministers to 'Whosoever They May Be,'" Colorlines, March 28, 2011, http://www.colorlines.com/articles/hivaids-30-edwin-sanders-ministers -whosoever-they-may-be.

23. "Core Values," Metropolitan Interdenominational Church, http://www.micwhosoever .org/about-us/core-values.html.

24. Allen McAlister, "Affirming Churches Welcome All," Out & About Nashville, July 1, 2007, http://www.outandaboutnashville.com/story/affirming-churches-welcome-all #.Vr4Ytxiw7wo.

25. Leslie Jordan, David Alan Leonard, and Matt Maher, "Hear the Sound" (song), 2012.

26. Rev. Greg Bullard, "Captive Captions," sermon, Covenant of the Cross, Madison, Tenn., January 17, 2016.

27. "Jan 19: Franklin Graham and Dr Dobson Q and A," Dr. James Dobson's Family Talk, http://drjamesdobson.org/Broadcasts/Broadcast?i=a3d573e3-9c9c-498a-860b -9c0d6f08ef3a.

28. Ibid.

29. Sher Watts Spooner, "Faith Communities Find Their Own Ways to Honor Orlando Shooting Victims," Daily Kos, June 6, 2016, http://www.dailykos.com

/story/2016/6/16/1539565/-Faith-communities-find-their-own-ways-to-honor
-Orlando-shooting-victims. The full version of Britt Cox's statement appears at her
blog: Britt Cox, "A Holy Place," Knot Your Average Pastor, September 20, 2016, https://
knotaveragepastor.wordpress.com/2016/09/20/a-holy-place/.

30. Sarah K. Burris, "These 7 Christian Leaders Showed Their Love by Celebrating
the Orlando Nightclub Massacre," Raw Story, June 14, 2016, http://www.rawstory
.com/2016/06/these-7-christian-leaders-showed-their-love-by-celebrating-the-orlando
-nightclub-massacre/.

31. Emily McFarlan Miller, "Christian Response to Orlando Leaves Some LGBT
Activists Cold," Crux, June 14, 2016, https://cruxnow.com/rns/2016/06/14/christian
-response-orlando-leaves-lgbt-activists-cold/.

32. "The Briefing 06-13-16," AlbertMohler.com, June 13, 2016, http://www.albertmohler
.com/2016/06/13/briefing-06-13-16/.

33. Dan Wooding, "Pulse Nightclub Attack: Billy Graham Rapid Response Team
Chaplains Deploy to Orlando Following Deadliest Mass Shooting in U.S. History," June
14, 2016, http://www.crossmap.com/news/pulse-nightclub-attack-billy-graham-rapid
-response-team-chaplains-deploy-to-orlando-following-deadliest-mass-shooting-in-u
-s-history-28682; KTV SkyAngelNetworks, "BillyGraham.TV: Rapid Response Team in
Orlando," video, July 14, 2016, https://www.youtube.com/watch?v=5hksT7OkUQg.

34. Mark I. Pinsky, "Prayers for Orlando," Orlando magazine blog, June 2016, http://
www.orlandomagazine.com/Blogs/Metropoly/June-2016/Prayers-for-Orlando/.

35. Matthew Vines, "What Christians Must Do in the Wake of Orlando," Time, June 13,
2016, http://time.com/4366465/christians-after-orlando/.

36. Ashley Carter, "Christ Church Orlando to Receive Recognition for Pulse
Response," News 13, January 21, 2017, http://www.mynews13.com/content/news
/cfnews13/news/article.html/content/news/articles/cfn/2017/1/21/christ_church_
orland.html.

37. "Cathedral of St. Luke, Orlando, Describes Pastoral Response in Wake of
Massacre," pastoral letter, Episcopal Café, June 17, 2016, https://www.episcopalcafe.com
/cathedral-of-st-luke-orlando-describes-pastoral-response-in-wake-of-massacre/.

38. Gal Tziperman Lotan and Alicia DelGallo, "Christopher Leinonen: Gay Rights
Activist," Orlando Sentinel, July 8, 2016.

CONCLUSION

1. Figures derived from 2010 Muslim adherent estimates. "The 2010 U.S. Religion
Census," U.S. Religion Census 1952 to 2010, http://www.rcms2010.org/.

2. Claire Cain Miller, "The Search for the Best Estimate of the Transgender
Population," New York Times, June 8, 2015, http://www.nytimes.com/2015/06/09
/upshot/the-search-for-the-best-estimate-of-the-transgender-population.html.

INDEX

Abernathy, Reverend Ralph David, 96

Above Rubies, 210–11

Affordable Care Act, 23, 31, 102, 104

African Americans, 45, 50, 59, 61, 110, 112, 125–28, 165–66, 226; congregations of, 29, 56, 79, 231; as Christians, 38; migration of, 74; students, 77; population of, 110, 220

African Methodist Episcopal Church (AME), 11, 26, 167, 170

AIDS. *See* HIV/AIDS

Alabama, 6, 23–25, 40, 75, 86–88, 90–91, 94–95, 99, 112, 133, 200, 222, 228; bishops, 90–91, 103; anti-immigration law of, 92–93; Catholics in, 178–93

Allen, Ivan, 114

American Civil Liberties Union, 35

American Culture, 2, 38, 212

Appalachia, 4, 10, 22, 15, 65–67, 177, 183

Arkansas, 23–24, 40, 86, 169, 200, 228

Arroyo, Raymond, 185

Ashley, Wendy, 20

Asuza Street revival, 73–74

Authority, 11–12, 28–29, 64, 88

Baker, Bishop Robert, 91

Bapticostal churches, 82, 165

Baptists, 7, 10, 20, 26, 40, 52, 68, 84, 108, 110, 129, 135, 137, 140, 149–50, 167, 175, 177, 183; churches of, 6, 8, 15, 68, 70, 77, 123, 126, 134, 174, 185; black, 6, 175; ministers, 52; white, 175

Barber, Reverend William J., II, 9, 95–96, 98, 100–101, 103

Barton, Bernadette, 221

Barton, David, 87

Baton Rouge, 110, 113, 135

Beck, John, 17

Bellevue Baptist Church (Memphis), 155–65, 170, 174

Belmont College, 212

Benedictines, 178–79, 182, 192; and Poor Clares, 192

Benedict XVI (pope), 188

Bentley, Robert, 90

Berry, Wendell, 211

Bible Belt, 24, 182, 239

Billy Graham Evangelistic Association, 238

Biloxi, Miss., 108–9, 131–32, 134, 137

Bird, Warren, 170,

Birmingham, 95, 87, 176, 193; church bombing, 61

Bishop, Father William Howard, 183–84

Black church, 19, 37, 124, 104, 148, 160, 165, 167, 225–26, 229, 238–39, 265; preaching in, 80, 169

Black Lives Matter, 61

Blessed Virgin Mary, 179, 182, 185, 186

Bob Jones University, 212

Boles, John, 18

Bond, Julian, 86

Bond, Sam, 44

Bonhoeffer, Dietrich, 33, 36

Breen, Father Joseph P. 195

Brewer, Greg, 240

Brockman, Holly M., 212,

Brown, Michael, 108

Bryant, Anita, 216

Buffett, Jimmy, 61

Bullard, Reverend Greg, 232–35, 240
Bush, George W., 108, 161

Calvin, John, 71, 120
Calvinistic ideas, 140, 145
Campbell, Nancy, 210
Cane Ridge revival, 70
Capital Punishment, 54, 57
Capito, Shelley Moore, 86
Carter, Jimmy, 86, 98, 117; Carter Center, 26
Cathedral Church of St. Luke (Orlando), 240
Cathedral of Praise Church of God in
    Christ (Nashville), 77–79
Catholic Church, Catholicism, 39, 112,
    120, 177, 181–85, 187, 189–90, 193–94,
    199–200, 237; in the South, 177, 190, 192,
    195, 199–200; traditional, 188–89; large
    Hispanic parishes of, 196; families in, 245
Cathy, Truett, 17
Cauthen, Kenneth, 68
Chapel Hill Harvester Church
    (Decatur, Ga.), 165
Charleston, S.C., killings, 59
Chattanooga Times Free Press, 65
Cheairs, Nathaniel, 43, 44
Cheairs, Susan, 43, 44
Cheairs, William, 45
Choby, Bishop David, 195
Christ Church Cathedral (Orlando),
    239–40
Christian Church/Disciples of Christ,
    70, 228
Christianity, various forms of, 4–8, 37, 70,
    243–47
Christian South, 39, 241, 246;
    homeschooling in, 10, 207, 209, 213;
    culture, southern, 17, 35; conservative
    Christians in, 29, 87, 211, 215; and
    southern virtue, 49; and liberty, 73,
    87, 205; liberal Christians in, 75; and
    Christian theology, 77, 172, 213; and
    redemption and grace, 130; Christian
    schools in, 203, 213; homophobia in, 218,
    221; marriage equality in, 228
Christ's sacrifice (atonement), 30, 196

Churches: nondenominational, 6, 12,
    70, 126, 176; contemporary, 12; family
    conception of, 17, 118, 158, 231; local, 24,
    140, 220; mainline Protestant, 32, 36;
    magisterial, 35; conservative Protestant,
    68, 158; old-time holiness, 72; new, 74,
    176, 218, 230; integrated, 133; small, 155,
    172–73, 175, 221; suburban branch, 157;
    large, 170–71, 175; gay-affirming, 216,
    224, 227–28, 232, 239; "whosoever,"
    230, 269; multicultural, 239. See also
    Megachurches
Churches of Christ, 4, 6, 12, 24, 70
Church life, reinvention of southern, 153,
    155, 157, 159, 161, 163, 165, 167, 169, 171, 173,
    175
Church of God in Christ (COGIC), 4, 11,
    72, 75–78
Civil War, 9, 42–45, 47–51, 53, 55, 58–59, 207
Clarke, Erskine, 7
Clergy, 94–96, 126–27, 137, 144, 148, 167, 193
COGIC. See Church of God in Christ
Commandments, religious, 86–87, 185–86,
    202
Confederacy (Confederate States of
    America, CSA, 1861–65), 44, 47–48,
    49–51, 53, 55–56; Confederate honor,
    42; generals, 44; battle flag of, 51, 55–61;
    chaplains, 51
Confederate Veterans, 47–48, 52, 55, 59,
    255–56
Conversions, 30, 49, 53, 75, 77, 183
Coots, Pastor Gregory James, 64
Coots, Pastor Jamie, 64
Covington, Dennis, 64
Cowan, Michael, 111–13, 119, 136
Cox, James, 132, 148–49
Creationism, 85, 112, 179, 203, 206, 209, 214–15
Crew Clay, Louie, 219
Cruz, Ted, 40, 255
Cullman, Ala., 178, 180–82, 194

Darwin, Charles, 68
Davis, Kim, 40
Davis, Sam, 53, 54

Democrats, 98

Denominations, 3, 72, 149, 172, 175–76, 225–27

Desire Street Ministries, 120, 140

Dickson-Rishel, Reverend Rod, 136–37, 147

Diocese of Charlotte, 191

Dobson, James, 204, 221; in *Family Talk* program, 236

Dye, Father David, 190

East Biloxi, Miss., 132–34, 149

Education, 201, 204, 207–8, 213–14; religious, 192

Egerton, John, 20–21

Eighmy, John Lee, 68

Elections, 78, 80–81, 84–87, 98, 161, 259

Ellis, Joseph J., 88

Elm Springs, 50, 53

Emanuel African Methodist Episcopal Church, Charleston, 56

Episcopal Church (USA), 11, 218–19; churches of, 6, 174, 227; members of, 92, 94, 110, 137

Equal Justice Initiative, 60

Evangelical Christianity, 89, 159, 206; preaching and preachers, 164, 174

Evangelical churches, 11, 174, 195, 232–33; gay congregations of, 10; contemporary, 232

Evangelicalism, 68, 159, 251; southern, 75, 104, 159, 212

Evangelical Lutherans (ELCA), 4, 227

Evangelical United Brethren Church, 15

Evolution, 85, 112, 203

EWTN (Eternal Word Television Network), 184–85

Falwell, Reverend Jerry, 89, 159, 162, 217, 221

Families, 18, 24, 54, 57, 90, 145, 166, 220, 222, 245, 210, 221–22; Christian, 77, 208, 223, 236; heteronormative, 221; of choice, 239

Family Research Council, 209, 244

Farley, Chaplain Alan, 53

Faulkner, William, 10, 42

Fear, in southern Christianity, 37–41

Federal Emergency Management Agency (FEMA), 107–9, 132, 134

Feed America First, 25

Figueroa, Hugo, 194

Financial Peace University, 162

First Amendment, 65, 91–92, 94, 103

Fischer, David Hackett, 17

Florida, 5, 7, 23–24, 54, 95, 131, 133, 177, 179, 196, 200, 217, 222, 227, 237, 240

Flunder, Bishop Yvette, 238

Food, role of, 16, 19–22, 24–27, 30, 37–38, 85, 91–93, 108–9, 130, 132, 137, 141, 149, 210; food banks, 11, 23; foodlorists, 20; food insecurity, 22; food justice, 25; food assistance, 124

Frampton, Reverend Donald, 116–20, 146

Francis (pope), 193

Franciscan University of Steubenville in Ohio, 187

Freedmen's Bureau, 44

Freewill Baptists, 15

Gaines, Reverend Steve, 158–60, 174

Gainesville, Fla., 95, 227

Gateway Rescue Mission (Jackson, Miss.), 35–36

Gathje, Pete, 28–30, 35–36

Gay persons, 10, 215–17, 219–21, 223–27, 229–33, 235, 237–41; black gay men, 224; ordination of, 224, 228; gay children, 236. *See also* Churches: gay-affirming; Lesbians; LGBT groups and persons

Gender, 38–39, 86, 244; identities, 215, 221; transition, 231

Georgia, 1, 21, 23–24, 51, 75, 85–86, 95, 100, 155, 161, 165, 175, 190, 200, 214, 217, 219, 222

Glenmary Home Missioners, 177, 183

Gospel, role of, 7, 31, 64–65, 71–75, 91–94, 108, 150, 169, 205; music, 79; prosperity, 155, 165–66, 170, 173

Government, 52, 56, 86–88, 97, 113, 135, 265

Grace, 37, 71, 130, 145, 153, 196, 206, 232, 234

Graham, Alice, 141–44, 148

Graham, Franklin, 236, 240

Granger, Gordon, 59

Grant, Ulysses S., 48

Great Depression, 31, 211

Guadalupe Catholic Church (Newton Grove, N.C.), 194
Gulf Coast, 110, 124–25, 139, 146, 150, 177–78, 243

Habitat for Humanity, 117, 119
Haley, Nikki, 57, 85
Hamblin, Andrew, 64–65
Hanceville, Ala., 181–82, 185–86, 192
HB 56 (Beason-Hammon Alabama Taxpayer and Citizen Protection Act), 90
Health-care clinics ministries, 24, 31–32, 241
Heifer International, 26
Heyrman, Christine Leigh, 68
Hill, Michael, 53
Hill, Samuel S., 6, 68
Hispanic Americans, 10, 165, 194, 199–200; Baptist, 32; as immigrants, 39, 94, 178; and Catholicism, 200, 192, 194; families of, 245
HIV/AIDS, 32, 85, 214, 220–21, 230–31, 269
HKonJ, 96, 99–100
Holifield, Brooks, 172–73
Holiness, 6, 11, 63, 65–67, 69, 71–73, 75, 77, 79, 81, 83, 187, 252
Holy Ghost/Spirit, 11, 65, 67, 69–73, 74–77, 79, 81–83, 202
Homeless persons, 22, 25–27, 29, 31, 34–35, 92, 94–95, 138; homelessness, 27, 33; shelters for, 35, 117; outlawing, 85
Homeschooling, 201, 204–5, 207–13; as movement and subculture, 203–4, 206
Homophobia, 221, 229, 268
Homosexuality, 215, 218, 220–23, 225, 230
Honor, 40–41, 45, 50, 53, 56, 68, 163, 167, 179
Hood, John B., 44
Hood, Ralph W., 67
Hospitality, 16–41, 92, 159, 219, 244–46
Huckabee, Mike, 2, 40
Humor, role of, 37, 47, 50, 81, 157, 163–64, 184, 235
Hunger, in the South, 20, 24–26; persons with, 9, 15, 22, 24–26, 31, 91–95, 108–09
Hunter, Pastor Joel, 239

Hurricane Katrina, 9, 59, 107–50, 243–46
Hyde, Archbishop George, 217–19

Iglesia Catolica Nuestra Señora de Guadalupe (Nashville), 194–98
Immigrants and immigration, 17, 38, 95, 102, 178, 193–94; undocumented, 91–92, 94, 193
Incarceration, 23, 26, 101, 112, 124–26, 128–30, 150, 229
International Pentecostal Holiness Church (IPHC), 39, 72
Irondale, Ala., 182, 185
Islamophobia, 244
Israel, 80, 125, 202

Jackson, T. J. "Stonewall," 31, 51
Jefferson, Thomas, 43, 88–89
Jennings, Willie, 37–39, 100
Jeremiah, 52
Jesus, 11, 26, 29–30, 38, 64, 66, 70, 75, 91, 95, 100–101, 118, 134, 157–60, 163, 196, 199, 202, 230–31, 235, 244–45
Jews, 100, 110, 113, 124, 126–27; as community leaders, 150
Jim Crow, 56, 74, 99
John Paul II (pope), 185
Johnson, E. Patrick, 225
Jones, Sabrena, 133
Juan Diego, 196–97
Juneteenth, 59
Justice system, criminal, 102, 130

Katrina. See Hurricane Katrina
Keane, Father Patrick, 194
Kentucky, 7, 20, 25, 40, 63–64, 70, 86, 95, 177, 200, 211, 222, 236
Kidd, Thomas, 51
King, Reverend Martin Luther, Jr., 34, 61, 92, 94–96, 101, 173, 230
Kintzel, Justin, 164, 165
Kmiec, Bishop Edward, 195
Krinks, Lindsey, 32–33, 36
Ku Klux Klan, 55

Landmarkism, in Baptist churches, 12, 70
Laney, James, 114
Latin America, 178, 193, 196
Latin American Sisters Exchange
    Program, 192
Latino/a persons, 39, 97, 191, 194, 239; as
    Pentecostals, 39; Catholicism and, 194;
    gay and lesbian, 237
Lausanne Covenant, 140
Law, natural, 113, 244; makers of, 24, 85, 98;
    unjust, 89, 92
Lee, Robert E., 48–49, 51
Lee, Robert G., 156–57, 163
Lee, Stephen Dill, 47
Lee University, 77
Leo XIII (pope), 198
Lesbians, 8, 10, 215–17, 219, 221, 223–24,
    232–33, 237–38, 239
Lewis, John, 86, 96
LGBT groups and persons, 10, 216–19,
    221, 223–24, 237–40, 268–69; pre-
    Stonewall southern, 217; gender-identity
    experience, 221; children and youth, 234,
    236; violence directed toward, 237–40;
    and Latin communities, 240. *See also*
    Churches: gay-affirming
Liberty University, 78, 155, 163–64, 212
Lipscomb University, 33, 212
Little Rock, Arkansas, 19, 26, 176–77, 192
Long, Bishop Eddie, Sr., 165, 170
Long Beach United Methodist Church, 110,
    136, 137
Looney, Bill, 206
López, Father Fernando, 196
Lost Cause, 4, 42–43, 45, 47–49, 51, 53, 55,
    57, 59, 61
Louisiana, 23, 86, 108–9, 121–22, 125, 128–29,
    177, 200, 228
Louisville, Kentucky, 176–78
Lourdes, 121, 185
Lower Ninth Ward (in New Orleans), 107,
    120, 124
Loyola University, 111, 136
Luther, Martin, 12, 217

Lutherans, 6, 26, 142, 203
Lynchburg, Va. 89, 155, 159–60

Mainline Protestants, 6, 11–12, 66, 104, 160,
    175, 193, 238; denominations of, 172, 224;
    conservative congregations of, 238
Main Street Missionary Baptist Church
    (East Biloxi, Miss.), 109, 132–33, 148–49
Manna House, 28, 30–31, 36
Marriage, 17, 40–41, 88, 172, 184, 189, 219,
    244; interracial, 39; marriage equality,
    40, 85, 90, marriage licenses, 40, 90
Marsh, Charles, 4
Mason, Bishop Charles Harrison, 74
Mason-Dixon Line, 48
Mathews, Donald, 68
Matovina, Timothy, 194
Matthew 25, as scriptural warrant, 21, 26–27,
    30, 103, 109, 173, 240
Maynard, Bishop Jerry, 78–81
McCallister, Davita, 226
McCrory, Pat, 98
McIntyre, Reverend Ingrid, 32, 35
McLean, Apostle Renny, 166
McLeish, Ben, 120, 123, 129–30, 135–36,
    140–41, 145–46, 149–50
Mead, Sidney E., 35
Meagher, Abbot Cletus, 179
Mecklenburg Community Church
    (Charlotte), 208
Megachurches, 3, 153–55, 157, 159, 161–63,
    165, 167, 169–75
Melo, Father Fidel, 191
Memphis, Tenn., 27–28, 30, 95, 155, 157,
    159–60, 167–68, 170, 174, 230, 254, 264–65
Mercy Children's Clinic, 31
Methodists, 6, 26, 52, 68, 71, 92–93, 149,
    175–77, 236
Metropolitan Community Church, 217, 227,
    232, 238
Metropolitan Interdenominational Church
    (Nashville), 229–32
Micah (prophet), 97,
Micah Project, 112, 124–26, 128

Mississippi, 1, 6, 9, 21, 23–25, 43, 47, 54, 57, 59, 61, 86, 99, 108–9, 124, 130, 133–36, 142–43, 150, 200, 222, 227–28
Mississippi Coast Interfaith Disaster Task Force, 143
Mohler, Albert, 238
Moore, Byron C., 169
Moore, Dorothy, 204
Moore, Pastor Johnnie, 164
Moore, Roy, 9, 87–89
Moore, Reverend Russell, 59, 238
Moore, Reverend Sharon D., 169
Moral Mondays, 87, 95, 98, 100–102, 261
Morgan, Bishop Hope Ward, 138
Mother Angelica, 182–90, 193
Murphy, William, III, 165

NAACP, 87, 99, 261
Nash, Diane, 96
National Baptist Convention, 4
New Birth Missionary Baptist Church (Lithonia, Ga.), 155, 165–67, 170
New Orleans, Louisiana, 9, 43, 107–8, 110–13, 115–25, 127, 129–31, 135–36, 144–46, 149–50, 177–78
Newsome, Bree, 57
North Carolina, 9, 22, 24, 28, 32, 37–40, 57, 63, 87, 95–101, 103, 141–42, 177, 191, 194, 200, 222, 225, 227–28; NAACP in, 96, 100
Nunnery, David and Leslie, 201–2
Nuns, 182, 188–89, 192–93, 199

Obama, Barack, 98, 161, 160
O'Connor, Flannery, 10
Old South, 42, 68
Open Table Nashville, 33–34
Orlando, Fla., 7, 237–40
Orlando Sentinel, 240
Osorio, Father Luis, 191
Ospino, Hosffman, 190
Our Lady of Fatima, 180
Our Lady of the Angels Monastery, 182

Paisley, Brad, 58
Palmer, Phoebe, 71

Parham, Charles, 73
Parker, Ray L., 52
Parks, Rosa, 40, 96, 112
Parsley, Bishop Henry, Jr., 91
Parton, Dolly, 188
Pass Christian, Miss., 108, 148
Paul (apostle), 52, 90, 201
Paulk, Bishop Earl, 165
Pentecostal and Holiness traditions, 67–68, 70–71, 74–76, 80–83, 76, 82; churches in, 63, 69, 72,
Percy, Walker, 37
Perry, Reverend Troy, 217, 219
Plessy, Homer, 112
Politics, 6, 8, 68, 161, 214; religion and politics, 84–104
Pollard, Edward A., 48
Pollard, Ramsey, 157
Poverty, in the South, 22–26, 29, 33, 48, 101, 112, 124–25, 129–30, 140, 150, 167
Prayer, 7, 18, 31, 52, 61, 73, 83–84, 103, 143, 159, 162–64, 174, 179, 187, 189, 196, 198; emphasized, 71; organized school, 203
Preachers, 18, 25, 73, 82, 85, 96, 147, 158, 164, 167, 173–74, 222–23, 235, 238, 241; practice of preaching, 73, 77, 100, 147, 157–58, 163, 168–70, 174–75, 222; old-fashioned, 99; prosperity gospel, 155
Presbyterian Church in American (PCA), 123, 140–41
Presbyterians, PC(USA), 7, 18, 26, 42, 51–53, 68, 70, 78, 110, 116–20, 148, 175–76, 220, 228
Priests, 61, 96, 177–78, 183, 187–91, 194–96, 217–18, 237
Prison, 22–23, 26, 92–93, 244; prisoners, 22, 109, 125, 243–44; visiting, 26; and death row, 29, 60; freed from, 130
Prosperity gospel, 165–66, 170, 173
Public schools, 85, 203, 205, 208
Pulse Nightclub shootings, 237–40

Racism, 39, 108, 124, 129–31, 150; systemic, 101; de facto, 125
Raleigh, N.C., 32, 95–96, 100, 176, 191, 195

Raleigh Diocese of Catholic Church, 191, 194

Ramírez, Father David, 198

Randall, Aaron, 17

Rasberry, Rick, 163

Ray, Brian, 208

Religion and politics. *See* Politics

Religious Liberty Commission, 59, 238

Republican Party, 38, 87, 98–99; dominance, in South, 38, 85–86, 87; Tea Party, 40

RHINO (Rebuilding Hope In New Orleans), 117–19

Rippavilla Plantation, 43–44, 46, 55

Riverbend Maximum Security Prison (Tennessee), 243

Robertson, Reverend Pat, 221, 237

Robinson, Reverend Kenneth, 160, 167, 169, 249

Robinson, Reverend Marilynn, 168

Rodi, Archbishop Thomas, 91

Rogers, Reverend Adrian, 157, 217

Roof, Dylann, 56, 58, 61

Ryan, Father Abram, 49

Sacred Heart Church (Cullman, Ala.), 192

Sacred Heart Monastery (Cullman, Ala.), 178

Sagrado Corazón (Nashville), 196, 198

St. Andrews African Methodist Episcopal Church (Memphis), 155–60

Saint Bernard Abbey (Cullman, Ala.), 179–81

St. Charles Avenue Presbyterian Church (New Orleans), 116, 119, 146

St. Edward Catholic Church (Nashville), 195

St. Luke Episcopal (Atlanta), 219

St. Roch Community Church and CDC (New Orleans), 120–23, 123, 130, 140–41, 145

Sanders, Reverend Edwin, 229–31, 240

Schofield, John, 44

Schwartz, Daniel, 124, 129, 144, 150

Segregation, 3, 6, 21, 99, 112, 159, 246

Segrest, Mab, 219

Serpent-Handling Christians, 63–67

Sexuality, 38–39, 189, 215–16, 218–22, 231–33, 237

Seymour, William J., 73

Sherman, William Tecumseh, 48

Shrine of the Most Blessed Sacrament (Hanceville, Ala.), 182, 185–86, 188–89, 193

Shuttlesworth, Reverend Fred, 96

Sims, Bishop Bennett, 218

Sin, 4, 8, 11, 20, 41, 77, 129, 135, 157–59, 184–85, 198, 206, 222–23, 235

Sixteenth Avenue Baptist Church, Birmingham, 100

Slavery and enslaved persons, 42–45, 49–51, 53, 55, 59–61, 90

Sons of Confederate Veterans (SCV), 47–50, 52–53, 58,

South Carolina, 22–24, 32, 38, 54, 57, 86, 95, 100, 119, 156, 200–202, 222, 228

Southern Baptist Convention (SBC), 4, 20, 155–56, 158; churches of, 20, 155, 196; members of, 11, 157, 173, 181; Ethics and Religious Liberty Commission of, 59, 238

Southern Christian Leadership Conference, 96

Southern Christians, 3–5, 7, 17, 21, 23, 26, 37–39, 66, 70, 114, 208, 216, 227, 236, 243–46

Southern civil religions, 48

Southern Foodways Alliance, 20–21, 253

Spanish-American War, 49

Starbucks, 58–59, 155

Stevenson, Bryan, 60–61

Stone Mountain, Ga., 51

Strobel, Father Charles, 26–27, 35

Syrian refugees, 193, 244

Tennessee, 22–26, 28, 31, 39–40, 43, 47, 53–54, 63–64, 72, 75, 77–78, 86, 95, 157, 167, 174, 195, 200, 210, 214, 222, 230, 232, 236

Thomas Road Baptist Church (Lynchburg, Va.), 155, 159–60, 162–63

Thumma, Scott, 170

Till, Emmett, 141–42